KT-226-577

ARTHUR MARSHALL

Life's Rich Pageant

Fontana/Collins

First published in Great Britain by Hamish Hamilton Ltd 1984
First issued in Fontana Paperbacks 1985
Fourth impression February 1989

Copyright © Arthur Marshall 1984

Printed and bound in Great Britain by
William Collins Sons & Co. Ltd, Glasgow

It was about a dozen or so years ago that I heard the highly agreeable comedian, Sir Harry Secombe, use a phrase that at once struck a chord with me. He said, referring to some episode or other, 'Never mind: it's all part of life's rich pageant.' I couldn't for the moment remember where I had first heard it (it has been on the lips of others since) and then it came to me that I had used the phrase in a gramophone record that I made for Columbia in the late 1930s.

As far as I know, I didn't borrow the words from anywhere else and no less a body than the compilers of *The Oxford Dictionary of Quotations* have since taken an interest in the matter. They have finally decided that the phrase, such as it is, was my own invention and it is to be credited to me. Let me assure you that this small feather in my cap has not gone, so to speak, to my head.

As the word 'pageant' appears in my title, I thought it appropriate to refer to the successive chunks of autobiographical experience as 'scenes'.

Contents

Illustrations

'A Chield's Amang You Taking Notes'

There is nothing like a morning funeral for sharpening the appetite for lunch and when, in July, 1941, we returned from Shaw Cemetery, Newbury, in the county that is now known as Royal Berkshire, everybody felt peckish. My mother had been able, despite wartime rationing and restrictions, to assemble a splendid spread of cold salmon and real mayonnaise and new potatoes and salad. From beneath somebody's counter a large Stilton had appeared. There were hot bread rolls. There were our own peaches, and with our taste-buds pleasantly activated by a glass or two of sherry ('Do let me top you up'), we all sat down and fell to with a will.

We had been burying, I am sad to say, my father and I mean no disrespect for the dead when I suggest how greatly preferable the aftermath of a funeral is to that of a wedding. The sense of relief is immense for the sequence of events has often been a trying one. Restful sleep is not easily come by in a house where a dead body still lies and the household, after a troubled night, has been early astir. A sketchy breakfast in funeral clothes has been followed by the arrival of elderly and distant relations not glimpsed since the last funeral ('Yes, it's me again: Edith Bagshawe'). There is anxiety about the efficiency of the undertaker until, and bang on time, the hearse is heard crunching up the gravel drive. Then it's into the cars with what the French so neatly call *visages d'occasion* and slowly off, while passers-by bare their heads and stand mute (do they still?). There are the excess of wire-tortured flowers, the service, the tear-jerking hymns, the heartrending words, the wobbly lowerings, the earth, the scattering, the turning away. It is a grim way to send somebody on their journey. Better far the brisk and hygienic crematorium and the simple bunches of flowers that can subsequently delight a hospital ward.

However, the môment the cemetery has been left behind, everybody cheers up. The cars increase their speed to normal and, within them, compliments fly: 'Very well arranged': 'How nicely Canon Whetmore spoke!': 'I oughtn't to say it, dear, but black suits you'. And there is, of course, lunch to look forward to ('Now, nobody's to rush off'). I have, incidentally, never been able to get either my tongue or my pen very happily round the word 'luncheon'. Although I do not mind it when used by others, I feel that in me it would sound pretentious. It reminds me of that memorable solo sketch (and there's another word I can't manage, the dreary-sounding 'monologue') called 'Fish for Luncheon' and written by Herbert Farjeon for Edith Evans to perform as an extremely uppercrust, county lady issuing a lunch invitation and patronising some less well-to-do neighbours ('We'll send the Lagonda to fetch you'). As to those who can find it in them to employ the doubtlessly useful word 'brunch', do they, I wonder, ever up-grade it to 'bruncheon'? This is the kind of question that I ponder on while waiting for the kettle to boil. The active mind is never at rest.

My father was admirably businesslike and on his death everything was found to be in apple-pie order. However, even the best-made wills often go wrong or cause unforeseen complications and though my father's will seemed, to the lay eye, to be clear as day, it contained a legal difficulty, eagerly pounced on by the lawyers concerned. We had at home, inherited from my Essex grandmother, a grey parrot of great age called Bobby. Somewhere along the line, somebody had taught him to say 'Enjoying yourself?' in a markedly perky and sneery manner, together, alas, with 'How are your bowels?' for which he employed a more solicitous tone. Visitors thus addressed found each remark disconcerting. He much enjoyed music and had quite a repertoire but he was unfortunately tone-deaf and could effortlessly manage two or three changes of key in a piece as short as 'Pop Goes the Weasel'. He would have been quite at home among the modish modern dissonances relayed at off-peak hours by Radio 3.

In his will, and more or less as a joke, my father bequeathed the parrot (with other things) to the maid who had tenderly looked after it and to whom, as to all of us, it was devoted. The legal minds then got to work and before probate could be completed, my mother was pestered with endless queries.

What was the value of the parrot? By that time, Bobby had, like many another, pulled out all his breast feathers and presented a scraggy bare bosom to the world. He had also developed a loud cackle (possibly caught from me), lived on grilled bacon and peas and not even the neediest zoo would have given him house room. My mother replied that the parrot's value was to us, limitless, but negligible otherwise. No good, and back they came. 'What would the bird fetch at auction?'. The conception of Bobby on a stand at Sotheby's enquiring after Peter Wilson's bowels we found to be diverting. Eventually, Bobby was mentally knocked down by us at a fiver, after which the keen legal minds brought themselves to bear on the value of Bobby's cage.

Although my mother loved my father dearly, and for life, she much disliked her own wedding at Ilfracombe on April 19th, 1906 (Primrose Day, and my father's 30th birthday), for after their four-year engagement, then a perfectly normal span, the maximum fuss was generously and kindly made by her parents. There is little to be said in favour of elaborate weddings, gatherings which after all kick off with the main item on the agenda ('. . . at 2 p.m. at St. Cuthbert's, Little Bedding, and afterwards at "Dormers", Great Bedding . . .') and which dwindle into anti-climax, a slow *dégringolade* of interest and event and with, to come, the endless hiatus while the bride disappears to insert herself into her going-away rig. There is little to delight the eye or ear – the new clothes (or if not new, crisply Sketchley-fresh), the unfortunate hats, speeches, telegrams, jokes, the examination of the presents ('I think I can just spot our kebab skewers behind that ghastly lamp'), the worryingly purple faces of some elderly guests and the tendency of everything and everybody to sag. Dotted about are middle-aged couples who, too, once had high hopes and who now have thoughtful faces. Meanwhile the marquee flaps on in the wind and the hired waiters are itching to be off ('Will that be all, guv?'). All too late one hears the glad cry of 'Ah, here they come . . !' The only crumb of comfort, for those of a mocking turn of mind, is the subsequent account, headed JOYFUL OCCASION, in the local paper: '. . . numerous and costly gifts . . . amusing "cracks" made by the groom's best man, Major "Bimbo" Gorringe . . . the bride's mother, Mrs. Tregunter-Jones, was in beige with elephant accessories . . . the happy couple emerged from the church beneath an

3

archway of nasal probes smilingly held aloft by laughing nurses as a tribute to the bride's work at Bart's ... the honeymoon venue is being kept secret but the name "Torquay" was being whispered!'

My father did not like young children and in due course found himself blessed with two of them, my brother Brian appearing in 1907 and myself in 1910. To say that he did not like them should not be taken to mean that he positively disliked them. He quite liked the idea of them, but simply preferred to be where they were not. Besotted parents, bewitched by every aspect of their young child – messes, smells, screams, dribbles, appalling expense, wind – will find this reluctance to mix a little inhuman perhaps, but I, who am not a parent, understand it perfectly. He worked hard (he was a consultant engineer) and when not working preferred to be either with my mother, whom he adored, or alone. In our house in Barnes, there were, on the top floors, splendidly isolated, a day nursery and a night nursery and a nanny, while he had to himself a small study on the first floor. As was customary in those days among many men of the middle class, he referred to this private bolt-hole as his 'den', a word about which I have never been entirely happy. He also had, at the end of the garden, a shed with a lathe and other mechanical contraptions for he was an admirable carpenter and metalworker, the pride of the as yet unchristened DIY. And the shed too, into which we were not allowed, was a valuable retreat.

There was a family tradition, if such it may rather grandly be called, for a parent not seeing more than was strictly necessary of his children. My father and his three brothers were somewhat taken aback one day when, on returning from some outing and about to enter the family house in the Lexden Road, Colchester, they found pinned to the front door a notice in their father's hand and in capital letters, the better to get the message across and avoid all misunderstanding. It said IN FUTURE BOYS WILL ENTER BY THE SIDE DOOR. This meant that they avoided the hall and my grandfather's smoking-room, a sanctum where he liked to muse and enjoy a cigar and read Dickens. The side door was near some fairly elaborate iron-barred kennels and led the banished quartet into a sort of hinterland adjoining the kitchen regions and featuring pegs with macintoshes and log baskets and umbrella stands and a servants' lavatory and the cellar door and some back stairs up which they could creep and disperse to their rooms. Three of the brothers were of a nature to accept this social down-grading in a docile manner, but my Uncle Vernon was a born rebel and I like to think that, as they crept in and up, he supplied some loud and derisive laughter designed to reach the smoking-room.

While on the subject of relations, let me say a reassuring word. I venture no further back down Memory's Echoing Corridor than to my Devon grandparents (maternal) and my Essex ones (paternal). As a devoted reader of autobiographies, I have long since come to dread passages which begin with 'The family hailed originally, I believe, from Cleckheaton', and back we go to the middle of the eighteenth century where, before long, there surges up a frightful old 'Character' called 'Grumps', first cousin to the Starkadders, who becomes the Scourge of Bradford and extremely bad news all over Yorkshire. Truly conscientious autobiographers scurry about the country, consulting parish registers and back numbers of local newspapers and cross-questioning oldest inhabitants. But not I.

I was by nature a loving little boy and was much saddened by this paternal aloofness and mild antipathy, clear to me from early on, for children know by instinct who likes them. I saw other children perched happily on their fathers' knees but the only time that I ever remember so perching was for professional photographic purposes and when I was recovering from whooping-cough in the healing ozone of Frinton, the East Coast resort made chic for a time by the presence there, on holiday, of Miss Gladys Cooper. The photograph still exists and shows no very contented percher. And other children were often, when perched, dandled, a nowadays unfashionable verb. To jog a child cheerfully up and down was well beyond my father and, as a friendly action, would have been abhorrent to all the adult male members of my father's family — a disappointing lot: not a dandler among them. My mother was of course aware of all this and increased her ration of love, which was already considerable. It needs no trick cyclist's fifty pound fee to announce the result of this emotional imbalance. It led to a determined search on my part for those who come out, I suppose, in the technical jargon of the couch as 'substitute father figures'.

I was a vigorous searcher. Even though I was only about

four, my affections were violent ones and no male over twenty was safe. An easy prey was my Cousin Willie Thomson for he was a push-over where children were concerned. He was in a Highland regiment and was sometimes on leave in London and there is a photograph of me applying to this handsome, smiling and kilted figure a head-lock which any all-in wrestler might envy, a head-lock with 'submission' written all over it. There were picnics with him in Richmond Park, with games of hide-and-seek and that running, swirling kilt swishing its way in pursuit through the ferns. I lived in dread that the rascally Germans would get him (we had patriotically destroyed all our toys with MADE IN GERMANY on them) but he survived and married and remains to this day a charming push-over.

To cover Willie's sad absences, I had acquired two under-studies. My father had a different pair of boots, each complete with shiny and three-sectional wooden boot-trees, for each day of the week and on Sunday morning a man came from somewhere to clean boots and shoes and, for they seemed in those days to need special attention, knives. He had been invalided out of the army and the war and was a moustached and stocky limper to whom I instantly took, increasing on his behalf my warm dislike of the Kaiser. I counted the days to Sunday, hoping that the boots would get themselves muddier than usual so that Albert would have to stay longer. I sat with him, all attention and gazing raptly, in an outhouse shed while he cleaned and polished and chatted.

Sometimes Sundays contained a double treat, for my parents were members of the Roehampton Golf Club and although they would neither of them have approved, even after attending Holy Communion and Matins in the Barnes Parish Church of St. Mary, of positively playing golf on a Sunday, tea was another matter and so if the day was fine we often piled into the car, a bright yellow Metallurgique, and made for the golf club's members' tea-room. Here a three-piece orchestra played 'Roses of Picardy' and selections from *Tonight's the Night* and *The Arcadians* and a bell-push on the wall and marked STEWARD summoned, when pushed, both tea and a steward who happily liked children and was suitably fatherlike and for whose arrival I waited breathlessly. Sometimes I was allowed into his private hinterland of sinks and crockery and glasses and could watch him washing-up. Once, and he must have been a kind fellow, he bought me a box of chocolates and, keen and greedy chocolate-fancier though I was, it was some time before I could bear to spoil its beauty by breaking into it. My father took all this quite calmly and seemed, more than anything, relieved that others had cheerfully shouldered that part of a parent's duties that he couldn't find it in him to undertake. I allot no blame, for the situation contains nothing blameworthy. It was just the way things were.

Although she loved me well enough and provided a constant flow of devoted support and comfort and encouragement, my mother disliked spoilt children of which there were then quite a number circulating in Barnes ('I simply *cannot* think why the Medlicotts don't do something about their odious little Winifred'). There was no risk of spoiling where my brother and I were concerned as she was the firmest of disciplinarians, usually considered a paternal responsibility but one which she gladly shouldered. I was allowed to get away with nothing. If, over-excited and jabbering, I went first through a doorway and preceded some adult, I was dragged back and the whole process was repeated. Failure to jump up when an adult entered a room meant awful trouble. I was rather given to sullen moods and pouts and there was an unfailing method of getting rid of a fit of the sulks: 'Go straight up to your room, wash your face and hands, and don't come down until you are looking altogether more attractive'. It took me some time to learn that at children's tea parties it was socially unacceptable to take a slice of cake from a proffered plate and then convey it, where surely it belonged, directly to the mouth. The cake must first be grounded and rest awhile on one's plate, thus wasting valuable eating time. As to punishments, I was seldom smacked and never sent supperless to bed or had my pocket money (2d a week) cut. There was in my case a much more devastating reward for poor behaviour. I was ignored. When I spoke to her, my mother did not appear to hear. Requests for something or other fell on deaf ears. She did not seem to notice my presence, sometimes for as long as 24 hours – a lifetime at that age. This soon brought me to heel, contrite and usually sobbing. As a weapon against obstreperous, rude and thoughtless children I warmly recommend it.

My Essex grandfather had died the year before I was born and so we all betook ourselves to my widowed grandmother at Christmastime. In the first world war years and in the 20s, very few Christmas cards were sent and they had not yet become the burdensome duty that they now are. Some people prefer to insert news of their intentions in the personal columns of papers and I admire those strong-minded enough to announce to the world that 'Nibs and Branwell Ointment are sending no cards this year and are subscribing instead to the NSPCC'. Absence of cards was latterly a great cause of worry to my mother and for days after the event she could be heard muttering 'I simply cannot think why I haven't heard from Gertie Comerford and Hilda Desborough'. The reason was usually painfully clear and the cards would have had to come a very long way: and by air.

I was deeply attached to my Essex grandmother, a lovely circular giggler who took little, except her religion and her good deeds, seriously. By the time the festive evening arrived, it had already been an exhausting day for her. She had, of course, attended Holy Communion, together with all the other adults in the house apart from my Uncle Oswald, a firm disbeliever and a provider of ribald jibes ('How was the wine?') at the breakfast table. She had, naturally, led us all to Matins at 11 o'clock, whence she had gone on to visit an old lady in her 'district', for she was a district visitor and one of those who took an interest in the needy and impoverished and helped them in a variety of ways, an activity which would nowadays be considered, I suppose, patronising and unacceptable and damaging to dignity but I doubt if the recipients of her interest and kindness saw it in that way.

At Christmas dinner, and seated near her, I used to watch with some anxiety the changing colours on her face. Although high blood pressure is by no means always revealed in a florid complexion, my dear grandmother went in for colour. Her pressure was said to be the highest in Essex and was even rumoured to have broken, during a test, Dr Bentley's apparatus, though the fact came from my Uncle Oswald, previously shown to be mischievous and not always a trustworthy informant. In her case the damaging pressure showed itself in her cheeks, now crimson, now mauve and settling finally, as her share of the succulent goodies disappeared, for a disturbing purple. I would like to report that, mindful of Dr Bentley's warnings, not to speak of his damaged contraption, she ate prudently and frugally but truth obliges me to say that she simply gobbled it all down. The word 'shovel' used as a verb neatly sums up her deft work with fork, knife and spoon. The menu was unvarying. There was turtle soup. There was fish, for to the Victorian that my grandmother was, no dinner was a dinner without it. There was The Bird, stuffed with proper stuffing (no chestnut rubbish) and with all the necessary and numerous concomitants. Then the lights were momentarily extinguished and my grandmother's parlourmaid, Emma (dead, alas, only recently and at a great age), proudly brought in, to cries of 'Ooooh!', the Christmas pudding, fully alight. There were mince-pies. There was Stilton. There were coffee and port and tangerines and chocs and Brazil nuts and a vast assortment of crystallised fruits, merely pecked at, so full were we, and which lingered on for weeks in an increasingly sticky and displeasing mess. Those readers who are sniffing slightly in disapproval and are thinking that we all made pigs of ourselves are quite correct. We did. Should we have been thinking of the starving multitudes elsewhere? Yes we should. Were we? No we weren't.

As there were children present, there were, of course, crackers which were then considered, perhaps as now, to be an indispensably cheerful part of the proceedings. They certainly looked, dotted about the table and with at least one within reach, very jolly and attractive (difficult to construct an ugly cracker, for its shape alone is agreeable and inviting). They contained, as usual, paper hats, none of which ever suited my grandmother and made her look either like Napoleon on a bad day or a member of the French Revolution en route for Versailles with a grievance. Sometimes there was an exciting box of Indoor Fireworks, for the enjoyment of which Emma brought in a large tin tray on which the various combustibles could be set off and for which, the better to see them, the room lights were again extinguished. There were magnesium flares which sparkled prettily in a twinkling star pattern. There were paper balloons which burst into flames as dramatically as the Hindenburg and then miraculously lifted themselves off the tray and sailed, in blackened ruins, to the ceiling and, after a bit, descended and usually on to something unfortunate – my father's immaculate starched shirt or my aunt's abundant chevelure or, indeed, the crystallised fruits. There were (IGNITE AND STAND WELL BACK) coloured pictures of some shooting scene or other, often a bearded Westerner picking off a Red Indian, and a large X at the rifle tip showed where a glowing match end must be applied, upon which, and with much spluttering and crackling, a line of fire extended from the gun to the fleeing native and reached him with a loud explosion. For these things my grandmother had her fingers in her ears ('Just tell me when it's over, darling') and wore on her mottled face an expression of intense suffering, probably not so much for the victim's demise as for the din of his passing. And sometimes, though these were usually in the crackers, there were Japanese water flowers which looked, being tightly folded rolls of paper, unpromising but which, laid on the surface of a glass of water, gradually unfolded themselves into entrancing flower shapes and colours.

From an early age I loved to laugh and in the field of laughter-provokers it is the serious faces that have often been my downfall. My Essex grandmother was, on her day, a prime chuckler and a great ally but she had too her glum and sober side. She had also an enormously wide correspondence with various friends and relations on whom life's misfortunes seemed to have crowded in to an extent that even the mildest person would consider unreasonable and it was her custom to read out at the breakfast table the latest bulletins from the different horror fronts. This was danger time for as a child of eight one could bear just so much and no more. There was one particular family ('My poor old Gunstons') who were in a permanent pickle. No 'flu germ avoided them, no rail crash occurred without them being on the train and at the very centre of the disaster. If a Zeppelin (it was first world war time) dropped a bomb, it landed near the Gunstons. The Gunston children caught, with hideous regularity, anything that was going in the way of croup or diphtheria or measles. If Mr. Gunston invested in shares, it was a signal for the bottom to drop right out of the market. We thought that the Gunstons had no more, so to speak, to offer, but no, for the eldest Gunston son had married and himself begat a series of children, all of them revelling in the family tradition and becoming from birth woefully trouble-prone. Fresh news of them came one disastrous morning. The first child had got rickets. The second child had swallowed a safety-pin. 'And the third child', gloomily read out my grandmother as she turned over the page, 'has a pronounced strabismus'. I did not then know what a strabismus was. I vaguely realised that 'pronounced' here meant that, as a strabismus, it was not to be sneezed at. But it was the sound of the two words together that I found irresistible. I choked on my kipper, burst into uncontrollable giggles and was in deep deep trouble for many days.

And before long I had another bad lapse, though this time I was much less to blame. My grandmother, like many of her age and generation, took a keen interest and pleasure in death in all its various aspects. Funerals provided many an enjoyable sortie. Hardly a week seemed to pass ('Dear old Kate Turner has gone') without my grandmother being seen in deepest black and about to set off, *visage d'occasion* in position, for a burial ceremony. On one occasion my mother and I were bidden to accompany her for we knew the victim ('Dear old Maud Laver') and, having frequently been to tea, thus became suitable funeral attenders. A hired car was engaged, for there was a mile or two to go, and my Uncle Oswald, who laughed fully as much as I did, volunteered fatally to accompany us. Seating himself beside the driver while the rest of us crowded into the dark and stuffy body of the vehicle, he discovered a small roller blind that separated the driving seat from the back and which could be pulled down and then rattled up with a satisfactory whirr and click. Knowing full well the effect it would have on me, he pretended to be a photographer and, using the blind as a camera shutter, kept urging us in the customary jargon to 'adopt a tasteful expression' and to 'look pleasant please' while the blind shot noisily up and down and my grandmother, who had long since assumed her funeral face, became crosser and crosser. This only drove him to further wild excesses ('Kindly moisten the lips and smile') and we arrived at the church in such a state of disarray that it was considered inadvisable for me to be present at the ceremony. I was sent home in the car in disgrace and poor old Maud Laver, who was a dear and wouldn't have cared a hoot, had to shuffle her way into the hereafter without me.

Grandmothers are not invariably known to their grand-children as grandmama or gran or granny or, in some sections of society, as nanny (such a muddle for foreigners to unravel). In many cases informality breaks in and a child's stumbling attempts at 'granny' become the chosen name. I have known of a 'Ginny' and even of a 'Gaga'. We called ours, for reasons now lost in the mists of time, Duzzy, or just Duzz. During the first world war, when we lived in London, the Zeppelin raids were thought to be having a damaging effect on my nervous system (actually, I rather enjoyed them and the Zeppelins that came down in flames at Cuffley and Potters Bar, both fully visible in the night sky from where we lived, were better than even the very finest Indoor Fireworks) and so my kind, anxious parents dispatched me to Duzzy and Essex for a recuperative three months. And once I had got over the traumatic shock of being separated for the first time for a lengthy period from my mother, we had a fine old time and formed a bond of close understanding and love that lasted until her death in the early 1930s.

And there was an instance of my grandmother's extraordinary and Victorian probity. Schooling was not neglected (I was seven) and I attended Miss Billson's co-educational academy, conveniently close, where in due course we began the art of subtraction in mathematics. Bringing home some elementary subtraction sums and puzzling as to whether I had subtracted 342 correctly from 696, Duzzy pointed out that a good way of checking was to add my result, 354, to 342, and see if it matched the original. She then looked very worried. 'Oh dear, perhaps I shouldn't have told you that. It might be thought to be cheating', and she wrote a note to Miss Billson making a full and frank confession of her wickedness. Some of the feeling of anxiety and evil rubbed off on me and, when I handed in my sums next day, I did not like to catch Miss Billson's eye.

My Devon grandmother did not much like me as in childhood I looked so very like my father, whom she positively disliked for was he not the interloper who had come to love, marry and remove her only child, my mother? She tried hard to conceal her distate for me and to sound jovial but her constant references to me as 'the dear child' ('Whatever is the dear child up to *now*?') were acidulous and her unloving eyes told all. She died while I was at Cambridge and it was no sort of surprise to me to find that she had left my brother a handsome four figure sum of money and nothing for me, but then he looked not at all like my father and, by a 365 to 1 chance, had the same birthday as her and could therefore be merrily referred to as 'my twin'. When as children we stayed with her, my brother and I shared a bedroom and sometimes she tried, while kissing us goodnight, to smuggle a sweet to him but not to me. She managed it so poorly that I always knew and at the age of six such exclusions go deep but I am six no longer and can provide an indulgent view of these matters. And as to sweets, I can now take them or leave them (usually the former).

However, I am grateful to her for one thing. She was a generous giver of presents and was good at choosing books that a child would enjoy – *Moonfleet*, *Treasure Island*, *Kidnapped*, the *Just So* Stories, and so on. Very early on she gave me, partly as a joke, *Little Arthur's History of England*, which I much liked and which is still worth, except for serious historians, a glance.

It kicks off with 'You know, my dear little Arthur, that the country you live in is called England', and we build from there. It is the work of a Lady Callcott and was first published by the wholly admirable John Murray – then, as now, of Albemarle Street – in 1835, the numerous further editions being steadily brought up to date, the copy I have forming the 1924 one and featuring as its frontispiece Their Majesties George V and Queen Mary, looking suitably solemn and in fullest Coronation rig and fig. Whether the subsequent additions, year by year, were still the work of Lady Callcott who, by 1924, must have been pretty long in the tooth, who can say? Certainly no other name claims any credit. *Le style*, thoughtful old de Buffon tells us, *est l'homme même* and one can detect not the faintest variation in her ladyship's style, a gracious mingling of serenity and simplicity and condescension, in the post-1835 sections and so perhaps she kept at it to the end.

Where, one so wonders, did she bone up on the facts of this vast historical panorama and what, one asks oneself, were her sources? Her judgments were, I fancy, all her own and she is fond of using just the one adjective or short and crisp phrase, often of a somewhat dismissive nature: Richard II ('not well. brought up'), James I ('mischievous'), Elfrida ('everybody hated her'), the Scots ('rude and wild'), Elizabeth I ('useful', and who can deny it?), Louis XIV ('grasping'), Queen Anne ('not very clever'), Edgar Atheling ('silly'), Bacon ('not without his faults'). Our authoress is as clear in her mind about the pleasures, apparently available to all, of life in the England of 1835, 'that dear country where God allows us to live and which He has given us to love', as she is about that dear country's very right and proper class structure and divisions. Whether born blue-blooded or blue-blooded by marriage or merely the marital appendage of a baron or a knight we do not know but she comes down very strongly on the side of the nobility. 'Perhaps you wonder, my little friend, if it is of any use that there should be noblemen. I think it is, and I will tell you why'. She does just that, and finds good reasons every-where. Look, for instance, at Magna Carta and King John ('greedy'), and there is a further point of interest: 'As nobles are rich enough to live without working for themselves and their families, they have time to be always ready when the king wants advice'. There now! Those who, with my little friend, were perhaps wondering about their usefulness are fully answered, and it is no surprise to find that nobles have 'next after the king, been the people we have loved best and who have done us the most good'. You see? And to banish any lingering doubts in Little Arthur's mind (he may, after all, have seen some nobles who were possibly being a little bit less useful than those in Lady C's orbit), she adds the reassuring words, 'When you are older you will understand this better'. Oh good!

My Devon grandmother's grim attitude to life never varied, even when away from home and on what might be loosely termed an excursion. It used to be possible a few decades ago, and perhaps it still is, to make sea-trips from the North Devon resort of Ilfracombe to various ports on the coast of South Wales in the Pembroke and Carmarthen areas. The boats that plied this forty or so mile passage were small and were always referred to as pleasure steamers, but the Bristol Channel was at that point more or less the open sea and choppy conditions and unpleasant swells meant that pleasure often swiftly left the helm and gave place to cries of 'excuse me, please' and hasty rushes to the rail.

My grandmother dreaded sea-sickness and in those pre-Kwell days the only known remedies were prayer and dabbing the temples with eau-de-Cologne, one as totally ineffective as the other. However, wishful to visit relations in Tenby, she once ventured courageously forth and was blessed with a calm sea and a radiant day. Having spent her entire life, when not in church, in vicarages, she could effortlessly recognise a vicar-age-reared girl when she saw one and she made friends on board with two Bishop's daughters, saintly sisters consider-ably younger than herself and in their early twenties. She wrote to tell my mother, by then married and fled the nest, of this inspiriting rencontre, detailing the girls' charms and their seri-ous, sober approach to life, for one never knew when a good example might not prove valuable, my poor mother being sometimes considered insufficiently serious and sober (in the sense of 'sedate') and getting herself frequently and reproachfully referred to as 'Miss Gadabout'. There was, alas, in my grandmother's letter one regretful and revealing sentence. It came at the end and after the recital of the girls' virtues, and it just said: 'But so sad – they had no work'.

By this melancholy statement my grandmother did not mean that neither of them was a trainee typist nor an apprentice coiffeuse nor preparing for a career in electronics. She was merely referring to the fact that fingers that should have been busy were idle – not a piece of embroidery in sight nor any intricate crochet-work. No knitting. No nothing. Dangerous, very. Victorians such as my grandmother always assumed, along with dreary old Isaac Watts who left us in 1748 and not one moment too soon, that Satan finds some mischief still for idle hands to do. Further Watts gems of an equally depressing kind include 'There's no repentance in the grave' and 'Hark: from the tombs a doleful sound'. We know that he wrote the stirring 'O God, our help in ages past' but that little number never seemed to me quite enough to offset the militant and insistent gloom. Not a fun person really.

Considering how deeply unfun-loving my Devon grand-parents were, my mother really did very well merely to survive their influence, let alone to become such a whole-hearted enjoyer of almost anything that promised laughs and a merry approach to life. They were both, of course, Victorian and my grandfather was a clergyman. Repton and Trinity College, Cambridge had had charge of his education and each had plainly skimped its work and had missed out on the lighter side of life. My grandmother, as was then customary, followed him in everything and took her tone from him. She knew nothing of Women's Lib and would much have disapproved of it if she had. They were kind to me for, I suppose, my parents' sake but it was clear to me from an early age that they disapproved of my smiles and gurgles and shrieks. They suspected me, and quite rightly, of being frivolous and of giggling during family prayers, a daily event at which my Cousin Madge was usually present unless she could invent a cast-iron excuse for absenting herself from the devotions and she made it her business, when there, to make me laugh, never anything of a task. She squinted, she made moustaches out of pieces of her hair, she raised her eyes to heaven, she pretended to nod off, and I loved her greatly. Morning prayers were after breakfast, and break-fast, interminable like all their meals, was at 9 a.m. It was 10 before the last lesson had been read (on bad days my grand-father embellished the text with reflections of his own) and the last prayer had been said and we rose, absolved and shriven and gone in the knees, to our feet to find the best part of the morning vanished.

Particularly distasteful to my grandparents was my passion-ate love of the theatre and of entertainments in general. This, as everybody knew, was the road to hell fires and damnation. Once when they came to stay with us in London, I proudly displayed my model theatre and announced myself as being graciously ready to perform for them the first act of Peter Pan. I had acquired some smallish doll-like figures about three inches high and these I hoisted about on string during the flying episodes in the Darlings' nursery and although, after she had completed some rather daring aerobatics during rehearsals, Wendy's head had come off and she had done a belly-landing, her head had been stuck on again with Seccotine and she was quite ready to resume her role. But the invitation to this stimulating treat was not accepted ('Some other time, dear . . .').

My mother was able to throw some light on this profound disapproval of theatricals. In about 1907, my grandparents, staying with, of course, clerical friends in London, were taken, apparently without being consulted or given a chance to protest, to a performance of a popular farce called *When Knights Were Bold*, one of those side-splitters in which the main character goes to sleep and wakes up several centuries earlier. Ever conscientious in my researches, I have before me the number of the *Play Pictorial* which dealt at the time with this lively piece and it is plain, from the photographs and snatches of dialogue, that it was a real stinker. The program-me, reproduced, reveals that in Act I (called 'Forty Winks') we are in Beechwood Towers, home of Sir Guy de Vere, Bart, who drops off after dinner. Then '710 years pass backwards' and we are on the Beechwood battlements ('A Dream of ye Goode Olde Times'), with Sir Guy still in modern evening attire and surrounded by knights in armour yelling 'By my halidom' and 'Yield, caitiff, yield'. There are jokes ('When is yonder door not a door?'). There is a terrible jester in cap and bells who keeps banging people on the head with his bladder.

Having nothing at all to compare it with, it can hardly have been the absence of merit that so upset them. Possibly it was the jokes, but in the main it was, I suspect, the actresses flaunting themselves, either as the beautiful Lady Rowena Egginton or as the comical Kate Pottleberry. A Baronet is never to be sneezed at and in Act I the ladies, five in number, cluster round Sir Guy ('On me life, you're spoiling me!'). One of them was a tomboy and not averse to hauling up her skirts (it was, after all, the twentieth century) and displaying legs. Can my grandparents' reckless hosts have sat them, I wonder, in the stalls, Row B perhaps, with everything so terribly close and so visible? Wherever they were sitting, their shudders must have rattled the seats.

My grandfather was a good bit nicer and kinder than my grandmother and we were all very astonished when, one rainy winter's day in about 1922 at Ilfracombe, he volunteered to take us all to the cinema, a suggestion that so unnerved my grandmother that she pleaded a splitting headache and retired immediately to a darkened room. Neither of them had ever seen a film and the nearest that they had ever got to anything of that sort was an illustrated lecture, with magic lantern slides, of the Holy Land. Perhaps my grandfather thought that it would be the dear old Holy Land all over again but in movement, with camels sloping along the skyline and heavily draped ladies filling pitchers at wells. It was not.

The chosen film was called *Orphans of the Storm*, the storm in question being the French Revolution and the orphans of the title were portrayed by two great stars of the silent screen, Lillian and Dorothy Gish. I recall a moment when the two young girls, standing in a Paris *rue*, got splashed with mud by the wheels of the king's coach, symbolical you see of purity meeting its opposite and hinting at future events. Alas, the main outline of the plot now escapes me but once more my painstaking efforts have produced information, in this case snaps of the affair nestling in that book indispensable to all movie buffs, *A Pictorial History of the Silent Screen*.

It is far from easy to tell from the photographs just exactly what is afoot. There are the sisters Gish just about to step into a coach obviously belonging to somebody of importance and drawn by eight horses (perhaps Louis had an eye for a pretty hitch-hiker and had given them a lift). There is Dorothy looking crestfallen in what seems to be a dungeon, while Lillian had obviously made it to the Court and, smothered in finery and with a large fan, is plainly just off to the Chelsea Arts

Ball. There are crazed revolutionary *sansculottes* revolving like anything and waving scythes, and I do now remember a sensational last-minute rescue from the guillotine, with thrilling close-ups, still then an excitement, of distraught faces, the blade glittering ominously above, Miss Gish (L rather than D – perhaps she had been mistaken for an aristo and rightly so after all that dressing up) in apprehensive tears, and every now and then a cut to galloping horses bringing the reprieve. Would it come in time? But of course. The front rows of the cinema, filled with small boys, broke into tumultuous cheers and my grandfather sat frozen with horror throughout.

It is always fascinating to see a famous professional at work and, in the strange way that things in life sometimes turn out, the chance came for me to observe Lillian Gish at close quarters. Kindly invited to be in the Michael Parkinson TV show, I found to my extreme delight that this goddess, worshipped all those years ago, was also to be on the bill. Well into her eighties and still as pretty as a picture, she was in every way charming and entirely modest, not the most prominent attribute in some stars that I could name, and we sat together while the first Parkinson guest was on, a distinguished film actor and director. We watched him on the TV monitor and Miss Gish at once sat up and clutched my arm. She was not happy about the way his face was lit, or not lit. 'No eyes!' she kept saying. 'No eyes. They haven't lit them enough. It's all in the eyes, you see'. And with memories of her own remarkably expressive eyes, staring in terror when she was trapped on that ice floe in *Way Down East* and drifting ever nearer to the dreaded rapids, one saw what she meant.

The entertainment world, of which I have been all my life an enjoyer and admirer and in which I have been an occasional executant, has played such a big part in my life and looms so large in the pages that follow that perhaps it will be as well to tell at once how I came to be in any way involved in it, a happening which astounded many, not least myself and my family. When, in 1934, I started to broadcast, my initial contributions including a somewhat unusual impersonation of a hearty schoolmistress leading her girls on a botany ramble, my father was very much puzzled. 'I simply cannot imagine where he gets it from', he would often say to my mother at lunch or at dinner. Although I was present in the room, for how else would I have known of his bewilderment, he spoke over my head and as though I were elsewhere or deaf or dumb and therefore unable to take part in the discussion that followed, a discussion largely sustained by my father. My mother, her mind often on other matters, was nevertheless a skilful provider of 'yes' and 'no' in the right places.

The 'it' to which my father referred, and one which bore no relation to the then popular 'it' invented by Elinor Glyn and indicating charm, might have been one of many things, some less reputable than others — my fondness for nougat: my tendency to laugh immoderately — but in fact it referred partly to my enthusiasm for the theatre and the entertainment world in general, and partly to the tiny mustard-seed of professional talent (I had had a demented and devoted amateur theatrical urge almost since birth) that had recently manifested itself and which, taken at the flood, had led me, although a schoolmaster by profession, to a modest fortune with the BBC and regular appearances in what was then known as Variety. The fact that a public school master should have got up to such tricks was pounced on by some of the less serious newspapers and I became the object of some quite friendly publicity, with its attendant misprints ('Arthur Marshall is, of course, a master at a pubic school').

Oundle School, where I was then on the staff, has always been a splendidly liberal and enlightened institution and novelty has been its life-blood. When I nervously approached the headmaster, genial Dr Fisher, for permission to absent myself temporarily from the classroom in order to take part in frivolous BBC activities, he just gave a loud chuckle and said 'But of course you must do it', followed by 'Let's go and tell Isobel', and off we went to inform Mrs Fisher, also a notable chuckler, of this forthcoming aural attraction. They and the school loyally supported me in all such subsequent undertakings and I am eternally grateful. Even when I began to write for the *New Statesman* they did not flinch. Could steadfastness go further?

Meanwhile my father's search for the bizarre family strain that had engendered my 'it' went on. Could 'it' possibly have come from my Uncle Wilfred, whom my father remembered to have had 'long tapering fingers' and who was thought to be 'artistic' but who, despite fingers and art, went to Sandhurst and thence into the Indian Army, rapidly perishing, not from a grumpy tribesman's kukri but less interestingly from typhoid fever? My Uncle Vernon, an unhistrionic figure and all his life a respected Colchester solicitor, was ruled out as being at any point connected with 'it'. What then of my father's third brother, my Uncle Oswald, a clever classical scholar both of Rugby School and King's College, Cambridge and who had, at one time, been a professional pianist? Perhaps the 'it' could be traced to him. My father was a modest man and regarded himself as an unlikely provider of 'it'. It was, probably, my mother who was the source but her family and herself were not discussed, my 'it' being assumed to be a male inheritance.

This boundless theatrical keenness had been fostered by a happy geographical fluke. We lived in Barnes and in a road called Castelnau down which the No. 9 bus bowled on its way to High Street, Kensington (alight for Barkers) and the wild world beyond. Every week-day from about the age of six, I boarded, with others, a No. 9, bound for what must have been the world's most welcoming school, the Froebel Institute, then situated in Colet Gardens, W.14, a school where everything was made both interesting and pleasurable. Soon after the bus had crossed Hammersmith Bridge, it turned right at the Broadway and then passed, on the left, the King's Theatre, well known to the No. 1 touring companies and to many West End performers, it being often then the custom to end a London run with a profitable week at Hammersmith and at the King's Theatre's exact counterpart at Wimbledon. Naturally, I always sat on the bus's left hand side (right hand side on the return journey), the better to read the billboards and to see what was on.

I was in the Kindergarten section of the Froebel and we all took lunch at the Institute, returning home about four o'clock, and it was at these wartime lunches that I formed a deep dislike of lentils. I am not speaking of lentil soup, of which by the time you have put in the stock, onions, carrots, dripping, potatoes, herbs and cream, the least important ingredient (take away the number you first thought of) is lentils. I speak of lentils *nature*, plain and untampered with and as they left their Maker. Even at home lentils had to figure from time to time on our menus so one was never safe from them.

The combination of the foreign words 'kindergarten' and 'Froebel' convinced one of my school friends that all the schoolmistresses were German spies but I was already enjoying the game of 'L'Attaque' and knew perfectly well what a spy looked like (a black-suited male wearing a large and broadbrimmed hat and imperfectly concealed behind a tree). Rightly informed by those in authority that our food, lentils especially, came to us, very bravely brought, over the seas, we sang every morning the same hymn 'Eternal Father Strong to Save' and intended to help those in peril on the sea. One sang as loudly as possible, feeling that it might help more towards the safety of the vital cargoes. And before my eyes there rose a vision of decks piled high with lentils and holds stuffed with the nutritious seeds. Even liners' cabins I suspected of being crammed with the stuff. Had the *Lusitania* perhaps sunk so sadly and so speedily because of lentils? For some time (I was quite young) I associated almost everything that floated with lentils. When we came, in the poetry class, to Masefield, I felt certain that, sandwiched in between the ivory, apes, peacocks, coal and pig-lead, were sack upon sack of lentils. How else to explain their unwelcome proliferation?

I was, I like to think, no greedier than the average child and, luckily for me, my parents both came from families which understood about good food and required everything to be just so. Mint sauce that had been insufficiently sweetened was briskly sent away to be rectified. Steamed puddings were, if necessary, removed and steamed anew. The larder contained great basins of proper home-made stock awaiting its little chance to shine in some sauce or soup. My mother would have been horrified by the modern tendency towards time-saving packet this and that.

Certain foodstuffs were, I was told, 'an acquired taste'. These words were often on my father's lips when he kindly tried to interest me, but at too early an age, in those two palate-teasers, mustard and what was apparently a species of black grit that fell from the bottom of a pepper-mill when gyrated. But other allegedly acquired tastes I immediately acquired without the smallest trouble. The first olive I ever ate, one of those large black ones that should be such a prominent feature of a Salade Niçoise, seemed to me delightful beyond words and I at once moved on to green ones, both with stones and without. The first oyster that ever came my way was at Rules in London's Maiden Lane, a restaurant made even more romantic to me by the knowledge that not only had it sheltered the then Prince of Wales (let in, it was said, by a private staircase) when giving supper to Gertrude Lawrence, lucky him, but also was a stone's, or pancake's, throw from the Adelphi Theatre's stage door where a maniac had once lurked and murdered a handsome actor called William Terriss. As to the oysters, I have ever since envied walruses and carpenters not to speak of East End dwellers of the Nineties whose normal daily diet included a number of these tasty bivalves, washed down with gin, a beverage wisely kept at a price within the reach of all and forming a useful numbing agent for the undoubted miseries of their lives. The first *bouchée* of caviare was mine in 1934 and in a small Monte Carlo *buvette* owned by a wildly Anglophil proprietor who, by way of encouraging customers at the cocktail hour to call for and indulge in the bubbly queen of drinks, put up a notice which read SAY ALOUD CHAMPAGNE COCK and, possessed of a pleasing tenor voice of a vaguely Tauberish kind, paraded the tables treating us empire builders to the Indian Love Lyrics in very nearly accurate English ('Pale hands I loved besides the Shali-mar').

Occasionally there was a diversion from work and play and in the first world war, nobody enjoyed a daylight raid more than my Cousin Madge. Zeppelins came only by night, and preferred a cloudy one at that, but aircraft sometimes ventured out by day to attack London and the sight, far above, of those German monoplanes with the curved-back and dovelike wings (they were called Taubes) stimulated her greatly as they circled in the sky. Once when she was staying with us, she volunteered to take me to an 'away' cricket match at Ewell in Surrey. Very mysteriously, I had been picked for a Froebel XI and I can only think that half of the school was ill and out of action. We set off by bus for Waterloo, travelling as usual on the upper deck and sucking bull's-eyes and we had reached Parliament Square when whistles began to blow and the bus came to a halt. We gazed upwards and there, way up and glinting in the sunlight, were aeroplanes wheeling and diving amid puffs of smoke from the anti-aircraft shells. We settled down to enjoy the spectacle, Madge expressing approval with her oft-repeated cry of 'I say, *what* a lark!' and we were much disgruntled to be, after a minute or two, firmly ordered downstairs and into an adjacent basement, missing all the fun. No bombs fell any-where near us and later we were allowed to press on to the station and Ewell where the cricket-match came as a sad anti-climax. Madge, who did not care for cricket, took herself off on a shopping trip and returned, characteristically, with a bag of buns which we happily munched on the return journey. The bus-ride home was rather tame, with not a Jerry in sight. When daylight raids happened when I was at home, I was encouraged to take cover, lying on cushions, under the grand piano in the drawing-room. The idea behind it was that the solid nature of the instrument would protect me from falling plaster and splinters and nobody worried about the fact that a collapsing ceiling might also bring the Bechstein, twanging protestingly, crashing down upon me. But it was a kind thought.

The King's Theatre billboards were a constant pleasure. It was still the days of the great touring actor managers. Sir John ('It is a far far better thing. . .') Martin Harvey, who had spent fourteen formative years in the Irving company, was frequently out on the road with *The Only Way*, alternating it with a fairly sickly Maeterlinck play called *The Burgomaster of Stilemonde*. Sir John was nobly assisted by his wife, Miss N. de Silva, a determinedly evergreen heroine who must hold the record for matronly Ophelias and who was still gamely hitting off that unfortunate girl at the good old age of 51. Sir Frank Benson, who indefatigably if unwisely continued to play Hamlet until he was over seventy, was a frequent visitor with his nursery of young actors and budding talents.

Most exciting of all was the billboard announcing *The Scarlet Pimpernel* with those two matchless hamsters, Fred Terry (brother of Ellen) and his wife, Julia Neilson, and the stage rang with cries of 'La, Sir Percy!' and 'Hoity-toity, Citizeness, what fly stings you, pray?' Their gifted daughter, Phyllis Neilson-Terry, found it a profitable plan to follow, the week after, her parents' tours with a play of her own and the closing words of Fred Terry's unchanging curtain speech became a treasured, and much imitated, theatrical memory: '. . . and please to keep a corner in yer hearts for me daughter Phyllis who'll be with yer next week in *A Butterfly on the Wheel*. Meanwhile me friends, good night, and God bless yer . . . all'. In the short pause before the final 'all', Miss Neilson would, out of the corner of her mouth, mutter the word 'curtain' to the stage manager, and down it would swoop to thunderous applause. What stage-struck boy could resist such fine, rousing stuff?

I first actually entered the King's Theatre in the early Spring of 1915 in order to see *Peter Pan* which, complete with the charming Madge Titheradge, had come on to us after its Christmas run at the Duke of York's. There could hardly have been a more enthralling introduction to the stage's possibilities and for months I thought of nothing else. And that Christmas there was a pantomime, *Sinbad the Sailor* and my first experience of a Dame in the person of Mrs Sinbad, come to say farewell to her son and his boat, the Saucy Sue, and falling about on the quayside ('Drat them bollards!') in a flurry of brightly coloured petticoats and vulgar jokes ('I have no money but my aunt has piles'). Later the action moved to a desert island, with the Porttown citizens now rigged up as dusky natives and where Mrs Sinbad miraculously turned up again and fell over (more petticoats) several times. She also supplied some jokes about coconuts which I, and just as well I dare say, did not at the time understand. The hit song of that war year was 'There's a long long trail a-winding', a poignant enough number rendered for us by a rather elderly male Sinbad, younger performers being usually away at the Front. And quite soon after Sinbad the D'Oyly Carte company arrived and we went three times (*Mikado*, *Pirates*, *Pinafore*) in one memorable fortnight.

By now I was theatrically and for ever hooked and my father kindly added fuel to the flames. He ran an engineering firm called The Pimlico Wheel Works, which was certainly situated near the river in Pimlico and which made, I suppose, wheels. One of his employees had an extra and evening occupation as a stage-hand at the Chiswick Empire, then a thriving music-hall, and it was arranged that one night I should be allowed back stage during a performance. Here indeed was a, to me, enchanted world and I took instantly to that rather weird theatre smell – a mixture of grease-paint, powder, size, fusty clothes, biscuits, sweat, dirt and, I am afraid, cats. I snuffed it all joyfully up. Though the front of the house was nice enough, the stage itself was paradise. I stood at first in the prompt corner but was later allowed to climb a ladder into the flies and gaze down at the acts below on the brightly lit stage.

The performance began, after an overture, with what was then a favourite opening number, a *siffleuse*, a description which looked on the programme more attractive than 'whistler' and which turned out to be a pretty lady in evening dress who whistled her melodious way from one side of the proscenium to the other and then, for an encore, whistled her way right back again. There was a trick cyclist, an 'impressionist' who did imitations of the great French star, Gaby Deslys, and of Marie Lloyd (with lightning dress changes in the wings), a conjurer, a baritone who gave us 'Friend o'Mine' and 'Drake Goes West', and the first half closed with some ballet girls wildly gyrating (I was astounded, then and later in life, by the tremendous din and the thuds that apparently thistledown ballerinas are forced to make and which the orchestra luckily masks). The second half of the programme contained the celebrated Harry Tate with his 'Motoring' sketch and although in the interval I was whisked away, one half being considered sufficient excitement for one day and it already being hours after bed-time, I was not greatly disappointed. It had been enough just to be under the same roof with Mr Tate, whose photographs and reputation I knew, and when we passed his dressing-room door on the way out, I felt, rightly, that I had been in the presence of greatness.

By the time I was about eight, my mother, ever indulgent, had started taking me to theatres in the West End (dear old No. 9 to Piccadilly and then we hopped out and walked, gazing raptly at the theatre photographs on display), and we continued to go right through the 1920s. It was the heyday of what is now scornfully called by some 'the commercial theatre', as though Shakespeare, Molière and Congreve all wrote their plays in the hopes that they would lose money. Theatrical delights were, in those days, everywhere and no theatre was ever 'dark' for very long. In *The Desert Song*, a contented and tuneful Edith Day was being nightly abducted at Drury Lane by the Red Shadow. The entrancing Binnie Hale was enjoying tea for two at the Palace. Noël Coward was on drugs at the Royalty and in *The Vortex*. Sweet little Winifred Shotter, every young man's pin-up, was scampering about in pyjamas and giving little squeaks of dismay in Aldwych farces, and in plays specially written for them and known in the trade as 'vehicles', Marie Tempest, Yvonne Arnaud, Marion Lorne and Lilian Braithwaite were being splendidly funny. The choice was wide.

I became deeply attached to a comedienne called Ena Grossmith, daughter of the famous George who cavorted in musical comedies and particularly merrily as an American sugardaddy in *No, No, Nanette* and we followed her about from play to play – *Tilly of Bloomsbury*, *A Safety Match* (a pleasing Ian Hay piece), *The Rising Generation*, *The Sport of Kings* and so on. She played gawky females of various ages and she had great clarity of voice and a crisp kind of comedic 'attack', the sort of thing that I was later to find in Cicely Courtneidge, who never fluffed a line or a laugh: and every instinct within me told me how vital attack and speed were in comedy.

We went in those days to matinées and we sat in the pit, for which it was necessary to queue. It cost a little less than the Upper Circle, where we could have booked, and the pit had for me the great advantage of requiring, for the best seats, our presence at the theatre a good two hours before the performance began. It was complete pleasure, so keen was I, just to be there waiting, and sometimes there was an exciting happening. Sir Gerald Du Maurier once strolled nonchalantly past us outside the St James's Theatre (we were waiting for his thriller, *Interference*), and Roy Royston did the same at the Pavilion, actually humming a song from the show. *That* was a moment!

There was an agreeable camaraderie among those who queued for the pit (it was long before the days of hiring camp-stools and letting the stool, with your name on it, queue instead of you). Although my mother and I were invariably there first, we were soon joined by other enthusiasts and sandwiches and theatrical reminiscences were exchanged. 'We went to a matinée of *Tons of Money* but Tom Walls was "off" ill, or so they said. Off to Ascot more likely!' 'We were at Gladys Cooper's first night and somebody in the gallery shouted "We love you, Gladys, but you *must* speak up". Well, she does mumble a bit sometimes'. Good manners, I like to think, prevented me from correcting incorrect items of information. 'Let's see now, Marie Tempest is 74 and married to Godfrey Tearle, isn't she? Or am I thinking of Gertie Millar? And they do say that this new girl, Edith Evans, has a glass eye and that's why her face is rather lop-sided'.

Although to go to the theatre was what I liked best, the cinema was an attractive alternative and I remember with joy all the pleasure I have had from films. There was a Hammersmith cinema much patronised by my mother and myself from about 1916 onwards and in those days, films divided sharply between broad comedy and stark tragedy. The half-way house got you nowhere. Silent celluloid transmitted poorly even such theatrical successes as *The Ware Case* and *The Second Mrs*

Tanqueray and films allowed such heroines as Lillian Gish and Mae Murray to be chased round and round a tree or a garden seat by a man either romantically inclined or who had other things in mind.

There was no mistaking which films were intended to be funny and which were not. The titles told all: *Mrs Plum's Pudding, Who Stole Pa's Purse?, Percy Wanted a Moustache* and *Oh! That Terrible Odour!* – these, if you are in doubt, were comic 'shorts'. Fatties were considered hilarious material, particularly Roscoe Arbuckle, bright star of the Keystone comedies who kicked off at 16 stone and whose salary rose with every precious pound of additional weight on which pies, crockery and sacks of flour could disintegrate and explode.

A popular Californian company called itself Phunfilms and physical merriment was everywhere. Deaf old gentlemen struck out with their ear-trumpets, trousers fell off right and left, black men shivered from head to foot at the sight of imaginary ghosts, bulky ladies stepped into deep puddles, bicyclists with fail-dangerous brakes went whizzing downhill and into china shops, and Ben Turpin's crossed eyes, at which everybody roared, were insured for $25,000. The sub-titles kindly kept one abreast of what was toward. Spectral shapes wandering mysteriously about in a dark and empty opera house were suddenly wiped from the screen and the words EERIE DOINGS AFOOT made all clear. Wartime aeroplanes indulging in 90 mph dog-fights high up in the blue were explained by FAR ABOVE THE TEEMING EARTH THEY FLIRT WITH DEATH.

In my youth my mother and father, fine examples of true parental care and conscientiousness in this free and easy world, used to ask around among their friends as to whether a certain film was 'all right' for me and in this way I was denied the pleasures of gazing at 'vamps' and in particular at Miss Theda Bara, though by some mistake I did manage to see her in her first smash hit *A Fool There Was*, which owed itself to a stage play based on Kipling's poem *The Vampire*. Hence the creation of the word 'vamp'. There was rather a lot of Miss Bara and she possessed several yards of jet black hair. Her forte was to gaze white-faced into the camera with what are called 'smouldering' eyes and look inscrutable. Her press agent put it about that, half French and half Arab, she was born in the shadow of the Sphinx but in point of fact she was née

Theodosia Goodman and the nearest she ever got to the Sphinx was Cincinnati. So rapid and complete have been the changes in fashions of beauty that to gaze now at the 'stills' of dear Miss Bara make one wonder whether she hasn't perhaps wandered across from Phunfilms.

From 1906 on, when they started married life in Barnes, my parents were keen theatre-goers and used, in the 20s, to speak warmly of what was by then the old-fashioned type of musical play with a middle-European setting – *The Merry Widow* (Marsovia), *The Balkan Princess* (Balaria), *The King of Cardonia*, with its hit song, 'The Wind of Love' – and as these were frequently revived by amateur companies, I was able to get a good idea of them and enjoy them too, though perhaps in a slightly different way. I was always very fond of the scene, set well down-stage to enable the glories of 'The Boldonian Market Square at Festa Time' to be erected and hung behind, in which the Grand Duchess Zaza, a lot of whose dialogue relied rather heavily on the letter 'z', summoned to her boudoir ('Zit down, *ma petite*') pretty little Melodie Metterling. A heroine has to be called something and the name Melodie alerted the public to the fact that she was, and quite soon, going to sing. One usually found that Melodie had rashly lost her heart to Igor, a penniless strolling musician (a Prince in disguise) with a fine tenor voice and the two best numbers in the play, 'The Way of Man with Maid' and a robust drinking song, 'Drain We Our Bumpers'.

The Grand Duchess 'seeks to dissuade', as the programme note had it, Melodie with the sort of dialogue that went 'Zis young man, Igor, vot do you know of eeem? Zese young men, zey are all the same. Zey lov you for a day, zey take vot you 'ave to give, and zen POUFFE, zey are gone'. Let me hastily explain that the explosive word POUFFE was constantly on the lips of middle-European Grand Duchesses and was accepted as indicating somebody or something that had suddenly vanished in a cloud, or puff, of smoke. The Duchess then croaked out her only number, a rambling account of her own disastrous love life and called 'Zere is Nozzing Left', after which there was a partially successful black-out in which dim figures darted on and removed Zaza's chaise-longue. Then the lights came suddenly and excitingly up and lo and behold, we were in the Market Square with crazed Boldonian villagers rushing in, singing violently and jigging vigorously up and down in a manner that could only be called unbridled. But it was, after all, Festa Time.

As time went on, my urge to become part of this magical entertainment world became fairly uncontrollable. Although I took every opportunity of acting in amateur productions at school and at Cambridge, it was the real thing, proper professional stuff, that I hankered after and by a strange chance it was, of all unlikely people, Angela Brazil who provided a key to the door. From a relatively early age I had been an ardent admirer of her girls' school stories. Miss Brazil had, of course, no comic intention when she started, in 1906, to write her books but I found them hilarious and I discovered, when I read out passages to friends and aimed to share some of the fun with others, that audiences were receptive and ready to smile and, even, laugh.

As an illustration, may I briefly outline for you a work from Miss Brazil's great Middle Period. The choice is wide but I suggest we have a look at *The Head Girl at the Gables* and note the gasps of astonishment that greeted, on the very first day of that autumn term of 1917, the announcement by Miss Kingsley that the head girl at this popular seaside school was to be, of all unexpected people, Lorraine Forrester. Competition for the coveted post had been pretty fierce. Although both Nellie Appleby and Audrey Roberts were considered to be in with a chance, the odds-on favourite had been Dorothy Skipton, even despite the fact that Miss Kingsley had 'several times caught her cheating', a crime which, one would have thought, ruled her out completely. Strongly fancied outsiders were Patsie Sullivan, Claire Bardsley (a name rich in ecclesiastical promise) and Claudia Castleton: but no! Lorraine ('very reserved' and huge brown eyes) it was, and the pulsating events of the term, and with Britain in dire peril, entirely justified the Headmistress's inspired appointment.

For it was Lorraine who 'focused her full mind on the Gables' and revived the Nature Study Union and the Jack Tar Club, the latter wisely involving contact with sailors only at a distance and in the shape of knitted garments sent by parcel post to Portsmouth. It was Lorraine who, diligently collecting ferns for the botany class, wandered by mistake into a forbidden Military Zone and got herself arrested by a special constable ('I shall report you'). It was Lorraine who 'kept slackers up to the mark', chivvied Juniors in the cloak-room ('Mona

Parker, put on your boots at once') and who, picking yellow ragwort on the cliff top, fell headfirst down the shaft of a disused tin-mine ('I want to forget about it if I can'). And above all it was intrepid Lorraine who unmasked the French mistress, a Madame Bertier ('flashing hazel eyes and carefully arranged coiffure'), as a German spy. The desperate woman spent her time, when not at the blackboard, loading oil-drums on to a U boat in a neighbouring cove and had aroused Lorraine's suspicions by her attitude to cricket ('Of what use is it *toujours* to hit about a ball?'). Could anything be more suspicious?

Miss Brazil always supplied two names, a Christian one and a surname, for her girls and for some inexplicable reason the two names together produced, when applied to a small, pig-tailed and gym-slipped girl of twelve or so, a funny image. One could hardly improve on some of Miss Brazil's own nominal inventions – Gipsy Latimer, Mabel Farrington, Loveday Seton, Tattie Clegg, Winnie Waters, Agnes Dalton – and if, after every name, you added, in bossy and schoolmistressy tones, the word 'dear' and pronounced it 'dee-ah', the effect was heightened. A sentence such as 'Blanche Doubleday, dee-ah, *what* are you doing?' implied that she was up to something forbidden, such as preparing an apple-pie bed for Mademoiselle or, at tea-time, secreting an extra doughnut in the elastic of her knickers.

This then formed the 'it' which so worried my father and which could really only be traced to myself rather than to three innocent uncles or to my mother. Anyhow, flush with 'it', which was merely an ability to see that by imitating the words of another and providing a little speed and 'attack' I could create a comic effect, I set to work. Between 1931 and 1934, not a day passed without my slogging away, either writing or rehearsing them, at my 3-minute schoolmistress sketches, or 'turns' as they were called (I knew better than to risk making them longer). And in 1932 I started to inflict them shamelessly on the public. No Women's Institute gathering or school concert or drinks party or garden fête was safe from my trying-out of at least one of the sketches, and preferably three or four of them (the slightest polite applause and off I went again). I never had, young and ambitious and bumptious as I was, the smallest doubt about their appeal and I must have presented an odious spectacle for visually I could add little to the business and the voice was all. The suffering audiences supplied invaluable experience about where the laughs, if any, came, and how to milk a laugh. There was also the great importance of 'timing' in comedy, though this, like tact in social life, is basically a thing that cannot be taught. It is either there or it isn't.

Desperately keen as I was to succeed, I buried my nose in various books on elocution and found myself at once in a fascinating world of physical technicalities. The writers were for ever encouraging me to open my mouth and, peering inside it with the aid of a glass, to feast my eyes on my hard and soft palates, my tongue, my glottis, my laryngeal areas, and, somewhere at the back, my 'little grape-shaped pendant', or uvula. Moving a bit further afield and in a southerly direction, there was my larynx going excitingly up and down, and my Adam's apple which, nowadays snugly enfolded, has not been on view since about 1948. Great stress seemed to be laid on the desirability of a musical laugh and the texts were thick with 'Ha! Ha! Ha!' on a rising or descending scale, or a hearty 'Ho! Ho! Ho!' right there on the very same note. Speaking was referred to as 'phonation' and the pages bristled with lively vocal exercises ('Hurrah! Hurry! Harry! Harriet!').

The rest of this self-absorbed and conceited tale is soon told. A BBC producer chanced to be present at a Cambridge party where I performed (invited to do so, for once) and soon I went for an audition with André Charlot, a famous London revue producer who had done so much to further the careers of Miss Lillie, Miss Lawrence and Mr Buchanan (undying respect for these Gods forbids me the use of their Christian names) and who was supplying every month on the BBC wireless a 'Charlot's Hour', which was a late-night, as we thought (10 pm), and fairly sophisticated entertainment in revue form, with an orchestra and a small audience. Mr Charlot (we called him 'Guv' behind his back) was kind and encouraging and took a chance on me for two of his 'Hours'. Three years of relentless performing and solo experience stood me in good stead and I got safely through. My fellow performers included Frances Day, Douglas Byng, Ralph Lynn and Nelson Keys, a great star in his day. I had made a start.

The 3-minute sketches were of the kind to sit comfortably on a ten-inch gramophone record and in 1935 Columbia approached me with an offer and I then made five records, which had a small success. The five records required ten turns but by then I had, goodness knows, enough of them ready. For some reason or other, the records had, and to my great delight, a special appeal for the theatrical profession and in January 1938, an invitation arrived from Ivor Novello, first to see his musical, *Crest of the Wave*, at Drury Lane, and then to go to supper afterwards in his celebrated flat in Aldwych, high up above the Strand Theatre. I was accompanied by a charming actress, Norah Howard, and I assumed that it was to be a supper party for six or so but as we walked from Drury Lane towards the flat, which was just round the corner, Ivor said 'Don't be alarmed but I've got a bit of a surprise for you. You see, it's my birthday and I've invited one or two friends. And we'd love it if you'd do your turns'.

The one or two friends turned out to be most of the theatre stars then in London, and among them many special favourites such as Marion Lorne, Dorothy Dickson, Zena Dare, Fay Compton and Miss Lillie herself, and, when I came to perform, Leslie Henson sat, but only literally, at my feet, while over to the right there was a young couple who had recently fallen in love, and their names were Vivien Leigh and Laurence Olivier. Actors make the best audiences in the world for they are generous and sympathetic and they miss nothing. I did three of my turns and then, by kind request, three more. I ought to have died of fright but I didn't, I just felt oddly confident and happy and some hours later I drove home on a cloud of bliss.

Those whose dreams have also come true will understand what follows. To be accepted as one of them and to be made much of by those whom I had so long admired was too great an emotional moment for me, and when I got into bed I was shaken by sobs and wept my heart out till dawn.

SCENE II

'We Are But Little Toddlekins'

I have sometimes wondered, though I never liked to ask them (it might have sounded ungrateful and unappreciative), just what considerations led my parents in 1916 to choose Stirling Court on the Hampshire coast as a prep school for, first, my brother, and then for me. Was it the proximity to the Solent and the bathing facilities? Was it the fact that the school specialised in entries to Osborne and Dartmouth and thence into the Royal Navy, whither my brother was bound until it was discovered that he was colour-blind? Whatever their reasons it can hardly have been the accommodation and food that swayed them. The choice of school was at that time very wide, for the early years of the century had seen a vast proliferation of such establishments. They popped up almost overnight, like mushrooms or, if your recollections are un-friendly, poisonous toadstools. Anybody who felt like it could start a prep school. You just bought a sizeable country house, thirty or so iron bedsteads, a few blackboards, engaged a staff (the one at Waugh's Llanabba Castle was a good bit less grotesque and improbable than might be imagined) and started in. Much depended on the personality of the headmas-ter and I think that my parents must have been greatly taken with that of the Stirling Court one – a jovial and captivating Scot, brilliant at teaching English and with, behind him, a record of solid scholastic achievement. Although his deafness was apparent to all, it cannot have emerged at their interview that he was also frequently awash with his country's national beverage, had very few years to live and, as regards supervising and disciplining his staff, had decided to let well alone.

My mother and father wisely thought that, before I went to a prep school, a year or so of a more formal education was a necessity for hitherto my schooling had been delightfully informal. The English branch of the Froebel Educational

33

Institute was founded in 1895 and its Kindergarten came constantly in for quite a lot of cheerful (and I suspect, envious) chaff, a Professor Graham Wallas writing:

> We are but little toddlekins
> And can't do much, we know,
> But still we think we must be nice
> For people love us so.

My two years there were an enchanted time. I remember no punishments, no rows, no squabbles. We seldom sat at benches or desks. Our schoolmistresses never frowned at us. All were sunny and in this happy and harmonious paradise we sang, we painted, we made cardboard models, we stuck chestnut buds in jam jars, we acted *Hiawatha*, we became Knights with shields and swords, we kept animals. We skipped on fine days and bowled hoops (and wherever have hoops gone to?). There were puppets and a water-tank and a revolving summer-house and a sand-pit for extreme toddlekins. There was a library (somewhere along the way I had learnt to read) and we were encouraged into it. One absorbed a great deal and almost without realising it. The building itself lacked beauty (it is still there) but we hurried to it in the morning with joy and left it at tea-time with regret.

My more formal education was undertaken by Miss Wright, headmistress of Ranelagh House looking out over Barnes Common, the common itself becoming at dusk an educational eye-opener for the older student. Miss Wright herself was a scholastic all-rounder who dispensed English, History, Latin, Geography and Scripture. She also taught me the piano and struck me with a pencil rather painfully on the knuckles whenever I played a wrong note. The obvious result? Nerves, and more wrong notes. Naughty of her, really, and deserving of one of the bad conduct marks which she herself distributed so lavishly. Maths and Algebra were in the capable hands of Miss Barrow. There were Gymnastics and Art and French (Madame Croxford).

We acted a great deal. On one occasion I had secured for myself, doubtless after a sickening display of ingratiation, the leading role in a playlet set in a doctor's consulting room but on the day of the dress rehearsal I was found to be, in the then popular phrase, 'running a temp' and was packed off to bed.

My mother informed Miss Wright by telephone of this major theatrical calamity and Miss Wright, in the spirit of 'the show must go on', rallied strongly, saying dramatically, 'Aubrey Pilton will take over Arthur's part but, Mrs Marshall, it will be *Hamlet* without the Prince'. This greatly amused my mother and for some days she called me 'Your Royal Highness', a joke which much mystified my father. But then such a lot did, not least my brother's and my references to Nanny's buffers. We were keen on railways and trains and Nanny's ample breasts seemed to us to be very similar to the buffers at the end of a siding. We were allowed, when she was pleased with us, to make loud steam and clanking noises and, pretending to be a goods engine, run with a thud into her buffers (what a feast this revelation would provide for a psychoanalyst). But to my father the word 'buffers' meant principally rubicund old gentlemen and some glorious confusions and muddles resulted ('Who on earth are these old men of Nanny's? Ought you perhaps to speak to her?').

Ranelagh House was co-educational and I formed a firm friendship with a charming girl called Mary White (she appeared, to my great delight, in my *This Is Your Life* and in a trice the intervening years, all sixty-five of them, sped away). Mary and I were in great demand as child reciters at Barnes charity concerts for some worthy cause (the war was reaching its climax). Our best piece, kept for the end, was Kipling's 'Big Steamers', done in the form of question and answer. 'Oh where are you going to all you big steamers?' Mary piped and I, dressed in a sailor suit, at that time quite an ordinary item of attire for a male child, supplied the answers. At the end of the poem, we bowed, hands on stomachs, to deafening applause. Mary then reluctantly left the stage (I never had to push her off but would have been quite ready to do so) and I then threw myself into a violent horn-pipe dance, taught me by Madame Croxford and with Miss Wright herself at the ivories. I rather doubt if the Barnes town hall had ever witnessed a more revolting spectacle. More thunderous applause and, on a good day, a box of chocs as a reward and a playful nip from the Vicar.

I had, I regret to say and disgusting it was, begun to bite my nails and I bit them, as I did everything in those vigorous days, whole-heartedly. When I complained one day to Mary that I had unfortunately come to the end of my nails and could find nothing more to bite, she sportingly offered me hers, which were long and invitingly biteable. I gratefully acknowledged the generous gesture and we repaired at once to Ranelagh House's sole lavatory and took a seat and I was just about to start biting when we were discovered by Miss Barrow. A tremendous fuss was made, it not being immediately apparent to adults that our combined presence in the lavatory had a more or less innocent explanation. Miss Wright was informed and I was given a bad conduct mark, which meant that in the end of term report my normal 'Behaviour. Excellent' was watered down to 'Behaviour. Very good'.

Mary gave me my first experience, though I did not know the verb until many years later, of gate-crashing. I had been invited by Denis Hovenden, a doctor's son, to take tea with him after school in their rather grand house (hard tennis-court, large garden, loggia) near Barnes parish church. Off we went, satchels swinging, only to find that Mary had tagged on in a determined manner. 'Mary, you have not been invited' Denis said at intervals, while I provided from time to time a discouraging 'Go *away*, Mary!'. However, the intrepid girl pressed on, got herself invited in and ate several éclairs. She landed, I am very happy to say, in terrible trouble later for not having gone straight home. The Hovenden family were to me an exciting household for the eldest girl, Valerie, was an actress and managed, in due course, her own little theatre just off St. Martin's Lane.

In the spring of 1920, I was told by my mother, and it was to me deeply unwelcome information, that we were to leave Barnes and were to build a house, and then live in it, at Newbury, a place of which I had never heard: 'fifty miles from London' it seemed, and remote indeed. My father's sphere of usefulness at the Pimlico Wheel Works had ended – one pictured countless locomotives and lorries fully equipped with his delightful wheels, their drivers bowling happily along in complete confidence – and he was now to operate in the vast paper mills that were going up at Thatcham, the next station to Newbury, and which still reveal a hive of industrious activity as the train flashes past them on that dear old Great Western line. My mother's kind reassurances that this would not mean the end of my London theatre-going gave some hope for the future and she herself, born with green fingers, was very contented at the thought of a much larger garden and country pursuits. She became very fond of point-to-point races and, oddly for her, hunt meetings and attended both on her bicycle, following the chase when the roads permitted.

And so, in the summer of 1920, I had two geographical upheavals, swopping Barnes for Newbury and Miss Wright's school for Stirling Court. A passing illness, probably of nervous origin, prevented me from joining my brother on the special train at the summer term's beginning. It went, as did so many, from Waterloo, preparatory and public schools being then able to order a special train to go anywhere and at any time. That, and not this, was 'the age of the train' and those silly advertisements are misleading. I had therefore to be inserted into the school a week late, no advantage at all, and I was taken by my father and by car. Over tea with the headmaster (there was quite a nice cake but I could munch nothing) the well-known clichés poured forth: 'I've brought the young man . . . soon find his feet . . . we'll keep an eye on him . . . nothing to be afraid of', only one of the clichés being correct. When my father left me and I was alone, fear in various forms was instant and homesickness was for a time a daily misery. Fortunately I knew better than to be seen blubbing. One had to wait, and there were others who waited too, until the night was well advanced and the more stout-hearted 'fellows' (our word for them) were fast asleep.

There are some jokes and comical occurrences that with me (and it must be an indication of something deeply unsatisfactory and feeble in my so-called intellect) simply increase, with every repetition, their power to please and among them I include the memorable visit paid by Lord Berners to his old private, or prep, school. He had been extremely unhappy there, as were all his fellow schoolboys, and as a result he had not been near the place since he left it, but he decided after many years to go back and have a look. There it all was, just as he had remembered it, with its buildings, extensive grounds and trees. However, as he strolled about he was at once struck by something strange that had certainly not been there in his day, namely an astonishingly happy atmosphere, with laughter to be heard and smiling faces to be seen on all sides. An air of frivolity was everywhere, and he then discovered that the school was a school no longer and had now become a private lunatic asylum. Many would find the metamorphosis in no way an elaborate one.

Wishful to stir memories, many of them quaint, and chancing to be passing through the district, I too paid a visit recently to the original site of my prep school (it has long since moved and had indeed, during the war, to shift its ground for defence reasons to inland and more suitable premises). In my case, however, very few of the past splendours were still to be seen. The main components, three red brick houses connected by corridors, still stood although the linoleum-clad corridors themselves had vanished and the houses had returned to being private dwellings. Gone was the gymnasium and with it the terrifying ladder, hung at what was for us a dizzy height and parallel with the ceiling and along which we had to progress hanging from our hands, an athletic achievement for which I have so far found no use in life, though it is still there when needed. Gone was the odoriferous boot-hole where a dear old overalled smiler called Bob uncomplainingly cleaned our shoes, when not stoking boilers or scattering tea-leaves prior to sweeping dusty floors. Gone was the large and hideously corrugated-ironed Recreation Room, known to us as 'the rec' and in which we relaxed after lessons, tried to recover from lunch, wrote letters, acted plays, read and squabbled and fought and dodged bullies ('Buzz off, you rotter!'). Gone (or, rather, now incorporated in the house gardens) was the gritty playground which we shared with the headmaster's wife's troop of Buff Orpingtons, discreetly wire-netted in a shady corner and trying to mind their own business but at daily risk from footballs and cricket balls (and how very satisfactorily they squawked whenever one scored a bull's eye). Gone. All gone.

And then suddenly, and miraculously still present and probably now used for housing gardening implements, I spied the shed in which we used to store our tuck-boxes, iron-bound wooden contraptions marked with one's initials and an absolutely indispensable part of pre-war boarding school life. They travelled from home to school by Luggage in Advance, a railway facility long since disappeared, I presume, accompanied by our large trunks, all of which were unfailingly delivered, no matter how remote the school, on the first day of term. The trunks, containing six pairs of almost everything and a Clothing List ticked off to prove it, were unpacked by Matron, gently perspiring in a giant cloud of tissue paper. We did the tuck-boxes.

As the term progressed and as the tuck-box emptied, which was pretty rapidly, for the school food lacked that really solid and satisfying quality so seldom present in prep school kitchens of the period, while the Buff Orpingtons' globular contributions seemed largely to be eaten elsewhere (it was known as the Private Side), the box got filled up with other things – killing-bottles in which netted butterflies breathed their last and pathetically fluttered out their little lives, and empty shoe-boxes in which caterpillars did whatever it is that they were programmed to do and in a smelly confusion of dying vegetation, leaves, twigs and ordure. The people involved in such activities were known as bug-hunters, and Lord Berners (and here we happily go again) relates an alarming incident when the headmaster discovered that some of them, innocently shortening the word 'bug-hunter' and suppressing the 'hunt' part, were heard to be referring to themselves as being keen you-know-whats. A dreadful pi-jaw followed.

It was, alas, at Stirling Court that I first became aware of the fact that adults, in addition to being either male or female, something that one had already grasped, divided up in another important way – those who possess tact and those who do not. On whatever grounds and for whatever virtues the Stirling Court masters were engaged ('Can offer handicrafts'. 'Prepared tackle "difficult" boys'. 'Said to be good mixer'. 'Some knowledge Hindustani'), tact was manifestly not one of them. At home I had become well aware of what constituted tact (my mother was an effortless practitioner) and its absence jarred. School instances abounded and I mention two of them, both of which seemed to me needlessly cruel.

Although by no means all of us were university-bound, we took for some reason an enormous interest in the Oxford and Cambridge Boat Race which greatly cheered up the end of the Easter Term, the school being roughly divided between light and dark blue supporters. We gazed admiringly at the snaps of them visible in newspapers and endlessly discussed the crews' rival chances. On the great day and in those pre-wireless times, it was difficult to come by an early result (intolerable to wait until next day) but the village post-mistress obligingly got busy on her telephone and posted up the outcome in her window, the thrilling news being collected by the sports master and disseminated to us, eagerly waiting in 'the rec'. And on this sad occasion, in he came and loudly announced 'OXFORD'.

There were deafening cheers from the dark blues, but then, to their consternation, he added with a smirk the fatal words 'HAS LOST'. Cries of disappointment and several boys in tears. It was, I suppose, meant as a joke ('Said to have witty personality'), but those horrified faces are with me still.

Another time, the mother of a boy called Parfitt and who lived locally announced a tea-party and bean-feast in her garden, an invitation extending, it was supposed, to the entire school, 64 strong. But then news came that, quite understandably, she could only, supplies of crockery, etc, being what they were, satisfactorily entertain about two dozen of us, the happy guests to be selected by Parfitt. It would have been possible, one imagines, to put up a list of those invited so that those unchosen could go away and blub in private. The method of selection favoured by the headmaster, however, was to line us all up and instruct Parfitt to walk up and down the rows, touching on the back those chosen. The suspense was unbearable among sheep and goats as Parfitt went to and fro. Faces drained of colour and tears were not very far away. Could anything have been less tactfully handled? You'll want perhaps, and in your kind way, to know whether I was chosen. Yes, I was (I had been sucking up to Parfitt in an odious manner for days) but here again the gasps of disappointment still ring in my ears.

Never imagine that children don't notice and remember everything. Our old chum, the poet Burns, had a phrase for it. 'A chield's amang you taking notes'. And, as you see, not always very nice notes, either.

If I seem to harp a little more often than is, perhaps, acceptable on life as it was lived in the early 1920s at my prep school, (proprietor, J. Macdonald. No fee-paying pupil ever refused admittance), it is because to have been removed from home at the age of nine and placed in cheerless and outstandingly unsybaritic surroundings was a traumatic experience that will be with me to the grave and beyond, if beyond there be. Macbeth who, when in the mood, could come out with some quite good things (thoughts on tomorrow, for instance), remarks on his very first entrance that he has never before seen so fair and foul a day. Plainly he was not educated at Stirling Court. There, sharp and rapidly changing contrasts of grief and joy, sunshine and shadow, pain and pleasure were the pattern of our every waking moment.

In addition to the ordinary privations and indignities and inadequacies inseparable from a prep school that, disloyal of me though it may be to say so, was not really absolutely in the first rank, there was a quite sensational amount of bullying and when I first went there, the school prefects (six of them, and aged a good old thirteen and a half) were allowed to administer beatings and called themselves the Star Chamber. The beatings were given, not with a cane in the normal manner but with something rather worse. Further along the coast there was a seaplane base and among the abandoned equipment and bits and pieces that were always lying around, somebody had discovered lengths of stout rubber tubing nearly an inch thick and of an elastic nature, and used, presumably, as some sort of shock-absorber. These were brought home and put into punitive use and managed to be quite extraordinarily painful. Nobody dreamt of complaining and you had to wait to blub until you were out of sight and sound of the others.

Another form of physical torment concerned hair. An older boy would come up and say 'Do you like champagne?' It mattered little what one produced by way of reply ('Yes', 'No', or 'Oh do buzz off, Phillips') for he then seized the pieces of one's hair that would one day be side-whiskers, tugged down on them and said, 'Sham pain' (get it?) and then pulled up on them and said, as indeed it was, 'Real pain'. This witty prank continued at regular intervals until, happy day, one was old enough and large enough to start doing it to somebody else ('Oh do buzz off, Marshall').

Prolonged unhappiness has never been either my lot or my line and gradually one accustomed oneself to the homesickness and to being away from gentle treatment and loving kindness. There was too a compensation in the person of a contemporary, a plump, smiling and fearless boy called Williamson who, when nobody else was brave enough to own up to this or that misdemeanour (madness to speak if undetected), frequently owned up for them, though entirely guiltless, and just for the fun of the thing, and he took subsequent punishment without complaint. A peerless chap. We spent much of our time laughing for our senses of humour ran along parallel lines and there was much in our scholastic life (Mrs Macdonald's Sunday hats, for instance) that seemed to us to be robustly diverting. Excessive laughter was, as I shall shortly be demon-

41

strating, by no means popular with the adults who ministered to us.

We were both, having been extremely well grounded previously, quite good at French. I do not now recall the name or author of our French text books but they, in the sentences they provided, had an old-fashioned ring and one disastrous day when we were in class and in the middle of a lesson, I saw Williamson's shoulders begin to shake (he had, in church, discovered in the prayer book a list of persons whom he was not allowed to marry, among them being his grandmother, and for weeks we had teased him with 'Proposed to Granny yet, Williamson?'). Pushing the book towards me, he pointed to a sentence in a forthcoming exercise and I read 'My sister cannot marry for her dot is but small'. Though we knew perfectly well what a dot, in this connection, was and had been told that no foreign girl could consider herself to be a satisfactory marital catch without a substantial dowry, the form of the sentence sounded irresistibly comical and suggestive and one began to twitch. In due course, we were required to translate it ('*Ma soeur ne peut pas se marier car elle n'a qu'une petite dot*') but it sounded just as risible in French. There was no hope at all of restraining or concealing our merriment and our laughter rang loudly out. We were reprimanded, sent to Mr Macdonald and cross-questioned as to the reason for our laughter. Williamson, of course, told the truth, silly donkey, and we were both subsequently beaten for 'nasty-minded sniggers'. Quite right too. However, to keep our parents happy, such shortcomings were never allowed to be mentioned in our end of term reports ('Arthur has had a good term and is developing nicely'). My father and mother were always ready with a kind 'well done, dear' while I tried not to look smug.

Looking back, I now suspect that the Macdonalds, both of whom seemed immeasurably ancient, were busily saving for their retirement for the school's outgoings had been thriftily pared to a minimum and virtually nothing at all was done in the way of entertaining. There was no Speech Day and no Prize Giving, prizes coming in the form of five shilling postal-orders to spend as we saw fit. No City buffer ever came down and addressed us. Occasionally we ran competitively here and there but there was no formal Sports Day, which might have required a marquee and, for the adults, a jug or two of claret cup. A number of activities were classed as 'extras' and had to be paid for (Hobbies Class: 10/-). None of the masters had, and no fault of theirs, been at a university and there was not a gown to be seen. They came and went, and some of them went in the middle of the term. The teaching of geography and history, both of them such easy subjects to make interesting to small boys, was deplorable. But, taking it all round, I was happy there. French, English and Mathematics were extremely well taught and caused no trouble later on. And furthermore I had something to look forward to, for I was to go on to Oundle, where I had already been taken by my parents and where I had already been captivated, as were so many, by the rosy charm of the headmaster, Kenneth Fisher. At our first meeting, when I was twelve, he assumed a mock look of horror at the sight of me and said, by way of being jovial, 'Oh dear, and when does this blow in?', an extremely unheadmasterly question which delighted us all and we remained firm friends for life. For me, a very happy happening.

At school and in the holidays I was a keen reader and fortunately the library of Stirling Court was well stocked. From such sources as bound volumes of *Punch*, which we also had at home, and the collected editions of the *Boy's Own Paper*, which went right back to its earliest days in 1879, I acquired an unusual hodgepodge of assorted facts, though immense gaps existed and especially in current, or recent, events. At school the only newspaper reading available was a single copy of the *Daily Mail*, taken, I think, for the charming children's animal, 'Teddy Tail of the *Daily Mail*' and loudly competed for ('Bags I!') after breakfast. One was lucky to get a two-minute squint at it.

Some Hull schoolchildren, examined recently on their knowledge of the last war and of Hitler, replied that he had a toothbrush moustache, made a lot of rather loud speeches and invented a political party called the Nancies. Well, yes and no. The Hull pupils did, in my view, rather well. In similar circumstances some 60 years ago one would oneself have fared a bit ignominiously. I knew, of course, about the Kaiser, all bristles and ferocity, who was going to hang everybody from lamp-posts. Then there were those remarkable Bernard Partridge cartoons in *Punch* which often depicted, against a shell-torn background, poor Peace, with the back of one hand across her eyes to shut out the horrid sights and sheltering plucky little Belgium in the folds of her robe, while in the foreground was to be seen a sturdy, female France, wearing a Napoleonic hat and apron and sensible clogs, holding out a grateful hand across the Channel to a prosperous-looking John Bull and saying something like *'Merci, mon brave!'*. A likely story. Further wartime information of a highly-coloured and doubtfully reliable kind came to me from a popular sort of fiction for boys, the rattling good yarns of Percy F. Westerman, author of *A Lively Bit of the Front.* From them one discovered that when not actually at the Front and in uniform, all German men were in England and imperfectly disguised as spies (you could tell them from their 'shuffling gait'), were apt to mutter *'Himmel!'* and *'Donnerwetter!'* when under pressure and were invariably unkind to animals, especially dogs. Need one say more?

Mr Westerman's rattling yarns appeared in the *Boy's Own Paper* (always known to its readers as the B.O.P.), a monthly magazine with an entirely wholesome tone (it was published under the wing of the Religious Tract Society). In it one learnt 'How to apply for a position as a lighthousekeeper', 'How to boil water in a paper bag', 'How to make an electric trumpet', 'What to do with addled hawk's eggs', 'How to catch ostriches' (put on an ostrich feather hood and so 'hoodwink' them, ha ha), 'How to stuff reptiles', 'How to make birdlime' (boil mistletoe berries to destruction) and 'How to keep spiders as pets'. There was a stirring article on 'How I swam the channel' by Captain Webb ('I rubbed myself all over with porpoise oil, dived in and struck out for Cape Gris Nez'), the gallant captain getting sharply stung by jellyfish (French ones, doubtless) and wading ashore to the strains of *Rule Britannia*. Though there was no article actually called 'How not to get into bad habits', the fear of private indulgence was everywhere expressed in feverish editorials. Take cold baths, sleep on a hard mattress, fling wide the windows, exercise vigorously with dumb-bells, turn in dog-tired, eat sparingly ('Fat makes duffers') and, if 'troubled' by sexual thoughts, on no account visit an art gallery. With a final warning about noses falling off, blindness, nervous twitches, insanity, the mad-house and suicide, we could pass on to less fussing matters such as what to do for the best with chilblains, bunions and blackheads.

In the B.O.P. there was, for some tastes, rather too much emphasis on physical punishments in general and beating in particular. There were articles such as 'Under the Rod' and

'Swishing Anecdotes' from the fertile pen of 'Cuthbert Bede', an alias of the Rev E. E. Bradley, the supremely wonky Lincolnshire poet, responsible for an unforgettable volume called *Passing the Love of Women*. There were 'Famous Floggers' (who was the headmaster who absent-mindedly caned six boys waiting outside his study, forgetting that they were intending confirmands who had come to hear him discourse on 'The meaning of the spirit'?). The description of the assembling, twig by twig, of a birch led one to suspect that there was somebody in the editorial office who had a problem.

Most important of all and wonderfully good were the serialised adventure stories, and in choosing their authors (among them, Jules Verne, Henty, Conan Doyle, Algernon Blackwood) the editors knew their business. How thrilling it used to be, reading away safe and snug and warm in bed, to be marooned on an ice floe, to come face to face with a Bengal tiger, to struggle with the sharks of Mauritius, or to fall off a cliff locked in a grizzly's hairy embrace, its hot breath on one's face and its great slavering jaws (see illustration) an inch from one's nose.

A regular and termly excitement was the scholastic intake of nourishment that used to be called a midnight feast, neither of those two words being strictly accurate and for 'midnight' read, roughly, 'twenty minutes to ten'. In the dormitories the lights (mantle-less gas flares) were put out at half past eight ('No more talking'). The food, now concealed in our chests of drawers, had been smuggled up during the day, a dangerous proceeding as the dorms were out of bounds other than at night in case, I suppose, one should come upon a housemaid emptying the slops (hand basins and *pots de chambre* abounded) and, inflamed by the presence of beds, swiftly ravish her, no easy task for a boy of eleven. After waiting in the dark, trembling with excitement and anticipation for over an hour, it certainly seemed like midnight as we furtively lit a candle, spread out the goodies and tucked hungrily in.

The menu of the feast contained but few items that would tempt a truly gourmet stomach but then anybody dotty enough to wait for solely gourmet food in prep schools of the 1920s would very rapidly have starved to death. There were Skippers sardines in tomato sauce, powdered sherbet in small paper bags and sucked up through a hollow liquorice tube, doughnuts, Chivers jellies which were chewed *nature* and in their solid state, ginger-beer correctly served from those charming brown bottles, Nice biscuits and a wide assortment of sweets ('Can anybody manage another peardrop?'). At Stirling Court we had a rather saintly boy called Paish who, kneeling nightly (as we all did) to say his bedtime prayers, remained in confab with the Maker much longer than the rest of us. At midnight feasts, pious Paish used to suggest, and get howled down, that we say grace before beginning, a prudent proceeding which might have got those Above on our side and ensured that we were not disturbed (we seldom were, as it happens) by Matron or any patrolling master.

And where, indeed, were the masters? Paid a pittance, they had dined on their own (and on what?) at 7.30 in their dingy common room that smelt of sweaty boxing-gloves and had then, presumably, retired to the bed-sitters that they inhabited and which were dotted round the small town. And then what? There was no cinema and no wireless and, too poor for pubs, they presumably corrected our exercises and then read a library book or just stared hopelessly at the wall, glumly wondering whether it had been worth emerging safely, as most of them had, from the first world war. 'There's a long, long trail a-winding', the song went, 'into the land of my dreams' (or was it 'unto'?), dreams blessed by, the lyric went on, the melodious tones of nightingales. But there were no nightingales at all in the rather skimpy grounds of Stirling Court, and the dreams were dusty.

As was the custom in all schools, we played every day, except Sundays (walks), some game, or boxed, or ran, or did gymnastics and I once, to my great surprise, found myself taking part in a cricketing 'stand'. In some ways the authorities at Stirling Court encouraged individuality, or perhaps it was simply because they got tired of struggling away, day after day, to make us conform to a pattern, and at cricket many of us had been at pains to acquire a little speciality that was all our own. A boy called Mould bowled sneaks of a really sensational speed and accuracy, varying them with lofted deliveries that appeared to descend from the stratosphere. A boy called Westmore used to pretend to have hurt his ankle and, playing at mid-off, limped quite a bit, encouraging members of opposing school teams to try to snatch a single where no single was (there were no fewer than five Run Outs in a needle match against Fairfields). I regret to say, but truth is truth, that

Murphy, who fielded at point year after year (our positions were never changed) had perfected a range of noises of a kind that I do not wish to discuss and which considerably unsettled prim batsmen from more sedate schools. My special friend, Williamson, was our wicket-keeper and, when called upon to bat, had developed, for use against umpires, a stare so compelling and imperious and disturbing that few ever dared to give him out even though, bulky as he was, he was plainly constantly impeding the straight passage of ball to stump. I freely confess that the cricketing tone of Stirling Court could not be counted among the best.

My own 'thing' was, and I cannot recommend it too highly for those readers who still indulge in our national game, to use the bat the wrong way round and present the triangular side to the ball. The results pass all expectation, the ball ricocheting quite unpredictably, now here, now there, and, as often as not, flying to the boundary to the amazement of all. During the stand of which I speak, I found myself at the crease with Williamson and playing, as so often, our great rivals, Dumbleton Park. Williamson had already survived four confident and fully justified appeals for LBW and one of the umpires had started to twitch nervously (another of Williamson's devastating ploys, anticipating Potter, was to request umpires, and especially after a No Ball, to 'speak up, please!'). On my going out to bat and join Williamson, he approached me and muttered a few words which I dare say onlookers took to be sage advice about which way the ball was swinging, or whatever, but which, knowing him, were probably a brisk run-down of the edible items that he later intended to purchase with his Saturday pocket-money. We then settled to our task, and Williamson's scowls at the umpires (he sometimes asked for an unusual guard: 'Off stump, please') and my wrong-sided bat produced between them 18 runs. This was, to us, a notable total and I expect that in the long winter evenings at Stirling Court they speak of it still.

At Stirling Court we 'did' Genesis in the sixth form (it was probably considered too sensational and disturbing for younger boys) and here Williamson came into his own for he had a splendidly enquiring and, when necessary, slightly dirty mind and was not at all! averse to asking questions, especially when he suspected, and how right he usually was, that the full truth was being, for some adult reason, withheld from him. He had already caused considerable consternation among the teaching staff by insisting on having the word 'whore' explained to him ('an immoral woman who sells herself for gold and I don't want to hear another word from you this lesson, Williamson') and he had followed it up with 'eunuch', which he mistakenly pronounced ee-unch ('a handicapped male person sometimes in the service of an eastern prince and come and see me after prayers, Williamson').

As soon as, in Genesis, we reached the Cities of the Plain and Sodom in particular, Williamson's alert mind spotted that we were not being told All. The story, as watered down for our youthful ears, was feeble in the extreme. Everything hung, as you'll recall, on a secondary meaning of the verb 'to know'. This, we were told by a young and blushing Mr Sinclair, just meant 'getting to know you' and merely indicated a chummy approach – one imagined a sort of exchange of names and visiting cards ('I'm Uz, and this is my friend, Obal'.) But why then the fire and brimstone and why, most revealing of all, these blushes? Williamson kept up a fine barrage of 'But, sir . . .', Mr Sinclair countering strongly with 'Oh do shut up, Williamson!' As soon as the lesson was over, Williamson flew to the school library and searching, in a high state of excitement, through Chambers's invaluable dictionary, found what he was looking for ('To have sexual commerce with') and next day a fresh persecution of poor Mr Sinclair began, by now in deep trouble over Lot's unconventional behaviour in the mountains behind Zoar. 'Please sir, what does 'commerce' mean?' 'It depends in what sense, Williamson. And why do you ask?' And so on.

Among the enticing literary treats that I have either had, through pressure of work or absence of time, to forgo or which have never, as in this case, come within my reach, a novel called *Apples of Sodom* ranks pretty high. It was the work of a woman, a Miss Mary Bramston, it was written about 1870, and she sold the world rights for £20. Somewhere there lurk, presumably, critical evaluations of the work ('Miss Bramston casts a bright and wholesome light on a dark corner of biblical history') but its chief interest lies in the fact that its authoress was, at the same time, governess to the children of those unusually bizarre Benson parents. It isn't every day that the Master of Wellington College, later Archbishop of Canterbury, marries a basically homosexual bride half his age and

48

they then produce between them, in conditions that the sensitive will prefer not to dwell on, three highly gifted and queer sons, among them E. F. Benson to whom we owe the marvellous Miss Mapp and Lucia books, and much else. There was also a homicidal maniac daughter. Believers in predestination will enjoy picturing God arranging all that elaborate little tangle, so very different from conditions at Oundle.

One does so wonder whether the oddities of the Benson background and the tendencies of her charges inspired or influenced to some extent the authoress of *Apples of Sodom*. Who, do you suppose, can be the main character? It can hardly be Mrs Lot of whom vivid details are really rather scarce and whom one sees as a somewhat shadowy and nervous figure, twitching a goodish bit and probably locking herself in a hidden recess while all that clamouring and banging was going on at their door ('Do see who it is, dear. Tell them we've got visitors. If you want me, I'm in the airing cupboard'), though she does of course in the end have her moment of glory as a Challenge to Cerebos. We know much more, rather too much in fact, about her husband and especially his last unfortunate days in that cave, though here his childless and incestuous daughters were much to blame and he, poor man, lying there in a drunken stupor, was literally more sinned against than sinning. None of these persons would, however, tempt the pen of a governess in the saintly public school household of a future archbishop, so the leading figure must have been somebody else. Or do you think that *Apples of Sodom* was in fact a 'modern' novel but with an, er, Sodom theme?

Twice a term, Matron would appear in the dormitories while we were getting up and deciding it was too cold to wash and, looking for her fairly ferocious, handed out brimming mugs of Gregory Powder, an appallingly explosive purgative. And in addition to this, we were all issued (6d on the bill) with an improving little booklet called 'Self Helps to Self and Fitness' which aimed at producing both the mind serene and the body beautiful. After a foreword on the importance of regular habits, the opening sentence of the main body of the work ran: 'On waking, trumpet vigorously to clear nostrils'. 'To trumpet', we learned, meant to snort noisily outwards. The author was a master at the school, a deviate giant who taught French extremely well and added to this ability various unscheduled extras when opportunity presented itself.

Whenever out in the open, he chose to trumpet and snuffle without benefit of handkerchief, finger and thumb to nose. I have seen others do this since and as a spectacle I haven't ever come to love it. With the aid of the Self Helps, we ran here, doubled there, threw this and held that, our minds sullenly unreceptive and by no means serene. We benefited, I don't doubt, bodily but I've never enjoyed being coerced into any violent physical movement, apart from those that come quite naturally such as running for a bus or nimbly dodging cars or playing Scrabble, and since leaving the school (it was 1924) and abandoning Self Helps, I've rather let that side of things slide.

Situated as Stirling Court was, it was natural for there to be a number of naval offspring and among them there was Tony Brand, son of a Captain stationed at Portsmouth. At the beginning of one summer term, he reported that during the hols (impossible even now to think of them as 'Holidays') and in conversation with his father's batman, or whatever it is that naval gentlemen have, he had been informed about a 'word' which was obviously one of deep significance to adults. It was, apparently, a verb but one which could also be used as a noun and as an expletive indicating dissatisfaction on the part of the utterer. If followed by an additional 'you', the word indicated dissatisfaction with somebody else and you arrived at it by trying to say 'Puck' with the corners of your mouth pulled wide with the fingers. Here was a pleasing novelty and although warned by Tony that it was a quite dreadful thing to say, we all immediately gave it a whirl and paraded round the room, mouths stretched wide and shouting the word that was so very nearly puck. It would have been a sensational moment for Matron to appear, waving a thermometer, and indeed our instructor became increasingly agitated, knowing full well that if authority arrived and posed the dire question '*Where* did you hear that word?', he would be forced to own up.

Much was made of Armistice Day and the two minutes silence. Whatever the day of the week November 11th chanced to be, we dressed in Sunday clothes and there was a feeling of dismal expectancy from breakfast on. There was a war memorial cross and plinth, with on it the names of the Fallen, on the front and near the pier and thither we marched in crocodile and in good time to take our places. The vicar and the parish church choir supplied a short service, after which we stood and waited. Eventually an official maroon went off, we removed our caps and bent our heads and looked thoughtful.

It was a trying moment for all, but worse for those, and there were a number, whose fathers or uncles or even elder brothers had been killed. Tears fell, and on one alarming occasion, the opposite of tears. An overwrought boy whose father and uncle had both died had a bad fit of hysteria. Starting slowly, his wild and maniacal bellows of a sort of laughter gradually increased in speed and volume – a dreadful and horrifying sound that chilled the blood. The boys next to him edged nervously away, but nothing could be done until another maroon announced that the two minutes silence (silence!) was over. The school authorities, never slow to criticise and punish, realised that here was a happening best left alone and the wretched boy was treated very kindly and was allowed home for a few days, though whether it was wise to expose him to a probably grief-stricken mother, who shall say? It is a saddening thought that there must still be a number of first war widows living out their solitary lives in, perhaps, parts of London (Sloane Square: Campden Hill: Holland Park) where once rents and rates were reasonable but now are reasonable no longer. Jewelry and the best pieces of furniture and 'Daddy's stamps' have long since been sold and soon the painful letter will have to be written, the one that begins 'Dearest Child, I am sorry to worry you but I was wondering whether you and Philip could find a corner somewhere for your poor old Mum. I would try not to be in the way . . .'

At school it was the custom to celebrate the end of the summer term by treating the parents and any local residents who hadn't been rash enough to accept a previous invitation (silver collection in aid of Dr Barnardo) to an entertainment provided jointly by the school staff and boys. The music mistress, gifted Mrs Wakefield, a resplendent figure in coffee lace, was perched at the upright, candles in holders illuminating her music, and got us off to a fine start with a tuneful selection from *The Gondoliers*, with much fancy fingering and elaborate crossing of the arms.

Then, to a jerky rattling of curtain-rings, the curtains parted to reveal four alarmed treble singers, nearly blinded by the bright, tin-encased footlights and who, by ancient usage, gave us what was always described as 'a traditional English air', quite often *Early One Morning*.

> 'Early one mor-hor-ning
> Just as the sun was ri-hi-sing'.

they warbled, Mrs Wakefield, all smiles, helpfully thundering out the melody.

With that safely, more or less, out of the way, our hearts sank. Again by old custom, item No. 2 featured the sports master, genial Captain Murray, in a baritone solo. For the four years that I was at the school, his song was the same. It told of the open road and the fine free life of the wayfaring pedestrian. I forget both name and composer but it started spiritedly:

> 'When you're jog-jog-jogging along the high road
> With your luck all upside down'.

Nobody could have jog-jogged more cheerfully than Captain Murray. For this melodious piece he wore tattered corduroy trousers supported by a leather belt and became, in a trice, the very epitome of carefree tramphood. With legs well apart and a thumb tucked into the waistband of the bags, he was, pictorially, the school's defiant answer to Peter Dawson. But there it ended. There was no trace of Peter Dawson's splendid rumblings about the Captain's voice. It was thin and scratchy and quite tremendously off key. The more musical boys winced and even Mrs Wakefield, the personification of loyalty, wore a strained look. I longed, though in vain, for him to do well (he had been gassed in the war, which shows which dreadful war it was) and I violently led the applause, anxious about my own dramatic contribution that was to come later.

One summer term, Matron electrified the entire school by coyly announcing that, if we would really and truly like her to, she would recite a poem which she referred to as 'The Daffodils'. 'By Wordsworth', she added, a positive mine of cultured information. She had 'done' it as a girl and had now refreshed her memory and was only too delighted to pronounce herself as being word-perfect.

Her offer was, naturally, gratefully accepted. One had never dreamt that such virtuosity would emerge from behind that crackling white starch, which normally only dispensed iodine, zinc ointment, lint, bracing talk ('I've had quite enough of your nonsense') and Gregory powder, which always sounded to me like a wealthy industrialist ('. . . and now I will ask our

chairman, Sir Gregory Powder, to make his annual report' –
rather a loud bang, I imagine).

With cries of 'No, no, I shall wait for The Night', Matron
refused to reveal her powers at any rehearsal, and so, with
Captain Murray's last despairing wails ('There's no luck
waiting along the high road for a vagabond like me') still
echoing round the hall, Matron, impressive in mufti, made her
stately appearance.

I only wish that I could report a dazzling triumph, with the
local paper, the *Gosport Sentinel*, describing her as 'a second
Siddons' but it was no such thing. She began quite well and
certainly wandered lonely as a cloud that floats on high o'er
vales and hills. She got through the milky way section and
seemed all set for booming out the finale but after 'For oft,
when on my couch I lie', disaster struck. Her voice tailed
despairingly off and she dried up completely. Of course, in
those days we didn't call it 'drying up'. 'Matron's stopped
speaking', we said. Pluckily, but how unwisely, she started all
over again, evidently with some idea of getting a fresh run at
the thing and bridging the gap. She wandered lonely as a cloud
once more, only to come adrift again upon her couch. The
headmaster tactfully led loud applause, Matron had the nerve
to take a bow, and the curtains rattled mercifully to.

By dint of being generally odious, whining all day long and
ceaselessly badgering poor Mr Riches, our compère, I had
secured for myself a solo appearance. My passion to display
myself was quite unbridled and so Mr Riches kindly sent up to
Samuel French for a suitable recitation and back one duly
came. It was entitled *The Single Hair* and described itself as a
Comic Monologue. To this day I can, Heaven help me, remember every word of it (a shining example to Matron). It began
with a strong comedic couplet:

> 'He was not bald, for on his shining cranium
> Remained one hair, its colour pink geranium'.

After several more equally hilarious couplets, the hair falls
off into his soup, is rescued and a taxidermist is called in. And
so to the payoff:

> 'And stuffed, within its case of glass installed
> It shows the world, HE WAS NOT ALWAYS BALD'.

To utter this risible gem, I was dressed in pierrot costume and the applause was tumultuous. Even today, I sometimes in dreams deliver the piece again and frighten myself awake, sweating with the horror of it all.

Although it was very agreeable to stay with the Williamsons and later, during Cambridge vacations, with other families, it was a sadness to me that I dared very seldom invite anybody back. Only very few of my oldest and most trusted friends could, I felt, be safely exposed to the eccentricities that awaited them, for the school friends would generally be deposited by a parent in a car, or a Cambridge friend would arrive in his own car: and cars were the trouble. My father, and for reasons that can only have been comprehensible to himself (who did not reveal them), to God (doubtless already pretty pre-occupied with the other and more important items on His plate) and to Freud (who would certainly have let out an understanding 'Ach ja!' and nodded his old nut off), used to attack motor-cars. Attack them physically, I mean. Not vehicles in busy motion, you understand, and scorching along the Hog's Back at a breathtaking 37 mph, but cars at rest and unoccupied and standing, irresistible targets, within easy reach of the front door of our Berkshire home. Motor-cars in the days of which I speak were by no means the sleek and streamlined roadsters of today. They had detachable lamps, large and bulbous motor-horns, tool-boxes clamped to the running-board, flapping talc side-curtains which combined with the hood to provide draughty protection in inclement weather, and spare tyres nestling in a sort of groove and held firmly in place by substantial leather straps. In cases of really de luxe machines, a speaking-tube looped its way from rear headquarters to the front line and permitted dowagers, cocooned in fur rugs, to give instructions ('Harrods first, Jenner') to their chauffeurs.

My father had discovered that some of these extraneous embellishments would, if given a vigorous enough push, become detached from their moorings and then fall, with a pleasing clatter, on to the gravel of our drive. Tool-boxes sometimes split open and scattered spanners about. Heaven! More fools the owners for not screwing them on firmly enough. Only themselves to blame! But if the various aids to travel all held firm, he would then, to make up for the disappointment, kick the car's tyres and wheels for ten minutes or so. One never knew, a puncture might develop.

Another anti-car pastime, when cranking a handle was mercifully abandoned and electric starters came in, was to climb on board, fail to switch on the engine, and run the battery down. He clearly found the steadily decreasing whirring sound, and the last few mournful chugs, soothing in some way. Friends arriving for tea had to be warned of this little risk (I can think of worse ones) and advised to leave their cars elsewhere than near the house, preferably camouflaged with branches of trees, and pretend that they had arrived on foot. This gave my father an opportunity of explaining to them that they had missed several valuable short-cuts. But at least their cars were undamaged. It was perhaps these little domestic embarrassments, for such indeed they were though I can now recollect them without rancour as in other ways he was a kind man, that have possibly made me on the whole a shade too chatty and over-effusive (a politer adjective than gushing) in my social life and always ready, at the merest hint in a guest of unhappiness or a sad silence or an awkwardness or the faintest trace of worry on a face, to rush headlong in with comforting (I hope) host noises and cries of 'Do I see somebody who can manage another macaroon?'

Another of my father's mild eccentricities was when we went away on holiday and the house was shut up, to close and lock the piano, removing the key. This always seemed to me to be hard luck on burglars who, after they had stuffed our silver and my mother's Persian lamb coat into a large bag labelled SWAG, might want tunefully to celebrate their haul with a few Chopin études or, in more thoughtful and grateful vein, a keyboard setting of *Bless This House*.

During the holidays at Newbury I had made a fairly racy friend of my own age, which was then about twelve. His name was Stanley and his attitude to life was enviably devil-may-care while I was a firm and priggish toe-the-liner. We made bicycle trips together and, if in the mood, he would remove his feet from the pedals and place them on the handle-bars, a difficult acrobatic accomplishment which seemed pointless but which I secretly envied. He also tended to sound his bell ('Oh do shut up!') overmuch. When one day we were planning a longer than usual ride to the far side of Greenham Common, at that time a non-nuclear and agreeable expanse of grass and heather and fern, he suddenly said:

'I'll have to ask Bill and Enid first'.

'Who on earth are Bill and Enid?'

'My parents, of course'.

'But do you *call* them Bill and Enid?'

'Certainly'.

'To their faces?'

'Naturally'.

'Do they mind?'

'Oh yes: they absolutely hate it'.

The mere idea of calling my own parents, at whatever age, Bertie and Dorothy was an inconceivable one. They would have shrivelled up with dismay, and even now I write their Christian names with diffidence. Perhaps parental shudders were what Stanley, a fine example of the deplorable sadism inherent in boys of twelve, wanted.

Our bicycle trips were usually arranged, as with most holiday activities, some time ahead. Stanley lived quite a distance from us and communication had to be by personal visit or by scribbled post-card, all postal items in those days being delivered promptly next morning, or, if the destination was reasonably local, on the very same day. The possibility that one's post-card might not be so delivered never crossed anybody's mind, or needed to. For some juvenile social occasions, printed post-cards were available and merely required filling in with the date of the festivity and its time and signature. There was one which said DO COME TO PING-PONG ON . . . AT . . . and supplied a bare clock face the hands of which you duly filled in (2.30 pm was the popular hour), and to encourage the recipient to accept the invitation there was, in the background, a coloured likeness of a group of rosy-cheeked kiddies smiling winningly and with their bats poised and at the ready. It would never have occurred either to Stanley or to me to ask to telephone to each other. Telephoning in those days was strictly for adults although, in a crisis ('I'm afraid that Stanley has got a bit of a temp . . .'), our parents would have been telephonically helpful. The easy familiarity with which quite young children now call each other up is well demonstrated in a *New Yorker* cartoon. A child of about six is shown comfortably seated on the desk in her angry father's study and saying down the telephone, 'I'm being scowled at. What's happening your end?'

A free-and-easy attitude to parents was not unknown in the 20s and I was to meet it again. My friend, Williamson, who went to a different public school but with whom I kept in touch and visited during the school holidays, had a regal way with everybody, his parents included. To him they became, and from quite early on, 'Percy' and 'Daisy' or, if referred to collectively, 'the Williamsons'. If he felt that he and I were reminiscing too much in their presence about life at Stirling Court (we were obsessed with the question as to whether the headmaster's wife, Mrs Macdonald, wore a wig, and the evidence for and against) he would say, as though they were backward children, 'I'm afraid the Williamsons are feeling a little bit out of it. We'd better try to drag them into the conversation'. We went frequently to the cinema, sometimes with Percy and Daisy and sometimes alone. On the latter occasions he would make all clear. 'We're leaving the Williamsons at home for this one. It's a German film called *Metropolis* and rather beyond your intellectual range, Daisy, so you and Percy can have a quiet little evening *à deux*. Don't get into mischief'. When first I heard this jolly chat going on I was very startled. Would they mind? No they didn't. He was an only child and they worshipped him. Also, he was never either rude or offensive or unkind and they were enormously diverted by this chummy approach.

I was slightly reminded of Stanley and Williamson many years later when Noël Annan, teasing me kindly for being so bourgeois and conventional and mind-the-step, announced that his parents (both of them among the world's charmers) were very liberal-minded and that he could discuss any subject in their presence and even, if he felt like it, swear loudly, a verbal liberation that would have been briskly discouraged at Newbury.

'What swear words would you use?'

'Anything. You name it'.

'Very well then, I dare you to say "Bugger!"'

'All right. I'm having dinner with them this evening in Bryanston Court. I'll bring it in to the conversation'.

On his return, I made haste to ask what had happened.

'Well, did you say it?'

'Yes, I did'.

'Did they mind?'

'Yes they did. They were furious with me. I was almost shoved out of the flat'.

It was very characteristic of his open and generous nature to

57

own up to having got things wrong for once and to have made a donkey of himself.

In my last winter term something happened that was profoundly to influence my life. In the course of a school debate, I said, and plainly by mistake, something or other that made everybody laugh, and laugh satisfactorily loudly and long. I blushed, of course, and I was surprised and delighted in equal quantities. I had suddenly become aware of laughter. What a splendid sound! And I had caused it, however inadvertently. I was anxious for more and since that time I have made laughter a prime consideration in life. I have read books and seen plays whose whole point was to provoke laughter. I have been lucky enough to have friends — and their name is legion — who have provided laughter in full measure. I have sought laughter out wherever possible. My ears are for ever cocked for it. Not a very lofty aim in life, perhaps, but I don't for one moment regret it.

I left Stirling Court borne high on a tidal wave of popularity, a popularity that owed itself, I am afraid, to food. It was the custom there, in your last term, to try to persuade your parents to give what we called a Bust-Up Tea, the main item of which was a large supply of those small little two-bite cakes that confectioners refer to as 'fancies'. They were the customary diet in those tea-shoppes, now largely and sadly replaced by beefburger joints, in country towns. These havens of refreshment often had fanciful names such as Pam's Pantry and ladies, settling down in them after an afternoon's shopping, would just order 'tea and fancies, please', the waitress subsequently arriving with her bill pad and the question 'How many fancies did you have?' The shops also sold highly-priced home-made fudge daintily done up in beribboned boxes..

When my mother and father, to whom I referred to at school as 'my people', came down for half term, I plied them with requests to give a Bust-Up Tea and they rallied kindly and strongly to this nutritional challenge. In matters involving generosity, they always passed every test. There was then in Newbury, and perhaps there still is, a cake shop that specialised in fancies and provided a dazzling array of small pink and yellow and white iced cakes, sometimes dotted with walnuts or angelica and sprinkled, for good measure, with hundreds and thousands and in due course my father arrived with the back of the car piled high with wooden tray upon wooden tray of assorted fancies (excited cries of 'Just *look* what Marshall's pater's brought!'). In addition to this, my adopted Aunt Violet, hearing of the approaching beano and being also an unfailing practitioner in open-handedness, sportingly weighed in with gingerbread and several large cakes of the cuttable kind. Never before had such a vast spread of desirable eatables been seen. I sat, every inch the genial host and graciousness itself, at the head of the table with Williamson, for once struck dumb with admiration, at my side. The Macdonalds momentarily joined us and were persuaded to take a slice of Dundee. Matron, all smiles, was indefatigable at the urn. I was Man of the Match with a vengeance.

I forget, after the feeding of the five thousand, just how many basketfuls of what must have been singularly unappetising left-over fish and bread were gathered up but my tea was equally miraculous and more attractive and we were able to have next day a mini-Bust-Up, a previously unknown feat. To crown all, there was a glowing reference to my feast in the headmaster's end-of-term speech, studded, as was his way, with Shakespearean quotations. I blushed suitably and assumed a falsely embarrassed look for I was far from displeased. And next day, accompanied by trunk and tuck-box, I departed for fresh woods and pastures new.

SCENE III

Willingly to School

It had been decided that I was to go to Oundle in the summer term of 1924, the summer being considered a more agreeable time for breaking the ice, an occupation that was sometimes and later in the year all too literally accurate on our perched-up little hill in the north-eastern part of Northamptonshire (there was said to be, in a straight line, nothing of equal height between us and the North Pole and the winter winds, blowing from that direction, supported the theory). It proved to be a particularly summery summer and I was instantly struck, and it is a condition in which I have remained ever since, by the beauty of Oundle itself and that part of the county in which it so happily sits. It, and the attractive stone villages and churches that surround it (Fotheringhay is but four miles away), make it seem like the Cotswolds only on a smaller and humbler and less hilly scale. And it has the advantage of being relatively unfrequented. Few would ever think of holidaying there. The world, and especially since the construction of so many grand new roads, hurries by quite oblivious of the beauty that lurks so close.

There was, that summer, a further advantage for me. The school was at that time expanding and working up to the creation of another, the eleventh, senior boarding house. This meant that a number of both new and junior boys were being temporarily lodged in the private houses of married masters (I assume and hope that they gained financially) and I and two others were handed over for a term to a biology master, Peter Hewett, and his wife, Elsie, a two-years married couple of great friendliness and by then complete with a brand new child, Sheila. They treated us like members of the family and were in every way agreeable. It was a very unagitating way of kicking off (observe how easily one slips back into the scholastic lingo).

We had our own sitting-room for work and reading and so on, and an airy bedroom on the top floor. Here I remember no homesickness for Elsie was motherly and spoilt us firmly. The housemaid, Jane, awoke us at 6 a.m. (school was not till 7 but the Hewetts also required their bathroom) and, to prepare us for the rigours to come when transferred to our senior houses, we were instructed to have cold baths, which we dutifully did. There had been no cold baths at Stirling Court where hot baths were weekly and communal and supervised by Matron and cold baths there would merely have meant a malfunction in the boiler. I did not at all take to intentional cold baths with their initial and severe shock to the system (one was on one's honour to stay fully submerged, like a U-boat at periscope depth, for a minimum of twenty seconds) and, on scrambling out and drying, I much disliked the sharp and tingling increase in body heat, that process that is known to some as 'glowing', or 'glowing with health'. I did not glow with either health or pleasure. Stuffy one felt. After dressing (Eton collars were a bother but obligatory for the first year), we descended, ate the biscuits and drank the cocoa that Jane had kindly prepared for us, collected up our school books and writing materials ('Lend me your bungie') and directed our shining morning faces towards school.

I truly loved everything. After the confined and manifestly inadequate conditions at Stirling Court, here was freedom and spaciousness and a more liberal outlook. To be allowed to go out of doors when we chose and just walk about was a joy in itself. Everywhere there seemed to be freshly mown grass and flowers. The school buildings were not *en masse* (in this respect, Wellington College always seems quite a bit forbidding) but were pleasantly dotted about in the town and elsewhere. I loved morning prayers delivered by Dr Fisher and the hymn that followed and which gave me a chance to exercise my piercing treble. The prefects were one and all father figures and I admired them enormously. Pettinesses and bullyings were no more. The food was fine (unlimited butter such a novelty!) and as I had in class been placed rather lower than I should have been (Common Entrance nerves had done me down), I found much of the work to be what I doubtless at that age referred to as 'potty'. I won a French prize and another for Mathematics and did not at all mind going up to collect them from the Headmaster at term's end. There was also a fortnightly check on work called Fortnightly Orders, when the top boy in each class or set marched up to Dr Fisher after prayers and handed over the Order and insufferably pleased with myself I must have looked.

As to games, the cricketing 'tone' was altogether better than at Stirling Court and after cricket there was bathing in the River Nene, a placid and muddy stream at which modern schoolboys would doubtless turn up their noses but which for us, splashing and diving and playing about, provided great enjoyment. To be able to identify those boys who could not yet swim and were at risk from drowning, non-swimmers wore brightly striped bathing shorts and were known as Mudlarks until they had passed the swimming test (100 yards up stream, and no toes on the bottom), upon which they became Blues.

In May, 1924, I became 14 and, for the benefit of the curious, I was by now physically altered and embellished and was experiencing surprising manifestations about which I had received no information or advice of value. However involuntary and natural the manifestations might seem, not to speak of the possibility of them being, later on, advantageous, to talk about them to anybody, or even to think about them, would have come under the heading of 'Smut', and Smut was harmful and to be avoided. So one just had to get along as best one could on one's own, occasionally puzzled and startled and guilt-ridden. My parents, always so helpful in every other way, fell down badly on the job, merely supplying disapproving frowns when anything remotely connected with the more interesting bodily functions floated into the conversation. Buttoned up they remained, and so where to turn? Nowhere, was the answer. Fearful as we all were of being accused of Smut, one couldn't begin to ask one's contemporaries how they too were getting along in this particular field. I cannot really say that I worried greatly about it all, for I was not then of a worrying nature, and in the winter term of 1924 I left, reluctantly, the Hewetts and was enrolled in Dryden House.

One of the many risks that one ran as a boy at a really ancient public school was that of being disadvantageously housed, to put it mildly. One did not expect de luxe surroundings but on the other hand there is a point when absence of luxury can safely be called squalor. Dryden House had started life as a coaching inn on a modest scale. Its double doors opened on to a cobbled, sunless, roadway between two lofty wedges of rooms and led to stables and a small, gravelly yard. Little, if anything, had changed from the days when the coaches came rumbling in, and in this very restricted area some sixty boys lived and ate and slept and worked. The tiny, airless and almost lightless changing room in which we prepared ourselves for games, and de-briefed ourselves after games, made the black hole of Calcutta seem by comparison like the Dorchester. The maids and the cook existed in a damp oubliette, in clouds of steam and smells of burnt porridge. For the first two years of life there, one's communal living-room looked out, like that of the Brontë girls, on to the churchyard. After that, we were moved to the three rooms above the horseless stables. One wag, providing for the yearly House Magazine an article on the house's origins, wrote 'the old inn accommodation has now been tastefully converted into spacious suites of rooms for boys'. This was considered satirical and was ill received by authority.

But there were, as always, compensations. We all remained quite cheerful and disposed to find merriment wherever we could. One was provided by the word 'Oundle', a town name that was then not at all widely known to the world at large. If the O was written with the faintest of wobbles, the name got transformed. 'Dryden' too could suffer metamorphoses. Writing to London for Gamages' catalogue, or to Gertrude Lawrence for a photograph, the answer sometimes came back addressed to A. Marshall, Dugden House, Bundle, near Peterborough. Bundle alternated with Durdle, a name by which Oundle is still affectionately known to many of its ex-inmates. Durdle occasionally became Dundee, which meant one missed a post (how many now?).

But the unsatisfactory building and the conditions in which we were housed were made bearable by the extraordinary personalities of the housemaster and his wife. Grey- and white-haired, they seemed extremely old but were, I see now, a mere 58 and 54. They were of the old world and graciousness personified. Elegantly attired at all times, they swished about the cramped quarters as though in a wing of Chatsworth, smiling to right and left and managing to remain as remote as Alaska. Nothing whatever could knock them off balance, not even when a boy, sensing the approach of an attack of malnutrition, was found trying to saw his way into the locked store-room beneath the stable rooms. The saw was removed

63

and they invited him to have dinner with them, quite alone. This totally unnerving experience soon shut *him* up. They don't make housemasters like that these days. And nor, thank heaven and for everybody's sake, do they have to.

The housemaster's name was H. O. Hale. There was then no official Second Master but had there been, he would have been it. Even in the 1920s it was still often assumed that many public schoolmasters were in holy orders and occasionally a letter would arrive addressed to the Rev H. O. Hale, which gave us pleasure. And one happy day a letter came for the Rev. H. O'Hale, allotting him a supposedly Irish provenance. But Mr Hale was in no way Irish. He was entirely English and therefore in a constant state of anxiety about our moral welfare, a matter which worried him a good bit more than us. There were a number of rules which he evidently hoped were a foolproof recipe for chastity. A boy could not speak to anybody a year older than himself. Smiles too were out, for smiling (and few human activities are pleasanter) spelt danger, a go-ahead to depravity. Conversely a boy could not speak to or smile at anybody younger than himself. A boy could in no circumstances mix socially with a boy of whatever age in another house. This was for some muddled reason thought to be especially perilous. I found it wellnigh impossible not to smile, never having been previously required to desist, and for a time I was considered to be rather 'fast'.

Every so often Mr Hale, a gifted speaker, delivered himself of a moral lecture designed to scare the pants off one and all. The lectures were given, of course, after evening prayers (everything disagreeable took place 'after' something) and if it happened to be your bath night, you missed the treat. By that time of day, Mr Hale was in a dinner jacket and once when a power failure had caused the dining room to be lit solely by flickering candles, he looked like some ancient prophet foretelling Doom. He had composed a striking opening sentence: 'This house is a midden'. Only the cleverer boys knew what a midden was (I was fourteen and unclued-up on middens) but the word's general meaning became clear as the pijaw progressed. The 'trouble' was, it appeared, not at the top of the house (the prefects, looking smug) or at the bottom of the house (the new boys, looking relieved) but slap bang in the middle of the house and an innocent, intelligent and clean-living boy called Milburn, feverishly totting up on the house list, discovered that he was precisely in the middle and therefore the obvious cause of all the bother. When all was over and we were dismissed, gifted mimics got busy on the speech and as we disrobed for bed, key phrases rang round the dormitories: 'This house is a midden': 'This thing wrecks lives': 'It is not the top of the house': in all, a robust reaction. The house proved to have been an oddly fertile seed-bed and among my contemporaries were a future Lord Mayor of London, the producer of *The Mousetrap* and my special friend, Gordon Fraser, who revolutionised the Greetings Card and brought great taste to this expanding world and to the printing of books.

One of the Hales' most agitating preoccupations was the importance of preventing parents, at Speech Days and half terms and week-ends, from penetrating into the boys' part of the house and observing how very little of material benefit they were getting for their money. The natural instinct of parents was to penetrate and peer ('We just wanted to see where Stephen sleeps . . .') and nobody thwarted penetration better than Mrs Hale, a figure reminiscent of Boadicea repelling a Roman attack: her queenly manner did not encourage parents to request to see beds. From time to time, Mr Hale asked for our help in anti-penetration activities: 'I do not wish to find your parents cruising unaccompanied in the upper parts of the house. Bring them to me as soon as they arrive'. And being so brought, found escape out of the question.

In my day, Dryden House was one of the few remaining so-called 'proprietary' houses at Oundle, a deplorable system by which a housemaster was given a yearly sum of money with which to run the house and make what profit he might for himself. As will be obvious, the profit to be made was the result of a struggle between the housemaster's conscience and his keenness on cash, sometimes nothing of a battle. The Hales provided good breakfasts and excellent lunches, but the rest of the day represented a falling off. Tea consisted of sparsely margarined and left-over hunks of bread, washed down by tea from an ancient urn (the tea-leaves were said to nestle in an old football sock hung from the lid). Supper at seven o'clock consisted of what is known as 'a cooked dish'. On one occasion a dashing and fastidious boy registered his disapproval of mince on toast by cutting up the toast and, with the mince, fashioning a word of four letters, beginning, I regret to say, with the letter S. The maid who waited on his table, outraged at this slur on a dish which she may well have helped to construct, bore the plate away to Mr Hale. The head boy was instantly summoned and the plate, bearing the rejected foodstuff, was held out to him to examine. Once more, a striking opening sentence was provided: 'What, may I ask, is the meaning of this noisome motto?' Not an easy question to answer acceptably. The culprit was, I need hardly say, soundly thrashed.

In my four years as a boy at Oundle, I do not remember a single instance of anybody trying to run away. Although some were happier there than others, Oundle was not a place that young people positively wanted to run away from. I do not possess a copy of the Guinness Book of Records and therefore do not know whether there is listed there the name of the boy who ran away most often from school, but at this late stage I would like to put forward a candidate. He lived in the Wirral and was a charming and unique friend of many of us. His name was Edward Bates, Eddie for short, and, brave as a lion, he was killed in the war while dropping low-level bombs on the odious Boches (one world war one might now just possibly forgive: two, never). Playing truant is now, I gather, an un-punished commonplace but in the early 30s to absent yourself at all, let alone run away, was a serious crime. Nerve and resolution were needed and, possessing a great deal of both, Eddie managed finely and did excellent pioneering work in this very exacting field.

The school from which he departed so frequently was Winchester College. He did not at all care for the life there, an aversion the guilt for which need not be laid at that august door for the public school does not exist that could have either pleased or contained him. His mode of departure was simple. No lengthy preparations. No food parcels and means of disguise. He stood not, obviously, upon the order of his going. He just went, and a Bradshaw enthusiast could tell us what was then (and there were some fascinating changes, I'll bet) the swiftest railway route to take him from Hampshire to the Wirral. Sometimes he left mid-morning, and after attending a lesson or two. Sometimes he was up and away before first light ('Anybody seen Bates?'). Sometimes the mood took him in the afternoon and he would make a hasty bee-line for the station.

His delightful parents, Sir Percy and Lady Bates, bore all

stoically. He was their only child and their first indication, often at the breakfast table, that their family of two was about to become once more a family of three and at full strength was usually a call from the lodge-keeper and his wife at the gates to the effect that they thought they had seen Master Edward walking up the drive, upon which information Lady Bates, for a mother is yet a mother, probably ordered more toast and another kipper, while assuming a suitably sorrowful and reproachful look. Eddie was allowed to remain at home for an hour or so, there were telephonings ('Yes, we have the young man here') and then the chauffeur, and latterly quite automatically I expect, started up the Daimler and a party of two, Eddie and his mother, set out south. I would give a lot to know the exact dialogue that subsequently went on between the absentee, his mother and the headmaster and housemaster, with the air thick with phrases such as 'But this just isn't good enough!' and 'Twice in a month is twice too often'. Did Lady Bates say 'Eddie is truly sorry for what he has done, Mr Popejoy?' I expect so. Mothers normally do.

I forget the exact number of Eddie's absences in one year, indeed the only year when he was, or rather was not, at Winchester, but if we say six we are certainly not overestimating, and he may well have reached double figures. He remembered with particular pleasure (I can hear his guffaws still) the final episode and the final return. Asked by Mr Popejoy, his housemaster, whether he would now give an undertaking to behave himself, Eddie gave a wild cry of 'No! No! No!' (one more than for Nanette) and, flinging out an arm, managed to knock over a small table on which reposed Mr Popejoy's treasured collection of bibelots and knick-knacks, many of them frail and made of china and all of which fell to the floor with a satisfying tinkle. And in due course the Daimler bore him away northwards.

Like many other recipients, some of the instruction that I received at school was patchy. It is possibly my fault as much as theirs that in my youth all those who strove to teach me history, strove in vain. I would not say that history was as detestable to me as Latin but it was, like Waterloo (and I seem to have learnt some history after all), a close-run thing. Anyway, the verb 'to teach' is surely all wrong for history, which ideally should be a subject requiring a shared enthusiasm rather than being a formal classroom exercise such as, heaven help us all, surds. At my prep school there was no enthusiasm for history, shared or otherwise. Formality reigned. Nobody ever read us a stirring account of, say, a Chartist rising or a nice massacre somewhere (the Armenians seemed always to be copping it, but how justifiably I cannot say). The Great War was only two years over and therefore ranked as history and could have provided horrors and fascinations galore but for us history stopped abruptly with the outbreak of the French Revolution, and even before those tumbrils started excitingly to rattle over the cobbles. Day after day we sat solemnly at our desks and learnt dates. I defy anybody to get a crumb of comfort or intellectual stimulus from 'English regain Madras (1749)' or 'Siege of Danzig (1734)'. When we had learnt enough dates for the time being, we learnt the terms of the Treaty of Ulm (1620) and I really cannot recommend them to you. Despair was everywhere, with not a laugh to be had and not even my friend Williamson, normally a determined chuckler, could manage a half smile when informed by the master that next day we were to 'tackle' Cromwell's 'Rump'.

And thus it is that the world's most sensational events – Death of Mahomet, invention of the Spinning-Jenny, De Ruyter's Fleet in the Thames (the *cheek* of it!), that business in Boston Harbour and stout Cortes conquering Mexico (pronounced, I understand, Mehico) – still leave me quite tremendously cold, but I do have to confess to a slight and perverse penchant for the mini-facts of history, those tiny happenings that for me have a piquancy all their own. For example, is it still remembered that when in 1889 the Queen of Hawaii was invited to a tea-party at Lambeth Palace with the wife of Archbishop Benson, she had to be dissuaded, by a warning gesture hastily made by an equerry, from dunking her sponge cake in her tea-cup. How delightfully the event relives itself in the imagination – the wafer-thin bread-and-butter, the splendid array of home-made cakes, the gleaming silver tea-pot, the 'Do try a piece of sponge, Your Majesty' from Mrs Benson (or did she, as hostesses sometimes do, say 'I can recommend the sponge'?), the steaming Earl Grey in the delicate Rockingham cup, the dusky little finger crooked and the sudden longing, for monarchs are but human, to dunk. Then the warning look and move, the anxious moment and the final and wise decision not to dunk, for nobody, queens or

68

lesser people, looks at their best while manipulating into the mouth a wedge of soggy and dripping cake.

I am very fortunate for I can truthfully say that I have never in my life been bored, however inviting the circumstances. The most severe challenge was, I suppose, provided by the chapel services at Oundle School in the 1920s but even here, though at maximum ennui risk and encased in sombre black and starched collar and feeling fairly Sundayish and dreary, there was always something to activate the imagination or to feast the eyes on – the School House matron's interesting new hat, the pleasing altar decorations (gladioli again), the boil scars on the neck of the boy in front, the sight of the fully vocal headmaster, kind and jovial Dr Fisher, with the possibility of his letting us off ('Sing up, everybody!') the dreaded midday Scripture lesson and an hour with those fearful Acts of the Apostles, the spectacle of various impressionable boys struggling not to catch the eyes of the other impressionable boys, the chief stinks master's cavernous yawns and wild myopic gaze, the very occasional misprints on the organ. And there was always the final hymn to look forward to and then the hurried pushing and shoving out into the sunshine to cluster round the gates and see whether Dr Fisher was coming through with a treat ('Well, you've all been good boys and you sang nicely and as we won the Uppingham match . . .'). Deafening cheers. Hard cheese on St Paul. Some other time, perhaps.

There was one hymn, under the prayer-book's 'Morning' section, for to sing it at eventide would have meant rendering its main message virtually useless, which we frequently sang and which kicked off with 'Awake, my soul, and with the sun Thy daily stage of duty run,' and, after a rather impertinent injunction to redeem the mis-spent time that's past (why assume its mis-spending?), we were encouraged to 'live this day as if thy last'. Though this obviously had a deeply pious significance, I and several of my more unholy school friends used often, over lunch (especially good on Sundays), to deal with this concept in a more practical manner and discuss how best to extract the fullest and most pleasurable value out of one's last day on earth. It was taken for granted that one's last day would be here at school and so, in my case and after an enormous breakfast, one changed into holiday togs, got into the headmaster's car, a stately Sunbeam, and was driven rather grandly by the chauffeur straight to London and to the Shaftesbury

Avenue area. Enormous lunch at the Café Royal. Matinée of *Mercenary Mary*. Enormous tea at Gunter's in Curzon Street. Evening performance of *Rookery Nook*. Enormous supper at the Savoy. Bed and finis. What a saucy little rip one was but what a very satisfactory way to wind things up before going rat-a-tat ('Anybody in?') at the pearly gates. I remember one of the impressionable boys above mentioned, when firmly cross-questioned as to his ideal last day, blushing painfully and announcing that he would 'like to go for a walk with Pendleton'. Loud and scornful shouts of 'Boo!', though some shouted more loudly and scornfully than others.

But unbored as I was and try as I may, I could never at school come to love and appreciate in chapel the First Lesson, and the words 'Here endeth the First Lesson' rang out like a benison. Apart from the occasional phrase that fell, in youth, so pleasantly on the ear – 'He smote them hip and thigh' always had such a pleasing and wholeheartedly destructive ring to it, and I was rather keen too on 'Curse God, and die' (Job, you know) – I do resent, even at this rather late stage in one's development, having had when young such vast chunks of the Old Testament read out at one. Not a day went by at school without some mirthless twaddle, for such it seemed, about unleavened bread or the wormwood and the gall or the little hill of Hermon or boils and blains (one stole a glance at Matron) or somebody's bowels being moved (ditto). Then there were unlovely sentences beginning with 'Woe to', followed by a whole list of things. And there were obvious impossibilities ('Howl, ye ships of Tarshish'). When a dog-collared divine, clutching the lectern, let fly with 'Who is this that cometh from Edom, with dyed garments from Bozrah?', a rhetorical question apparently for answer came there none, one was quite frankly nonplussed, apart from noting the fact that the dye used seemed to come from squashed grape skins, as far as one could gather, and the garments would therefore presumably be either Burgundy-red or Beaujolais-purple rather than a dull Hock-white. And then, where was Edom and where, as though one cared, Bozrah? And why was almost everybody in the Old Testament permanently ratty and disagreeable, with God (whom we were constantly thanking for this or that) by far the rattiest of the lot? It didn't make sense then and, by golly, it makes a great deal less now.

The names of the characters too bristled with problems. I

don't mean simple and relatively pleasant names such as Jacob and Joseph and Sarah and Ruth. It is things like Ham. My O T section of the biblical 'Told To The Kiddies' series informs me that Ham means 'hot' (one's mind flies at once to gammon steaks and pineapple slices) but I still would find it difficult to call to it out of a window and tell it to come in to lunch. However, at least Ham is short. The trouble with names begins quite soon after the Flood when, with Noah 599 years old, the ark was grounded and his three sons have branched out on their own. Japheth and his family decide to settle along the European coasts of the Mediterranean (one tends to picture them, basking in the sun and covered with olive oil, at Nice or Cannes). Shem heads for the south-west of Asia (after oil of a different kind, possibly), and hot Ham for Africa (pineapples). And before we know where we are, poor old Job has turned up with friends most unfortunately called Eliphaz and Zophar and Bildad. And here is the puzzle. Are these names surnames or are they what we must, I suppose, call pet names (as we are in BC 1996 or thereabouts, we can hardly call them Christian names). Was Eliphaz, for example, married to Muriel Eliphaz and did they have two lovely girls called Dawn and Cindy Eliphaz? The problem becomes even more acute later with a name such as Jashobeam (apt to linger in barley fields and slay 300 Philistines before lunch). This cannot, surely be a pet name and was there therefore Prudence Jashobeam, mother of Annabel and Tracy Jashobeam? Nobody can tell me that Mephibosheth is a baby's name, to be whispered to the robed priest at the font side, or whatever went on by way of a naming ceremony. Nor is Og, a displeasing name if ever there was one. And you can add Jehoshaphat, jumping or not.

Well then, I'm sorry to have to go on complaining about this but how deeply unattractive are some of the place names. With mouthfuls like Bethshemesh and Ramathaim-zephim to cope with, one comes to the conclusion that the shorter the name the better, but even then that produces Tob and Uz and Ur and Nob, and also Ai which, with a diaeresis on it and an added 'e' is surely what the feeble frogs scream when somebody sticks a pin into them. Although my 'Told To The Kiddies' informs me that Abel-shittim means 'the Meadows of Acacias', one of our rarer and more attractive trees, it remains a name that I personally could never be permanently happy about. I would not, for example, have been at ease when writing to a friend to announce a change of address ('We've had this offer of a bungalow at Abel-shittim. Huldah and the children are over the moon about it, and a change from Gilgal will do us all good. I did have my eye on a semi at Michmash, but it looks now as though we'll land up in Abel-shittim').

Choral singing, much approved of by Fisher, was an important feature of Oundle musical life and I enjoyed it immensely. Every year we sang the *Messiah* or the *Christmas Oratorio* or *Elijah* and two years running everybody plucked up courage and we sang Bach's *B Minor Mass*, an extraordinary undertaking which amazed the musical world and caused great critical excitement. The entire school took part. There was an orchestra of, roughly, fifty, strengthened here and there by professionals. The senior mathematics master played, brilliantly, the organ. The choir proper consisted of about 250 boys, and the 350 remaining formed the so-called non-choir. The latter learnt, at the daily practices after Prayers, the important themes of Bach or whichever composer it was, and then, at a given moment, joined their willing if untrained voices to the tenors or basses and just let fly. 'Everyone suddenly burst out singing' and the soloists, unprepared for this unbalancing vocal onslaught, nearly jumped out of their skins. The performance was always on the last Sunday of the Michaelmas Term, a vast corporate effort that was much relished by all. It meant that boys on the way to bed or to have a bath could be heard happily humming Bach, which can't be bad, and the Mass stayed with them for life. It also inspired interest in other composers and the afternoon voluntary Musical Appreciation classes (gramophone records and chat) filled up.

My keenness on singing had not gone unnoticed and that and my apparent musicality encouraged an over-enthusiastic music master to enter me for a choral scholarship at Caius College, Cambridge. I was doomed from the start but although I knew I hadn't a chance, it meant a day and night away and an opportunity of seeing Cambridge, where I was soon to go, and so I fell in with the plan and, equipped with a signed exeat from the headmaster ('Where are *you* off to?'), copious instructions, journey money, sandwiches, overnight necessities and a packet of good-luck Luxivox Voice Pastilles from Matron, off I set.

To get by rail from Oundle to Cambridge it was necessary to change trains a time or two and one of the changes provided an eye-opener for at one point I found myself on the small and deserted platform of March station in Cambridgeshire. Reassured by a kindly porter that my onward train would chug into view any minute, I made for the gentlemen's lavatory, conveniently close indeed and primly obscured by laurels. Here I found myself face to face with, though I didn't realise it at the time, my first specialised sexual graffito, fully visible in all its incomprehensibility. 'Why don't we form a So Club', an excited hand had scratched on the wall, 'and meet here on Thursdays?' I was later to discover that the word 'so' when applied to male amatory abnormalities derived from the German phrase '*Er ist so*' and was the equivalent of the then fashionable 'He is one of those'. But at the time I merely wondered what the letters SO stood for. Sanitary Orderlies? Station Operatives? And why on earth choose such a whiffy trysting place, and what was so special about Thursdays (early closing day, perhaps)? No time was mentioned and so wouldn't they have to hang about (indeed) for hours? I was just seventeen and in those relatively wholesome days it was possible to remain innocent for quite some time.

On arrival in Cambridge I was made welcome and comfortably housed in Caius and, though I suppose I should have been gargling and 'resting my voice', ho ho, I had accepted an invitation from an Oundle friend who had preceded me by a year or two and had kindly asked me to dine with him in Clare. He was an agreeable and, to me, worldly character who had always had more pocket money than the rest of us, had an elder brother who flew about in a private aeroplane, and had once asked me, during a holiday outing, to send a telegram to his home announcing that he would be late back. This seemed to me tremendously dashing. Telegrams in my own family circle were productive of gasps and ashen faces and hands pressed to bosoms. One neither sent them nor was ever late back.

And so it was no surprise to find in my friend's rooms a very smart red leather HMV portable gramophone and the latest musical comedy records, a drinks table, copies of *The Bystander* and several framed photographs of girls, shingled and marcelled to within an inch of their lives. We discussed theatres. He had recently been to Seymour Hicks's play *Mr What's His Name*, with the attractive actress, Benita Hume, in it, and when she had had to lean over a sofa, her breasts had (Phew!) bulged excitingly forward. He was going, he said, the very next evening to London to 'do a show' with Monica. I asked, of course, what show. Well, Monica couldn't make up her mind between Gershwin's *Tip-Toes* at the Winter Garden or Jerome Kern's *Sunny* at the London Hippodrome. 'Which is it to be then?' I asked. 'I don't know yet', he said, 'so I've bought tickets for both of them'. I was thunderstruck. 'But that means that whichever you go to, there will somewhere be two seats unoccupied'. 'Of course. What of it?' he said, vigorously shaking a white lady (the cocktail).

I was terribly shocked at the wicked waste. And, innocent again, I assumed that every night in every London theatre every seat was full. What if the entrancing Dorothy Dickson, in the middle of dancing her heart out and singing the tuneful 'That Certain Feeling', should peer down into the stalls, spot the two deserted seats and consider herself virtually alone in the theatre? What if the supremely talented Binnie Hale, reaching for a high note in Kern's 'Who?', should look into the audience and see emptiness not fifteen feet away? But I do, in retrospect, sympathise with Monica's predicament. Her indecision is like that game, of which there are many variations, when you imagine yourself in a balloon losing height over dangerous, tiger-infested country. You are in distinguished company but whom do you expel from the basket, Dickens, Proust or Balzac (as far as I am concerned, it's out goes Marcel)? Or on an over-crowded life-raft in tropical waters, whom do you feed to the sharks, Wagner, Beethoven or Mozart ('Sorry, Wolfgang, but there just isn't room!')?

Next morning I had, to coin a phrase, to face the music. There were six candidates and while I waited my turn I heard some of them fluting melodiously away. The examination consisted of a set Handelian piece, scales, sight reading, and Song of The Candidate's Own Choosing and for this I had settled on that charming setting of the Thomas Moore poem, 'She is far from the land', which I had ceaselessly practised and enjoyed rendering. I had arrived at the currently over-worked 'Moment of Truth' and had soon to reveal the fact that my voice, although in tune and extremely loud when needed, was brassy and altogether horrible, with a defiant and grating ring to it. And furthermore I looked, while singing, repulsive.

When I was ushered into the examination room, I found there a piano and three judges, one of whom was the famous Dr 'Daddy' Mann of King's. They smiled politely and, skipping Handel for the moment, requested scales. 'How high can you sing?' Dr Mann asked. I named a note. He struck it. I obliged. 'Go on', he said and so up I squeaked, ever higher and into regions where only dogs could, poor things, hear me. It can only have been kindness and consideration for the young that stopped the three of them stuffing their fingers into their ears. I then did about a quarter of my Handel ('Thank you'), smartly failed the sight reading, and was being speedily shown to the door when I remembered my Song Of The Candidate's Own Choosing! 'Oh, er, yes . . .' Dr Mann said, and so back I went and wailed it out ('Thank you'). When I returned to Oundle, the madcap music master wanted to know how I had fared. 'Do you feel you've pulled it off?' 'I don't *think* so', I said.

I had made at Oundle a friend, Maurice Johnson, who was as dementedly keen on the lighter side of the theatre as I and during the Christmas and Easter school holidays we always met in London for a theatrical jaunt. Our trysting-place was invariably in front of the London Pavilion and just to gaze, while waiting, at the photographs from the latest Cochran revue was a treat in itself. My father sportingly and uncomplainingly stumped up the necessary cash for these expeditions. It was possible, a fact which becomes increasingly hard to believe, in those days to 'do' a matinée, as racy people phrased it, at a cost of slightly less than £1, a sum known, again only to the racy, as a Bradbury, or 'Brad' ('I say, old bean, lend me a Brad'), after the Treasury official who signed the note and promised the bearer to shell out, on demand, 20 shillings. The lopped-off monosyllable reminds me happily of a winning entry in a long-ago *New Statesman* competition for monosyllabic advertisements: 'Prog. coup. wish meet prog. coup. view share hol. bung. Sex ab. no ob.' We must, I fancy, assume that the 'ab.' is a shortened form of either 'aberrations' or 'abnormalities'. 'Ob.' is, of course, 'objection'.

But to our £1's worth, and the year (around 1926). The return railway fare to Paddington (crumpled travel) was 6s 9d. The cost of the bus to Piccadilly was negligible (3d, I suppose, if that). The four-course lunch on the first floor gallery of the Café Royal (and what a rip one felt!) came to 3s 6d (waiter delighted, apparently, with 6d). An upper circle seat for whatever Binnie Hale or Cicely Courtneidge or Gertrude Lawrence happened to be in at the time was 5s, programme 6d.

Even with a reckless order of tea in the interval, you were about two bob in hand on your return home, ears still a-tingle with melody for those were, indeed, the days when, emerging from any popular musical entertainment by Gershwin or Coward or Richard Rodgers, there were in your head at least three tunes that refused for weeks to dislodge themselves.

On my return from one of these matinée jaunts a piece of unexpected good fortune came my way. I was seated alone in a compartment of the 6 pm out of Paddington and we were barely rattling through Ealing when there entered from the corridor somebody of about my own age (17), followed shortly after by two older men of a *louche*-looking, race-going type. Suspicious. As we went whizzing through Slough, they invited the younger one to play, at a Bradbury a time, what I think is called Spot The Lady or the three-card-trick – the identification of the back of the Queen of Spades from two other cards juggled swiftly about. In next to no time the young man had won quite a tidy sum.

The performance was, of course, being set up for my benefit. The three of them were in league. I suppose that I looked, sitting there in my tidy, grey pin-stripe theatre-going suit, affluent and fully fleeceable. Soon they turned to me. Would I care to have a go? 'Yes', I said, greatly daring in view of my remaining two shillings but knowing that they always encouraged victims with an early win. I picked out without difficulty the queen and was handed a pound note. 'Here we go again', they said. 'Thank you, no', I primly replied, 'I have played sufficiently'.

Amazement, disbelief, realisation, anger, fury and those looks that are called 'ugly' and promise fisticuffs. I was contemplating tugging the communication cord (£5 for Improper Use, and what use could be more proper than mine?) when the guard happened to pass along the corridor and I nipped quickly out and engaged him in animated conversation, subsequently locking myself in the lavatory. Disreputable behaviour all round, really, but it meant a free matinée next week (*The Last of Mrs Cheyney*, if memory serves, and worth every penny of the serious risk to life and limb).

About half way through my time at Oundle it had become clear that I was to be Cambridge bound and although my parents' final goal for me, that of schoolmastering, was abhorrent, I greatly took to the idea of Cambridge, whither a number of close school friends were also going. Like many another, I wanted to go to King's but my Uncle Oswald's time there had not been without incident and he had fallen foul of a humourless but distinguished don called Clapham (pause for a dear old *Punch* joke of my childhood. Muddled old gentleman to railway porter: 'Tell me, porter, does this train clap at Stopham Junction?') It was thought wiser therefore, in case the family connection should be discovered, to enter me for a more modest college and so Christ's was settled on, if a college could be called modest that had produced Milton and Darwin. A mystery remains. I took no college entrance examination. I was summoned to no interview. I had no connection with them at all and not even a post-card was exchanged. I can only suppose that Dr Fisher and Mr Hale and my form master, Mr Bray, all wrote such fulsome letters of recommendation that the college authorities, completely dazzled by my merits, were hypnotised into accepting me sight unseen and sound unheard and abilities untested. I didn't, I like to think, actually disgrace the place but I do rather wonder if, with hindsight, they would have welcomed me as warmly, if remotely.

My parents had another admirable idea. As I was to read Modern Languages, why not remove me from Oundle a term early and send me to spend the summer with a French family where I could attend the summer course for foreign students at Grenoble University? This plan too, although it seemed to make a pedagogic career ever more unavoidable, I fell joyfully in with for there were some aspects of an Oundle summer term (early school: Higher Certificate exam: OTC camp) that I would be happy to miss. And so, in May, 1928, I and two others set off for a Grenoble suburb called La Tronche and a French house which catered for students and was run by three spinster sisters called Rolland.

There is usually something odd about sisters that come in triplicate. Consider pretty little Cinderella and her ugly and dance-mad relations. Consider Chekhov's trio, high and dry in the provinces and longing gloomily for Moscow. Consider Macbeth's friends, bent keenly over the cauldron and intent on passing that Culinary Test for the Advanced Student. The Sisters Rolland were no exception to the rule. There was poor, frail Mademoiselle Alice, a middle-aged poetess who had in her youth evidently ranked as the Sweet Songbird of Savoy and possessed printed books to prove it. She was forced by a chest complaint to remain bedridden in a downstairs room but registered her presence with little moans and wails and splutters and, on her better days, croaked out advice and encouragement through a half-open door. Very occasionally she was well enough to receive a visit and we went timidly in for coffee and cakes, and once she very touchingly read us some of her poems – echoes of Lamartine and Alfred de Musset. Then there was Mademoiselle Cécile, a sad victim of dental decay and toothache who sat, also wailing and usually fresh from the dentist's chair, with a hand pressed to her jaw and a repetitious cry of '*Ah, que je souffre!*' Sympathy for the two sufferers was frequently required but beyond '*Pauvre Mademoiselle!*', what to say? Flowery embellishments were not easily assembled. The robust physique of the third sister, Mademoiselle Berthe, was, I suppose, Nature's way of redressing the balance. As I had recently been involved in Oundle games, Berthe put me in mind of a second-row rugger forward, constantly capped for France and a real devil in the loose. Amazement at her sturdy build was only equalled by amazement at her appetite. She provided me with my first experience of oil-soused lettuce being eaten as only a really hungry Frenchwoman can eat it. A giant forkful of foliage was pressed to the mouth, suction was applied and a loud plop! sound showed that suction had succeeded. Any outlying fragments were helped in with the tongue – pity to waste anything – or, if in dainty mood, with a little finger tastefully crooked. Cécile and Berthe presided at mealtimes (food tip-top) and were tactful and conscientious in correcting mistakes and in suggesting useful French phrases, for example '*Il n'y a pas de quoi*' when acknowledging expressions of gratitude and corresponding to 'Not at all' or, in some circles, 'Pray don't mention it', or, more familiarly, 'Don't mensh!'

By day we attended lectures, wrote French proses, jabbered away in French, wrote home, played tennis ('*Merci pour la balle!*') on courts crowded together in a line, swam, bicycled through the beautiful, and often sensational, countryside, and generally absorbed what I suppose I must call culture. We went to art galleries and museums and found here and there pleasurable moments not intended by the authorities. One particular museum concentrated on the older type of antiquity and as there were many British students about, they obligingly provided English explanations of the artistic treasures on display.

Thus it was that a rather chipped and armless Roman female bust, correctly described underneath as *torse d'une jeune fille*, was presented to English visitors as MAID'S TRUNK.

As we all, of course, know, the French word for legacy or bequest is *le legs* and the museum was rightly keen to acknowledge its grateful thanks to its various benefactors of the past who had remembered it in their wills, one of whom had been a member of the ever generous and public-spirited Rothschild family. And so it befell that the lower section of a sort of mummified Egyptian body, two brown and wrinkled stumps somewhat lacking in charm but apparently of enormous importance, interest and value, was described to the public as *Legs de Mme Rothschild*.

My mother and father kindly came out to visit me and we made happy trips to the Grande Chartreuse monastery, to Aix-les-Bains and to Annecy, and in due course I returned to England to prepare myself for, though I didn't know it then, what were to be three of the most pleasurable years of my life.

SCENE IV

A Horse to the Water

I approached Cambridge with mixed feelings, one of which was apprehension. My brother, a clever boy who was well liked, had preceded me to Stirling Court and to Oundle, where he won a minor scholarship, and so I knew in advance, more or less, the ropes, but Cambridge was, to me, virgin territory though my Uncle Oswald was helpful. To give me a good send-off and to install me safely, a double carload of relations was assembled and off we went, my Essex grandmother and my Uncle and a raffish friend of his being grandly chauffeur-driven in one car, and my parents and I and my Cousin Madge, indispensable on occasions of family importance, in the other. We inspected my lodgings, deposited my luggage (in those days, of course, still a large trunk) and then lunched on roast pork at the University Arms Hotel, the raffish friend disgracing us all by asking for 'another portion of crackling', the kind of embarrassment that worries one when young and stays in the mind for life. One of his other physical indulgences was, apparently, to step into a hot bath fully clothed in a dark blue pin-stripe suit. My Uncle was ever a rum picker.

When the time came for them all to go, I was emotionally overcome. My parents, though not poor, were in those days far from rich and there had been sacrifices in order to send me to Cambridge. They gazed at me with loving expectancy while I gulped and was silent. 'Now it's up to you, darling' my mother said. They had such high hopes for me and I knew only too well that they were to be disappointed. They had mistaken diligence for brains. At Oundle I had managed to win the Modern VI form prize but this success had been due entirely to an ability to slog. Even up to the almost last, it was hoped, not only by my parents but also by the Oundle languages staff, that I would do so well in my first year that the College, Christ's, would be sufficiently impressed to give me an award. Their faith and their blindness amaze me still. A university award requires more than slogging. I was just not up to it, a completely unscholarly type, as I have since made abundantly clear, and I briskly began to let everybody down. From about the age of four to eighteen, I had been a model of conscientious endeavour (I dearly loved being handed prizes, eyes modestly down) and I had had enough of it.

On the evening of our first day at Cambridge, Maurice Johnson came round to my rooms and we set about trying to join the Amateur Dramatic Club, or ADC, which had its own small theatre, dressing rooms and club room in Park Street. Would they allow us in, we diffidently wondered? Would there be an audition (that dreadful Macbeth dagger speech perhaps, or an imitation of Henry Irving going melodramatically dotty in *The Bells*, a vignette well beyond my powers)? The club had started life in rather grand circumstances and with an upper-crust membership and among its former Presidents was the Prince of Wales, later Edward VII: indeed the club's eye-catching and virtually unwearable tie owed itself to the Prince's racing colours. And so, would we pass muster? Maurice came from Thames Ditton and I from Newbury. Had I better suppress Newbury and speak of living 'in Berkshire', implying spreading acres and parkland?

I worried needlessly. Maurice had discovered that the club's secretary was a Trinity undergraduate called Robert Eddison and thither, after hall, we repaired. Approaching his rooms, we were greeted by the sound of piano music and, on knocking and being bidden to enter, we found Robert seated at an upright, rippling away and giving his musical all to, if memory serves, 'La cathédrale engloutie', a tuneful treat which may well have also found its way into the ear of A. E. Housman who 'kept' not far away. Robert seemed immensely tall, welcomed us warmly, was reassuring about membership and audition requirements and generously shared with us the tray of coffee that the buttery had supplied for him after hall, a facility of which one then thought little, unmindful of the fact that a servant would have had to trudge over with it and accepting it, as one did so much else, as one's due. I shudder even now at the memory of one's complacency. And so, in due course we became members of the club that rapidly came to be my daytime home for most of my happy three years. Just to stand on our own stage and look out into the auditorium (it seated 150) was an unfailing pleasure. Teas and drinks and light lunches (usually boiled eggs) were available and came lurching up on a rickety lift from the basement where the admirable caretaker, Mr Talman, and his wife lived. I walked on air down Park Street and into the premises.

A printed card, with date and time filled in by hand, summoned me to a first meeting with him who for my three years up was to be my tutor. He provided details of supervisions (usually two or three persons gathered together and studying the actual language) and of the lectures I should attend, lectures dealing with history and literature. He had only recently become a tutor and was everything that a tutor should be – conscientious, polite, kind and hospitable. In your first year you bicycled out to Grantchester for tea and agreeable paper and pencil games with his friendly wife. In your second year you went to breakfast with him in College, breakfast parties being then quite a popular social occasion. In your last year you were invited to lunch. He was unfailingly courteous and it was no fault of his that to me and many of my friends he seemed a fearfully cold fish. He appeared to be very senior but can only have been in the mid-30s. He had side whiskers and wore starched winged collars. He had one of those pairs of spectacles for looking over the top with, if you follow me and will forgive syntactical imperfections. What is the opposite of *joie de vivre*? *Douleur de vivre*? He was an authority on Ibsen, no fun figure, and some of the *douleur* had rubbed off. For our three years association, he called me 'Mr Marshall', which was accurate but in itself discouraging. Those who peer over the top of spectacles impart no very pleasing expression to the face. It would, I think, have greatly distressed this good man if he had realised (perhaps he did) the cold douche effect that he produced. Even now and fifty years on, if I walk through Christ's and look up at what were the windows of his rooms, I have a feeling of unease. Sad.

In my first fortnight I busied myself visiting old Oundle friends in other colleges ('Care for a gasper?') and there then arrived another little printed card inviting me to call on my tutor at the socially productive hour of 6.15 p.m. Hooray, I thought, envisaging a small party for fellow freshmen, with glasses of sherry and kind enquiries ('Well, are you young chaps finding your feet?'). Not at all. I was the only one so summoned and, uninvited either to sit down or sip Harvey's best, was informed of College Rule No. 273 (c), or whatever, which forbade undergraduates being out after 10 p.m. more than three times a week. I had, it seems, been out six times in each week – the complete social butterfly – and must now toe the line ('You are here to work, Mr Marshall'). Chastened and dispirited, I left the forbidding presence, subsequently discussing this tiresome embargo with others who lived, or 'kept' as we phrased it, out of college. Some landlords, I discovered, could be coaxed or bribed to sign their charges as having been in by 10 p.m. when they were all too obviously out, but my landlord, who worked in the College offices by day, was a model of probity and one couldn't even, nonchalantly clinking silver coins, open a parley that would have been profitable to both ('I say, I was just wondering if we couldn't come to some arrangement . . .'). The College Rule aimed, of course and how wisely, at producing diligent evening work and close attention to books and essays, but in this respect I had defiant news for the College, and it was 'You can lead a horse to the water . . .'

Geographically I was finely and centrally placed for my rooms were in Hobson Street and in a handsome Queen Anne house which stood conveniently at the back gate of Christ's. A minute's walk brought me to the brightly lit Central Cinema; two minutes to the Dorothy Café, known to us as 'the Dot' and justifiably renowned for the extreme lightness and feathery texture of its meringues. Miller's music shop, with its gramophone records of *Oh Kay* and *Mr Cinders*, was close by. Within four minutes I could be in the ADC, these locative details showing where my frivolous interests were to lie. Most of my friends were in King's, John's and Magdalene and no distance away and, like everybody else, I bicycled to and fro. The bicycle which I had had for some years was nearing the end of its active life and was anyhow now rather small for me and my father proffered his own machine, which he no longer rode, and I did not like to refuse it. It was an extremely heavy one but was happily equipped with a three-speed gear. It had a patented and stoutly reinforced frame and, with it, there was an embarrassment. Where the ordinary man's bicycle had that straight horizontal bar which extended from the saddle to the front, my father's dipped down appreciably into a 'v' shape, not as far as a lady's bicycle but certainly half way there, giving it the appearance of being neither male nor female. As a result it became rapidly known to my friends as 'the hermaphrodite'.

'You arrived on the hermaphrodite, no doubt' they would say, pouring sherry. I bore the teasing stoically and the bicycle had at least one advantage. Nobody would have been seen dead on it and it never got stolen.

I sampled a lecture or two, just to test the ground. The accepted procedure among the non-diligent was to attend the first lectures of the year, when a piece of paper was passed round on which we wrote our names and our Colleges, and then to attend no more. In my day the general standard of lecturing in modern languages was deplorable. Some lecturers just read out typed sheets of stuff. Others mumbled and twittered. Few had any theatrical sense and could present their subject attractively. Some were painfully shy, and shyness in lecturers is a disaster. There were however two glorious exceptions and the only lectures that I never dreamt of missing were those dispensed by two women – Miss Pernel Strachey, a lady who had inherited that family's failure to be boring and who spoke on the writer Constant and others, and Professor Elsie Butler, an entrancing pint-size bundle of wit and erudition who early won my heart by referring to Goethe as 'poor old Goethe', an opinion that I had long shared. And when she added on the words 'poor old Schiller', I was at her feet for evermore. She became, luckily for me, a friend and when, later on, I reminded her of 'poor old' this and that, she gave a happy laugh and denied ever having said any such thing. But she had.

These two splendidly lively and intelligent ladies were a real eye-opener for me, for the ordinary and comfortable middle-class Berkshire circles in which I was then living contained no intellectual ladies of any sort. Nobody narrowed their eyes at one and talked about Proust. Tea-table chat did not include a mention of the Russian Ballet designs of Bakst. Modern composers, if spoken of at all, were referred to as 'freaks', an opinion with which, in some cases, I am still inclined to agree. There was, it is true, a rather forbidding lady whom one met going in and out of tobacconists (perhaps she smoked a pipe) who wore gentlemen's hats with a feather in them and sported a collar and tie and a well cut jacket. She certainly looked intellectual and indeed narrowed her eyes quite a bit but may have just been, and why not, something else.

There was no incentive to work for I found to my dismay that in French literature we were to concern ourselves yet again

84

with the plays of that dread couple, Racine and Corneille and during my last two years at Oundle we had done little else. And Oundle had had an advantage which Cambridge had not, namely a teacher called A. C. Bray, who took the Modern VI. He was in every way dynamic and I owe him much. With his decibels mounting *pari passu* with his blood pressure, this stimulating master, whose noise alone rendered it impossible to snooze even if one had wished to, boomed out the French classical plays in such an effectively dramatic manner that one could fancy oneself positively at the Comédie itself. His exertions frequently caused his nose to bleed, upon which he lay flat on the floor and carried right on with *Phèdre* from the prone position. Have Racine's liquid lines ever before come up from below and swirling round dusty desk legs? I very much doubt it. He had, not the only possessor of an awkward nose, a special affection for *Cyrano de Bergerac* which came to electrifying life, duel scene and all, before our very eyes. When, at the end of that most romantic of plays, the heroine, Roxane, now retired to a nunnery where the autumn leaves are gently and symbolically falling, realises at last that the old nobleman, wounded and dying hideously before her, is the man she has really loved all her life, Mr Bray could be seen, struggling to get the text audibly and clearly out, to be weeping, and the less hard-boiled of us wept with him.

I very much doubt the wisdom of exposing youngish persons to the plays of Racine and Corneille. It is possible to take the view that the plays of Racine and Corneille lack interest and attraction, and if Racine and Corneille knew any jokes, they kept them to themselves. The plays' characters were too remote from life and one longed for Bérénice to come rushing on, looking distraught and saying that she was fresh out of darning-wool and could anybody remember whether Thursday was early closing? Furthermore, Racine and Corneille were presented to us as being Godlike and unapproachable figures. If only somebody had reminded us that, when not actually writing plays, Racine and Corneille went, just like anybody else, to the lavatory, picked their noses, snored, yawned and, after unwise eating, belched noisily. In German too, Goethe and Schiller were pedestal figures who lived on air, remote from platefuls of Sauerkraut and Steins of beer and worries and wives.

Once a year, and in the summer term, my mother came to

stay. Her visits coincided, intentionally, with our ADC summer production and she stayed for three or four days at the Blue Boar Hotel, still happily in existence in Trinity Street. When she used to come with my father to Oundle Speech Days and half term, I was always in a state of anxiety about her hats. Would they, as one hoped, blend into the background or would they startle the eye? Although the one crime that was socially taboo at all schools was in any way to mock openly a chap's people, one felt sometimes that a chap's people might be being mocked in private, and ladies' hats, so ostentatiously perched up and visible certainly provided mockable material. I recall a wide-brimmed brown straw, with attendant roses, in 1926 that should have been left ('It suits Madam perfectly') right there where it was chez the modiste. But by Cambridge days I was past such childish embarrassments and when my mother, in her kind way, gave (hatted) little lunch parties for my friends, I was just very proud of her, hats and all. She could make the dullest people become less dull and, above all, be happy and her ability to please was unfailing.

My father came to Cambridge just the once and in my last term, by which time I was President of the ADC and very pleased with myself. I sometimes wondered, in the preceding three years, why it had never occurred to him (he worked then in London) just to jump on a train and come and see how I was getting along. An amicable lunch, out of the blue, might have brought us closer together. But in his case no visit could ever be undertaken at short notice. Every trip was arranged weeks in advance, 'then you know where you are' (a favourite phrase), and where he was was only once Cambridge. Perhaps it was just as well for he would undoubtedly have found me between cinemas, with no sign ('Where are your to-day's lecture notes?') of work being achieved and with my rooms littered with film and theatre magazines. He was never a person to try to trip one up or catch one out (cinemas again). He would have thought it ungentlemanly and dishonourable. Elsewhere, however, cheerful Dads were to be seen bouncing in and out of friends' rooms, often arriving with a hamper of tuck (perhaps the May Races would be on) and one was bidden to share both amenities: food and Dads, I mean, rather than Races.

I had a sense of loss and I was getting rather short of father figures. I had outgrown my Cousin Willie, now far away in Trinidad and profitably immersed in oil (the managerial side), and outgrown too both stewards and bootmen. Christ's College was then a bit bereft of dons who filled the bill, and anyhow, intellectual ability rather militates against the type, and the Christ's dons were long on brains. There was one dear old fellow, very distinguished and widely loved, called Tibby Marshall (no relation, as we frequently discussed) who wandered about the college accosting anybody who looked ripe for chat, but he was rather more of a maternal presence than anything. And so it was to London that I turned for somebody to hero-worship and my dramatic leanings led me, naturally, to a famous theatrical person.

I first saw him many years before. One September evening in the last year of the first world war, my parents had decided on a beano. Perhaps it was an anniversary celebration – their engagement day, their first sight of each other, the first trembling word – or perhaps it was to rejoice in the turn of the tide on the Western Front with old Jerry on the run at last. My brother was away at Stirling Court but I was included in the festivity, arranged well ahead and with everything, taxi, dinner and theatre booked. We were to dine first at the Savoy and then go to a revue called *Tails Up* at the Comedy Theatre and it was there that I got my first sight of that elegant star, Jack Buchanan. He sang, leaning nonchalantly on a stick, a number called 'An' everything' ('She's got a little bit of this and that an' everything'). Impossible, as with Gertrude Lawrence and many others, to describe the spell such performers cast. Mr Buchanan danced in a lissom manner that was called 'lazy', sang rather nasally and not very well, and acted hardly at all but in the theatre his presence was magical. His musical comedies were light, bright affairs with memorable tunes (the theatre orchestra continued to play them while the audience left the theatre, and kept on until there was nobody left). They ran a year or so and then another one bobbed up. Films, of which he made many, suited him less well. The actual physical presence was what counted.

And so, in my second term and with the sort of brash and impertinent confidence not uncommon in a youth of eighteen, I wrote Mr Buchanan a letter asking if I might call on him for advice about my future and a polite answer soon arrived and said 'I hope to see you when next you come to the theatre'. Hastening up to London for the next matinée performance of *That's A Good Girl*, I presented myself, with letter, at the stage door. Mr Buchanan's manager was called for, received me politely, calmed my apprehensions and fears of having been too impetuous ('Mr Buchanan quite understands') and then conducted me into the presence. Nothing could have been kinder than the way in which I was received, or wiser the advice I was given. Having started at Cambridge, why not stay the three years and get a degree? Then see what happened. I must have looked fairly callow and hopeless sitting there in my best suit, hair glinting with brilliantine, but at no point did Mr Buchanan try to discourage me or appear to think me and my hopes futile and negligible. When, after ten minutes or so, we parted, he gave me an agreeable smile and said 'Keep in touch'. Of course I never again dared to do so but it was nice of him to say it, and I shall always be grateful to him. No wonder he was so well loved.

I was meeting, and it is one of the points of a university, a great many new people. I find it very difficult to describe on paper my friends' characters and gifts accurately and in the way they deserve, and in the case of my closest friends I find it quite impossible. Their virtues are to me so superabundant and their vices so negligible that no sensible picture of them would emerge. Nor could I ever manage to describe faces and physiques that would make them in any way come alive. Maugham, who should know, said that this latter ability was among the rarest in a writer's armoury. It is certainly beyond me. I shall attempt nothing along these lines. Just take it, please, that the less I say, the more I mean, though words come more easily when writing of George Rylands, known to all as 'Dadie', a don at King's, a producer (as in those days we called a director) of plays, a lively scholar of English literature who blew away all the dreary dust of scholarship, an animator and encourager who, for me and many other undergraduates before and since, opened endless doors. My Cambridge and subsequent life would have been bleak without him. Most of us suffer, to a greater or lesser degree, from egomania but he had none at all and I never heard him utter a dull sentence. But like all such fascinators, he had a cross to bear. Over the years the circle of the fascinated becomes ever larger, the fascinator's energies diminish, and in the end the charm ration will hardly go round. Those denied their customary and pleasurable whack become at first despondent and then tetchy. There is no solution to this. Noël Coward, who was constantly finding himself in a similar pickle through over-fascinating, used just to hop on a ship and sail away. But Dadie was, luckily for his friends, tied hand and foot to Cambridge and there was for him no escape.

Cambridge undergraduates in my day had a wonderful advantage, the presence in the town of half a dozen or so married ladies, wives or widows of dons and so forth, who kept open house, involved themselves in university activities such as acting, were endlessly hospitable and kind, took an interest in what one was up to and were, though nobody in those unsophisticated days thought of them as such, a kind of mother substitute for those of us who had developed rather more slowly than others. There were, I am happy to say, three in my life – Mrs Salzman, Mrs Pryor and Mrs Gordon – and I can only hope that at the time one displayed (the young take so much for granted) as much gratitude to them as I now feel. They lent one books, provided coffee and cake, gave parties, remembered birthdays, mended clothes, listened sympathetically to one's troubles, produced pretty girls for the more romantically minded and, if one were keen on dancing, were ever ready, for it was the usual thing to do, to roll back the Axminster and put on the portable. The husbands in these cases were vague background presences who, though perfectly polite and pleasant and well disposed to all this lavish hospitality, managed to keep out of the way and to find occupations of their own.

Every so often, one's own hospitable instincts, entirely dormant in childhood and fairly so in youth, awoke at last and one gave either a lunch party (whitebait, cutlets and crème brûlée) or a tea-party (tomato sandwiches and Fuller's cake). As ladies were to be present, flowers seemed to be an essential part of the affair and I had no idea at all how best to manage with flowers, apart from buying them and then sticking them in a vase. I can remember to this day the sight of a vase of giant size delphiniums dominating the table, rendering visibility difficult (dear Mrs Pryor, small in size, was at a great disadvantage) and shedding their petals into the butter. Lupins too presented a problem and were inclined to disintegrate before one's eyes. I dare say the fact that they had travelled from the flower shop to my rooms in my bicycle basket had discouraged them and they were making their floral protest. Did the ladies seem to notice one's various gaucheries? Not a bit. They chattered, bless them, blithely on and I send them, across the years, great waves of gratitude.

It was in my Hobson Street bedroom that I had my first, though not my last, experience of becoming intoxicated, a quite unplanned venture into the world of the tipsy. I had been invited to a dinner party thrown by an affluent friend in an excellent Regent Street (the Cambridge one) restaurant. We were eight in number and we wore our dinner-jackets, as there were to be no ladies present: otherwise it would, unbelievably now, have had to be tails. Cocktails were offered. I drank. With the soup there was sherry. I drank. With the fish there was the then inevitable Liebfraumilch. I did not refuse it. Claret appeared with the meat, and brandy with the coffee and, jabbering away, I imbibed with the rest. The party was a success for we all knew each other well and most of them were ADC members. Noticing nothing amiss with my constitution, I duly returned on foot to my rooms and went to bed about midnight, upon which the foot of the bed rose from the floor and hovered, swaying, in the air. Much mystified, I switched on the light to see what was up and, finding all normal, I tried again to sleep, rapidly becoming once more air-borne. Eventually I kept the light on and by staring fixedly at it, hypnotised myself into fitful sleep. A fearful headache next morning encouraged me to take things easy and have a restful day (only one cinema).

For theatrically inclined undergraduates, the main event of the Lent Term was the Marlowe Society production, usually of a Shakespeare play, and in my first year it was *King Lear*, with Peter Hannen, son of Nicholas Hannen, in the title role. Peter was a brilliant actor and already, though only 20, unusually mature, and I was very excited when the Society secretary came and offered me the part of Cordelia. She finally enters, you will recall, dead and in Lear's arms, but as in those days I was very small and slight and slim, the transportation question was nothing of a problem. But my tutor, alas, discovered a College Rule which prevented me acting more than twice a year. I was enormously discouraged by this, but was determined to help in some way, and so I asked him if I could prompt. Apparently there was no College Rule about prompting, though I dare say he tried to find one, and I was allowed to undertake this important task, during the course of which I came to know the play rather well.

However, there was also a lesser theatrical event, namely the annual Smoking Concert of the Amateur Dramatic Club. It was known as 'The Smoker' and there was one performance only before an all male audience neatly attired in dinner jackets and full of glasses of wine and expectancy. It was all male because one of the main points of the production was to supply mild indecencies and sauciness, provided the indecencies were considered funny. The Smoker was really a sort of revue – songs and sketches and so forth – and a characteristic item, thought to be hilarious, was one announced on the programme as 'Recital of Water Music by Sir Philpott Knightley' and in which a delightful Oundle friend, Randulph Barker, extracted hymn tunes from a row of chamber-pots. The pots were arranged in an ascending scale and according to the note they sounded, as in a xylophone, and Randulph collected them that morning from members' bedrooms and tuned them up with, I trust, water. The final effect was very pleasing as, smartly dressed in tails, he banged out tunes with drum sticks and 'Lead Kindly Light' had to be encored. And no smoker was complete without two performers supplying, in a cross-talk act, a string of non-sequitur jokes:

A. I'm learning to play the trumpet. The high notes are difficult but yesterday I got up to G.
B. That's nothing. Last night I got up to P.
A. Excuse me but are you feeling hysterical?
B. No. He's feeling mine.

Competition was fierce, not only to acquire tickets for the performance but also, among the members, for opportunities to display, in lighter vein, their talents. In your first year you couldn't expect to shine very much and I felt myself honoured to be permitted to render, in a garden-party dress of my mother's, a popular number from an early talking film, a number which seemed to possess a suitable double entendre:

When you're feeling all at a loose end,
Just remember me,
For I'm at a loose end wanting you
So we're two little loose ends with nothing to do.

Normally, however, an insignificant and non-speaking role was all you could expect and in this connection I like to remember the experience of Geoffrey Toone, a Christ's friend and as keen on the theatre as I. He, in his first year, was allotted a minor part and, on the appointed day, mounted his bicycle at

7 p.m. in New Square, arrived at the ADC, dressed himself as a female, carefully applied make-up and, at the given moment, made his entrance on to the brightly lit stage where Lionel Gamlin, an experienced actor, was in the middle of a sketch in which he played a lascivious theatrical producer busy rehearsing a play. Geoffrey looked quite fairly unlikely as a woman but Lionel, seeing him there, moved on to a section of the dialogue aimed at creating a dirty laugh. The script ran as follows:

(*Enter Miss Arbuthnot*)

Lionel: Oh there you are, Miss Arbuthnot. I shall be running through your part in a moment.

(*Exit Miss Arbuthnot*)

The laugh duly came and Geoffrey then exited, removed female clothes and make-up, put on jacket and bags and macintosh and gown, mounted his bicycle and, having pedalled his way back to New Square, settled down for a bedtime Ovaltine, and with, within him, a warm glow, not only of Ovaltine but a glow from a sense of theatrical achievement. He had not been long, it is true, before the public but it was undoubtedly a beginning (he has done very well since). He had helped, limited though his contribution had been, to carry forwards and onwards the sacred Thespian torch and who knew, next year he might actually speak.

Most of my contemporaries were given by their parents an allowance of money for the year ('It'll do the young man good to learn to stand financially on his own feet') and as a result were often in a terrible state of anxiety about bills, but my father kindly preferred just to pay all college and university accounts and leave me without worry, though every vac I was expected to hand him a list of my petty cash disbursements. The items required careful doctoring for he would certainly have disapproved of many of them and so I quite shamelessly and dishonestly disguised my frequent cinema visits as 'Offertory money', 'Subscription to RSPCA.' and 'Trip to Ely Cathedral'. My parents were both admirably businesslike and efficient over money and accounts and all sums, great or small, were written down and totted up. Then 'you knew where you were'. I did once strive to emulate them in this respect and to that end I bought a small account book. I have it still and it has got just the one entry in it.

Account book 1s. 6d

Some of my friends were more affluent than others and entertained lavishly. One of them was an American who bore the name of Charles Bedford Sutton Shope. He gave frequent dinners at the quaintly styled 'Scotch Hoose' café in the Market Place and used to startle the waiter, unused to the ways of the world, by ordering a bottle of claret and saying 'Be sure to *chambrer* the *vin*'. Another was the excellent and musically-gifted Ronnie Hill, also at Christ's. He was a warm-hearted chap with a wide acquaintance and on going in his second year into College, decided to give a large party, a sort of house-warming affair for everybody that he knew and we all received impressive and gilt-edged and copper-plated invitations to the beano. Wishing to leave nobody out, Ronnie hospitably sent an invitation to the tutor, who was his as well as mine, but received a chilly rebuff ('While acknowledging your invitation, I must draw your attention to College Rule No. 483 (b) . . .'). Parties above a certain and rather small number were only allowed on official occasions, or if it was a gathering of this or that reputable Society. So poor Ronnie's merry little 'do' was off, a non-event, a failure, a cancellation, but the spirited fellow slightly got his own back and soon afterwards we all received another communication, again elaborately gilt-edged and copper-plated. It read, OWING TO MY TUTOR POINT-ING OUT TO ME COLLEGE RULE No. 483 (b), I MUCH REGRET TO SAY THAT THERE AIN'T GOING TO BE NO PARTY. Did he send one to our tutor? I can only hope so.

One fine May morning in my last summer term at Cambridge, I withdrew from the Bank the sum of Three pounds (then quite an item: it would have to feature in my term's petty cash account as 'Replacement for stolen bicycle pump' and 'Book by Canon Sheepshanks on Early Brass Rubbings'). I was dressed in my best suit, which was at that time a lightish fawn with thin red pin-stripe and constructed for me by a City tailor, and I set out by train and without permission for London. I had been informed, and the information had been confirmed by Peter Hannen, that a number of members of the theatrical profession were often to be seen at lunch at a restaurant called the Ivy, situated right opposite the Ambassadors Theatre, with the St Martin's only a few yards away. On arrival at Liverpool Street station, I telephoned and booked a table and in due course and trembling with excitement, I pushed open a door that I was eventually to push open a good many more times.

It was one of those enchanted days when everything goes right. If I could have chosen the first people I was to see as I walked into the Ivy it would have been Gertrude Lawrence and Beatrice Lillie, and there they miraculously were, seated opposite the door and talking animatedly. I, of course, stopped dead in my tracks, lowered involuntarily my jaw and just gaped at them but they were soon spared a continuation of this clumsy impertinence by my being led away to my table, happily surprisingly near. I gazed about me and saw, in that corner behind the door which he made very much his own, Nöel Coward giving lunch to Marie Tempest. Dotted about elsewhere I could see Lilian Braithwaite and Owen Nares and Ivy Tresmand. Next to my small table there was another one, as yet unoccupied. Who was it to be? I had already seen *Bitter Sweet* twice and there, walking towards me and sitting down within touching distance, was its great American star, Peggy Wood. I suppose that at some point I had ordered some lunch but I have no recollection of doing so. I stared so intently at poor Miss Wood that in the end she stopped eating her melon, put down her spoon, gave me a delightful smile and just said, 'Do eat your lunch. It's getting cold'. I hurriedly ploughed my way through whatever it was, and when I had got it down, Peggy Wood smiled again and said 'Well done!' I cannot think that this was her first experience of demented fan behaviour.

I stayed on drinking coffee until absolutely everybody had gone, took a bus to Liverpool Street and returned to Cambridge unrepentant, entirely satisfied. Next day I bought a gramophone record of Miss Wood singing 'I'll See You Again' (it would have to go down as 'Repairs to tennis racquet').

Lucky chances and a good fortune which I have done nothing to deserve have sometimes brought me into contact with a number of gifted people and now and then a passing acquaintanceship has blossomed happily into friendship. For one such rewarding sprouting, one of the best of my life, the seeds were sown long ago, and in the theatre. During my years at Cambridge, my Uncle Oswald lived in the then popular type of residence known as a 'service flat' in London, where domestic stress was eased by the fact that servants and meals could be whistled up as required from the lower regions and were the manager's responsibility. There was therefore no tiresome interviewing of prospective housemaids ('How long exactly were you with this Mrs Slowly-Jones?') or wrestling with menus ('Are you getting sick of mutton?'). During the summer long vacations and before I went off to stay with a German or French family, I used to spend a few days with my uncle and in 1929 and after one such whistled up dinner, we set out for the St James's Theatre to see a play called *Caprice*. Great things were being said of a couple newly arrived from America and who were making their first married appearance in London. Their name was, it seemed, Lunt and Mrs Lunt was an English actress and her stage name was Lynn Fontanne.

It was indeed a night to remember. The house lights went down, the curtain rose and one saw at once that a miracle had occurred, a revolution in comedy acting. The Lunts' impact was an astonishment. Never before had such playing been seen. In the plays of the period, lines and speeches were holy material and especially when written by Galsworthy, Shaw, Barrie and Pinero (no dead wood there). Words, even when provided by lesser dramatists, were given their full weight and actors waited to speak until somebody else had finished. It often irked them, but they waited. The dialogue in Coward's plays certainly went at top speed and was in short speeches and frequently in single lines, but even there they waited for each other. The Lunts turned all that upside down. They threw away lines, they trod on each other's words, they gabbled, they whispered, they spoke at the same time. They spoke, in fact, as people do in ordinary life, a theatrical innovation that nobody seems to have tried before (Lady Macbeth cutting Macbeth short would indeed be a novelty, welcome to some). The result may sound chaotic but it was not. The essential lines came across and they extracted from what was fairly light stuff (well, look at the title) laugh after laugh. And they had the ability (Marie Tempest had it too, and in some dreadful plays) to make the audience feel that they were enjoying themselves equally. They were a supremely elegant pair (Lynn made her first entrance in a stunning red and yellow dress) and they took their curtains with a style and panache that enraptured everybody. I returned to the flat in a dream.

Forty years later I went to stay with them in America. I had met them first in Edith Evans's Albany rooms towards the end of the war. They had come over to appear in *There Shall Be No Night* and had very courageously taken the dangerous air passage from Portugal that had already cost the life of Leslie Howard. I was introduced to them by Hugh ('Binkie')

Beaumont, head of the theatrical firm of H. M. Tennent, and was immediately bewitched. Lynn who, had she failed as an actress could well have become what we must call 'a leading coiffeuse', had entwined in her beautiful hair a bunch of violets and she asked me to look at them and tell her if they were wilting. If so, should she water them? Perhaps I could give them a sprinkle? She then said that their bed at the Savoy Hotel was higher at the sides than in the middle and how very agreeable that was for this irregularity tended in the night to throw them together. They came rolling down the sides, and Bang! She added, with a faraway look and *à propos de rien*, that it is very difficult to keep up a quarrel in a double bed.

Alfred was equally engaging and, as is the way with most actors, relished stories against himself and when disaster had struck. There had been a performance of *Elizabeth The Queen* when, playing the Earl of Essex, he had buried his face in Lynn's bosom, her strings of pearls had burst and gone flying all over the stage, and he emerged from this passionate embrace with a large pearl stuck up his nose. My cackles rent the room and we became friends and after that I saw them whenever they were in London. We went to theatres and, very occasionally, a film. We had meals, or just sat and talked: and laughed: and laughed.

They came twice to stay with me in Devon (they were fascinated by every aspect of English village life and loved meeting people) and reciprocal visits to them in Wisconsin had been often and kindly suggested and at last, in 1970, I was able to accept. I would not at that period have found an expensive journey very convenient financially but all that was generously and tactfully taken care of and I started off in what was for me an adventuresome manner. I went to Liverpool and set sail on an Empress liner for Canada, proceeding from Montreal by Greyhound bus round the lakes and so into America by the back door. The sea trip took six days and my social standing was not great for, on my passport and opposite the slot requiring details of 'Occupation', I had put, and as requested in capital letters, the description WRITER but I had written it poorly and at first, and even second, glance it read WAITER. Faces fell when I presented it at the purser's office, despite my attempts at a scholarly air and my depressingly la-di-da voice, and I was allotted a very un-grand cabin, sharing with three.

Sad to find that waiters, so happily associated with food and drink, should be ranked so low.

I had, as it happened, never intended to cut a dash and the role of life and soul of the boat was immediately taken over by a hugely jolly party of nuns returning from a European visit to the religious and other rigours of Saskatchewan. Never were there such madcaps. The continent had gone to their coiffed heads with a vengeance. The barbolawork-encrusted panels of the dining saloon resounded to their shrieks as they tucked wildly in. They pressed their noses excitedly on the glass doors of the cinema, wishful to be first in for *The Wizard of Oz*. They were the last to retire to bed (I followed them about, anxious to miss nothing), lingering long over the advertised Late Night Snack in the Windsor Lounge. They were the joy of our Social Hostess, a Miss Warboys, for they played shuffleboard, they threw deck quoits, they entered for every fancy dress competition and no Bingo session was complete without the imposing presence of the Mother Superior (she never quite mastered the rules and kept screeching 'Bingo!' way ahead of time). When nearing Newfoundland and icebergs were sighted, they were first in the field with bad taste jokes about the *Titanic*. They attended every concert and took a particular liking for our resident pianist, 'Reg', whose periods at the keyboard were announced on a notice headed Today's Doings. '8 pm Chopin and Reg get together in a big way'. Waiter or not, I had a lovely time.

For travellers contemplating passage on Greyhound buses, the essential decision to make is to abandon all normal thoughts of day and night and of the activities connected with each. The finest buses leave about midnight, and marvellously cheap and safe and comfortable they are. There is a lavatory on board (faces politely avert themselves as you make your swaying way up the gangway and into it) and there is a halt every two or three hours. One snatches a hamburger here, and a catnap there. Every now and then I got off altogether and put up for 24 hours in a hotel. I expected, and got, nothing very de luxe. The scenery was becoming increasingly reminiscent of story-book illustrations in *South With Wolfe* and as we went further west an occasional fellow passenger was the dead spit of some old aunty of Hiawatha's.

In the middle of the lakes I stayed for three days at Sault Ste Marie, where ships are transferred in giant locks from one lake to another, and then pressed on round the north of Lake Superior and to Duluth in Minnesota. Somewhere near Fort William I crossed the frontier and less than agreeable it was for both Canadian and American officials eyed me with suspicion. Why was I in this remote spot? Where was I going and why? What money had I? Unfriendly they were, especially the Canadians, whom I was about to chide in ringing British tones until I thought better of it. I doubt if 'I say, look here!' would have cut much ice. However, on their demanding to know the name of the host at this house to which I alleged I was going, I spoke the one syllable 'Lunt', upon which the atmosphere briskly altered for the better and they stamped every document in sight. Lynn, wonderfully garbed and looking highly incongruous in the bus-station, met me by telephonic arrangement at Milwaukee and whizzed me away by car to the considerable pleasures of Genesee Depot.

It had been Alfred's family home. There were lawns and woods and parkland. There was the splendid old main house and, dotted about the grounds, two other houses in one of which Alfred's agreeable sister and husband lived when not in Chicago. There was a large studio standing on its own, with emergency bedroom and bathroom. There were flowers everywhere and, inside the house, beautiful objects, Lynn among them, whichever way you cared to look. There was exquisite china. There seemed to be five separate sitting rooms. There were oil paintings of Lynn at various stages of her career. My bedroom was a haven of comfort and prettiness. And there was, goodness me, welcome on the mat and I stayed a whole month.

It was summer and in the afternoon I swam in the pool where, on sighting my naked body, the engaging little chipmunks, cheeks bulging, decided that I must be some new type of walrus and, abandoning their initial nervousness, crept nearer and ate their tea. I walked daily to the small village, a single street with a bank and liquor store and shops and indistinguishable from a Hollywood set. Polite greetings of 'Hi!' were to be heard and as I have never been able to manage 'Hi!' with conviction, I settled for 'Good afternoon'. This, uttered in my prim English accent, gave much pleasure. In shops, old grandmothers were hauled down from upstairs to hear me speak. I was asked if I knew the Queen. 'Only to wave to', I said, and they clearly had a picture in their minds of Her

Majesty cheerily rattling up a Palace window and waving back as I strolled, waving, up the Mall. In the chemist's I had a happy find, an aid to sleep called Caramalt Slumbertight. I do hope it came Wodehouse's way.

In the mornings I worked at book reviews and BBC talks for Woman's Hour and letters. For this, Lynn and Alfred gave me the freedom of the studio, also full of attractive items and with, on the walls, the originals of various *New Yorker* drawings, in particular the Helen Hokinson ones that referred to themselves. In one of them a lady director is seen rehearsing an amateur cast in an old Lunt-Fontanne play and saying to a man and woman clutching each other nervously on a sofa, 'This is where the Lunts *rolled*'. My hosts warmly approved of industry and liked to see me busy. There was an alarming story of a visit paid by the distinguished American play-wright, S. N. ('Sam') Behrman. He was working on a play for them (I think it must have been *The Second Man*) and, as he had arrived at tea-time, they naturally hoped that he would waste no time in starting and with this in mind they ushered him to the studio so that he might do an hour or two before dinner (one such author, similarly trapped, swore that they locked him into the studio and wouldn't let him out until he had produced at least four pages of work but I don't believe it. I think.) But Sam said that he thought that perhaps on this occasion he would work better upstairs in his bedroom and so off he went. 'And after a short while,' Lynn said, recounting the affair to me, 'Alfred and I took a little walk and by chance we went up that raised path at the back of the house and after a bit I suddenly said to Alfred, "Good gracious, do you realise that we've got to just that point in the path from which you can see straight down into Sam's bedroom!" And so down we looked and do you know what he was doing? Not working at all! Just lying on the bed reading the newspaper'. I assumed a deeply shocked expression at such idleness, dishonesty even, while marvelling aloud at the coincidental nature of their walk pattern. 'Yes, wasn't it a coincidence', said Lynn without a flicker. I dare not catch Alfred's eye. I had to be rather careful with my laughter for Alfred's sense of humour was by far the sharper of the two and I did not want to show my awareness of this and cause unhappiness. Sometimes, if Lynn (and she was after all a good bit older, ten years being the general view) were slow in understanding something, Alfred

99

would refer to her as 'my idiot bride': but it was said with love.

There was an admirable cook and enormous trouble was taken over the food but on some evenings Alfred liked to cook for us himself. It was a hobby (vegetable growing was another) and brilliant he was at it. After one of their London runs, he and his excellent dresser, Jules, had gone over to Paris and taken the full Cordon Bleu course. This ended in an examination. The necessary ingredients were put out and some complicated dish was demanded, 'and do you know, I was far more nervous even than on a first night. In fact, my hands were trembling to such an extent that I had to ask the nice lady next to me to switch on my stove.' They had both passed the test and the results were a joy to behold and to eat. And while we ate, the reminiscences and the fun poured forth – Steffi Duna's Hungarian mother saying 'I 'av ze most awful craps' (it is thought she meant 'cramps'): Violet Vanbrugh, a non-comedienne if ever there was one, becoming so startled at getting a laugh in a play that she swept down to the footlights and took a bow: and, though perhaps this was on a later occasion, Dean Martin saying to the actor in *Airport* who went to the plane's lavatory and blew himself up with a bomb, 'Boy, when you go to the john, you certainly go to the john'.

Memory is an unreliable faculty and most of us over the age of seventy get some things wrong. Sometimes at Genesee a muddle was made and I treasure a snatch of dialogue that was spoken one day at lunch. 'Al-fred'. When addressing him and in that beautiful English voice that never revealed the slightest trace of her fifty years in America, Lynn liked to allow a small interval between the two syllables, creating a slight and affectionate drawl. The reply was unvarying.

'Yes, Lynnie dear, what is it?'

'Alfred, you remember that time when you went to New York to have lunch with Mozart . . .'

'With whom?'

'You know, Mozart'.

'Oh, I don't think it can have been Mozart, dear'.

'Alfred, it was Mozart'.

'But surely . . .'

'It was Mozart, Alfred'.

The discussion continued for some time with Lynn sticking valiantly to her guns and repeating the improbable name until it finally appeared that she was intending to speak of the author of their famous 1924 success, *The Guardsman*, a Hungarian dramatist called Molnar. Not Mozart, but foreign anyway and so what's the difference?

Another muddle concerned something rather more English and nearer home.

'Al – fred'.

'Yes, Lynnie dear, what is it?'

'Alfred, you remember when during the war we were staying with Ivor at Redroofs and he was composing 'We'll Gather Violets' . . .'

'Yes dear, but I don't think it was violets . . .'

'Alfred, it was violets. I'd been walking in the garden with Ivor and he suddenly said "I'm going to write a song called 'We'll Gather Violets'" . . .'

'But violets wouldn't . . .'

'Alfred, it was violets'.

This time I was drawn into the discussion and I said, placatingly, that although gathering violets would have been equally lovely and evocative, I thought that what Ivor really wanted to gather was lilacs, which had the added advantage of having only two syllables instead of three and therefore fitted the music better. I also pointed out that the verb 'to gather' was surely rather too ample a one for tiny violets, suggesting great armfuls of them. However, none of this was allowed and so in the end we settled for the fact, if fact it was, that Ivor had originally intended to gather violets but had switched, for reasons unknown, to lilacs. It was good to have the matter finally thrashed out.

A strange thing. I have never in my life, either in America or England, heard anybody refer to Lynn as 'Lynn Lunt', which she assuredly was. To servants and shop people and, of course, in the theatre, Alfred always referred to her as 'Miss Fontanne', a name which he also used when lovingly teasing her about unpunctuality ('Well done, Miss Fontanne. Only sixteen minutes late'.) 'Miss Fontanne' helped Lynn to preserve her individuality for, odd as it may seem in such a single-mindedly orchestrated pair, there was always an affectionate rivalry between them. Discussing past successes, Lynn would say 'That was Alfred's play' or 'That was my play'. Did they tot up the number of their respective lines? I wouldn't entirely rule this out. Such was their extraordinary modesty, they were both always convinced that if only they had tried a little bit harder, the plays would have been so much better. A constant subject for discussion was their sensational 1935 American production (alas, we never saw it in London) of *The Taming of the Shrew* which they turned into a brilliant knockabout pantomime, endlessly inventive and funny. Whose play had that been? One suspects that they had mutually decided that it had been Alfred's play, for a small grievance remained, even after 35 years.

'Alfred, I still think we were wrong to cut those lines in Act IV . . .'

'Oh no, Lynnie dear, it was a tiresome little scene'.

'Alfred, there was a laugh there'.

'Oh no, it was much better out of the way . . .'

'I could have got a laugh, Alfred'.

'But it held up the action'.

'There was a *laugh* . . .'

And so on. They told me, and acted, various bits of business that they had contrived, all of it hilarious, and there was a marvellous entrance for Lynn. She was shown returning from a shooting expedition, her beaters bearing with them a dead property cow hung upside down from a pole, with its udder flopping about. Arriving centre stage, she raised her gun and blasted loudly off heavenwards and in a few moments a very large dead bird fell heavily from the skies and landed right on Bianca's head. Not much fun for Bianca but a hilarious moment for the audience. Remembering it all, Lynn gave her famous laugh, a widely spaced and perfectly controlled 'Ha. Ha. Ha'. Alfred's play indeed!

One morning an idea came to me for another of my solo turns. I had always enjoyed hearing one lady writer discussing, enthusiastically or otherwise, the literary work of another and this seemed to be a profitable subject, especially if I were to use a sort of Rose Macaulay voice (the letter 's' presented a difficulty and came out as rather more of a 'sh': and 'soft' was apt to be 'sorft'). The two new invented works under discussion were *Crimson Her Chariot Wheels* (a Portrait of Boadicea) and *Lust Is Silent*, a novel. I worked hard at the sketch – it was only about 2½ minutes long and not unfunny – and rehearsed it well and one day after lunch and when Lynn had gone to rest, I informed Alfred of my creation. 'Arthur, you're to get up and do it at once' he said (I have to confess that

My mother displays her young

My mother's parents

Unwillingly to a wedding – my Essex grandmother

With my father, at Barnes

Oundle School, 1926.
Member of winning house
rugger team!

1934. At time of first
broadcast in BBC's *Charlot's
Hour* (*photo Kenneth Collins*)

With W. Somerset
Maugham, 1936, Villa
Mauresque

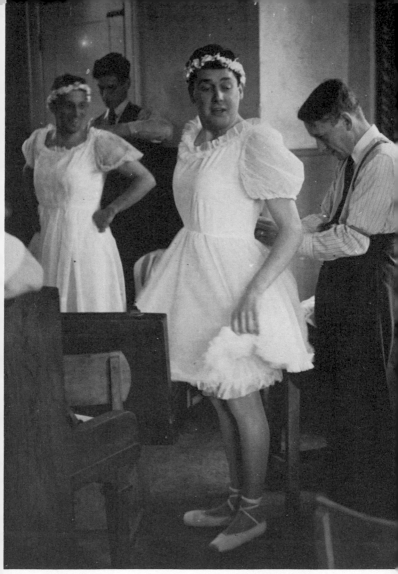

1938. Ballet preparations — Oundle School Masterpieces

1940. Lt Marshall,
Intelligence Corps
(*photo Howard Coster*)

1943. Inspection
of Combined
Operations HQ by
King George VI.
'My turn nearly next'

1954. On leaving Oundle School

Call My Bluff: Frank Muir, Robert Robinson

At 'Myrtlebank': with Larry Grayson

In the garden

Where the work is done
(*photo Ted Coleman*)

they liked me to perform, regularly and as a sort of domestic cabaret, my turns to them and so I felt no embarrassment at reporting the presence of a new one). I did as I was told and spouted it out. 'Do it again', Alfred said. I did so. Alfred left the room and knocked at Lynn's door. There was a distant wail of 'Alfred, I am resting'. Further knocks, and 'Lynnie, come out at once'. 'I am resting, Alfred'. 'Do you hear me, Lynnie? *Come out!*' She dutifully emerged and joined us. 'Arthur, do it again'. I did so. The new turn was then discussed at some length and Alfred kindly suggested a tidier and better ending for it. I mention all this in no boastful spirit but simply as an indication of their interest in any performance anywhere. Though deeply concerned about their own careers, there never was theatrically a less self-centred pair. Acting was all, no matter who was doing it. I had recently seen Carol Channing's solo (well, more or less) act at Drury Lane. She was a great friend of theirs and they begged me to tell them every detail. Every item was treasured. Questions were asked. Their eyes shone. And when in London we went to plays together – the all-male *As You Like It*, *Cowardy Custard*, *Hadrian VII*, *Crown Matrimonial* – we sat up into the early hours discussing them. They were, and how very profitably for the world, obsessed.

At dinner we often talked happily of London friends – Joyce Carey, John Perry, Adrianne Allen, John Gielgud – and one evening when we were discussing the plays of Winifred Clemence Dane, I was bold enough to mention, for I knew that Alfred would enjoy them, some of Winifred's more indecent remarks. These were famous and entirely innocent. The physical side of life had passed her by, together with the words, slang and otherwise, that accompany it. She had no idea at all why people laughed, or tried tactfully to conceal laughter, as time and time again she settled for an unfortunate word or phrase. Inviting Mr Coward to lunch during the war and when food was difficult, she boomed encouragement down the telephone: '*Do* come! I've got such a lovely cock' ('I *do* wish you'd call it a hen', Noël answered). Asking her friend, Olwen, what items she had managed to secure for a summer picnic, she was heard to yell up the stairs, 'Olwen, have you got crabs?' Wanting, for one of her plays, to write about an important new vitamin, she naturally chose Vitamin F. When staying at Binkie's and descending for breakfast, she said how delightful it had been to see outside her window, on waking, 'a row of tits'. And in the evening and finding that she had run short of writing paper, she turned on the stairs on her way up to bed and cried 'Now, who's going to give me a block?' To use correctly, in a literary sense, the words 'erection', 'tool' and 'spunk' was second nature to her. When wishing to describe herself as being full of life and creative energy, she chose, not really very wisely, the word 'randy'. To hear a large and imposing woman of fifty announcing to a roomful of actors that she felt randy was really something. She never cottoned on to the fact that the name 'John Thomas' had a hidden significance and she was heard one day expatiating about the different sides to a person's nature: 'Yes, every man has three John Thomases – the John Thomas he keeps to himself, the John Thomas he shares with his friends, and the John Thomas he shows to the world'. 'Of course, Winifred' people said, when they could speak.

I trotted them out, and all seemed well, but next morning I had slight misgivings and asked Alfred whether all this had been tactless and too much for Lynn. 'Don't worry', he said. 'Lynnie heard such things in her cradle. It is babytalk to her. She croons it in her sleep'. So that was all right.

Alfred was diffident and even very shy on occasion. Self-confidence was never his. Whenever you went round to see him after a performance you found that you had seen the play on the very worst night of its run. He sat slumped and despondent in front of the glass. 'I wish that you'd come on any other night. I was *awful*'. To the amusement of his many English friends, the word 'awful' was always pronounced as though it were 'offal' and this description of his performance seldom varied. Tosh, of course. He wouldn't have known how to begin to be awful. He merely provided varying degrees of brilliance. Lynn was more self-assured and Alfred happily relied on this strength in her character. 'You know, whenever salaries are being discussed or there's money trouble, I just send in Lynnie'. One would hardly have cared to be a manager facing a Miss Fontanne who had just been informed that her salary was to be cut. They both had a horror of drunks, having seen so much of the damage done, and an occasional drunk in their company was not unknown. It was Lynn who was left to give the karate chop to an actor who was found lurching about the wings during a tour of Canada. 'When you sober up', she said, 'just remember that Alfred and I loathe your guts. We're through with you for ever'. It makes an alarming picture – the sodden performer, the angry actress with her colour rising and her eyes flashing.

She had great determination and I became unwillingly involved in a display of this characteristic. One very warm evening in Genesee we were sitting, after a delicious dinner, drinking our coffee. I had had a whisky sour before dinner, and a glass or two of hock with dinner and was feeling well contented. Then dialogue began.

'Al-fred'.

'Yes, Lynnie dear, what is it?'

'Alfred, Arthur would like a liqueur'.

This was news to me for the subject had not been mentioned and I had not been asked nor had I shown any eagerness for more drink. And with the temperature in the 80s, the thought of a sticky liqueur was in no way alluring. Alfred was as surprised as I.

'Arthur, do you really want a liqueur?'

'Well, I . . . you see . . .'

'Arthur would like a liqueur, Alfred'.

There followed a discussion about what liqueurs, if any, they still had, and an uncertain picture emerged, together with considerable doubt about where, in that huge house, the liqueurs might be hiding. Nobody seemed to have set eyes on liqueurs since they didn't know the day when and I hoped that this would end the matter. Not at all.

'Alfred, give me the keys'.

'Oh, Lynnie dear, you really can't go poking about at this time of night . . .'

'Arthur wants a liqueur. Give me the keys'.

They were handed over and, equipped with keys, Lynn and I set forth on our needless expedition. We entered the kitchen regions, unlocking and opening cupboards as we went. We searched larders and pantries and still-rooms. We ransacked the cellar. Sometimes keys fitted locks and sometimes they didn't and we had to work our way through the bunch before a door creaked open. We then mounted to the dining-rooms (there were two). More openings, more creaks, more key clanking. I was a half-hearted searcher but my hostess was full of vigour and high spirits and eventually got her reward – a dusty bottle half full of Cointreau lying in a wine cooler behind a screen. She poured me a liqueur glass and we bore it back. We had been away the best part of half an hour. 'There!' she said triumphantly. I tried to look grateful and started to sip. Alfred gave me a wink. 'As you see, Arthur, in this house if you want anything you've only got to ask. It can be provided in a twinkling. Well done, Miss Fontanne, you've been like lightning'.

On another occasion, and far away in Florida, her determination brought an altogether less successful result. We were staying in furnished country club apartments in a small town called Naples on the Gulf, looking out on the Gulf of Mexico, where my safety razor had decided to develop a malfunction. Needing, in order to preserve my well-groomed English appearance, a replacement, I made my way to the chemist's shop near by, Lynn kindly accompanying me. My accent produced the customary polite smiles, after which the lady assistant displayed her razor availabilities, each of them being, in the modish modern fashion, fixed to a piece of cardboard backing and protected from dust, air, corrosive influences and all things harmful by a firm, transparent, plastic covering. One could admire the razor but not, in the shop, actually touch it, but then, who needed to? I chose one and was about to pay for it when a voice spoke. 'Mr Marshall will want to hold the razor in his hand before he buys it. Will you please take it out of its covering and let him hold it'.

I wanted no such thing. The razor looked to be of a type virtually indistinguishable from my defective one and I was happy to take the negligible risk of it being not what I required. The assistant rightly stood her ground. 'I am afraid that it is not possible to extract the razor from its covering before purchase. It is not our policy'. 'Mr Marshall will not be satisfied until he has touched it. Kindly remove it'. I muttered little half sentences and made noises indicating that I really would be perfectly content to abide by the shop's policy. As policies go, it seemed splendid. 'I can only repeat that I must keep to our ruling on this point. It would be very difficult to re-insert a rejected razor that had been extracted and handled. Customers prefer the article to be in pristine form'.

Well, some people are defeated by this kind of sales talk and some are not and I saw Lynn, to my horror, lift up the cardboard backing in her left hand and with her right hand start to pick with the nail of her fore-finger at the plastic cover. She picked, as she did most things, intently and vigorously and

I saw the plastic shift slightly. The assistant, looking outraged, moved closer. I could bear no more and, eyes averted, edged my way slowly down the counter, pretending a lively interest in the other products on view and sale. And shortly afterwards there came the sound of a loud slap. Lynn had, once again, got her reward. She decided not to notice her little reprimand and after I had paid, and stammered an apology, she sailed out of the shop with the greatest serenity. And later there was an episode in an Edinburgh antique shop . . . but enough! She did not wholly dislike a mild fracas, a disturbance, divergent views, ruffled feathers. They were stimulating.

When Lynn had time on her hands she was apt to suggest to her women friends that they might find her skills as a coiffeuse useful and, on receiving the slightest show of encouragement (perhaps the encourager did not like to appear to be discouraged), would seize scissors and combs and start in. With promising heads of hair the results were often miraculously successful, for she had a real gift. On one occasion, however, when they were both staying in Switzerland with Noël Coward, she started on hair that markedly lacked promise. It belonged to Rebecca West. It was a good, solid and fairly crinkly mass of hair and it served its purpose, but that was about all. Lynn worked away, snipping here and curling there, with little of value to show for it. In the end she put down her implements, sighed and said 'There's nothing I can do really. Never mind dear. You've got quite nice eyes and so that's something to be thankful for'. Dame Rebecca, later relating this incident, gave a delighted chuckle and said 'What a splendid woman!' True.

Now that they are both gone, they live again a little for me in their letters, of which I possess a large number. They contain nothing startling (they were not at all given to waspishness about fellow performers, much preferring everybody to be successful) but they may one day be of interest to an American university or student. They were both of them admirable correspondents and when not playing, and somewhat isolated in Genesee Depot, longed for the postman's arrival and, above all, for news from England. One could not write too often.

Their letters are characteristic. Lynnie's are charming and loving and full of practical details about their visits to London, or friends' visits to them — times of planes, accommodation needed, best route to take and so forth. Alfred's seldom fail to display his sense of humour, which had a strong schoolboy streak in it. He wrote to say that when Noël was staying with them, he had one day rushed to the piano and concocted another version of Sullivan's 'Lost Chord': it began 'Seated one day on my organ, I was jumpy and ill at ease'. He knew that I disapproved of an English singer (I will call her Marigold Myles) for she never sang the melodic line of a song, even when Jerome Kern had written it, and warbled away in highish regions of her own, and so a PS would say 'Marigold sends her best' or 'I've written to Marigold Myles and asked her to come and live with you'. He collected newspaper cuttings for me: an advertisement for 'The Jesus Christ Power and Light Company': a film announcement of 'Sexual Practices in Sweden (Kiddie Matinee Sat 3 pm)': an account of a night club singer of vast size and called Miss Baby Dumpling. The last communication that I had from him, shortly before he went into hospital, was a post-card of two huge lions basking in the African sun. They have just had an enormous meal – bones and other evidence are lying about – and their contented expressions tell all. On the back was written 'Whatever became of Marigold Myles?'

SCENE V

Unexpected Usher

Let me admit at once that I tried everything I knew not to become a schoolmaster, the career that my parents had plan ned for me many years before and which was the reason for my presence at Cambridge. The whole idea of it depressed me, especially the thought of returning to Oundle in a magisterial capacity. I had had no sort of training as a teacher and dreaded the whole business. In June and after I had come down from the university, warfare broke out between me and my parents and there was another Battle of Newbury. I behaved as badly as I knew how. I whined, I moaned, I shuddered, I wriggled. I showered Royal Academy of Dramatic Art brochures on my adversaries and promised that, if I were to become a RADA student in London, I would live as frugally as possible. I made constant mention of two Cambridge friends, Robert Eddison and Peter Hannen, who had both been allowed to take the theatrical plunge and were doing splendidly. I had got, and without the smallest difficulty, a poor degree, though an Honours one. At one time I had, in my despair, contemplated dishing myself finally as a schoolmaster by getting no degree at all and following the spirited example of a contemporary, Douglas Cooper. When, at the end of his first year, he was faced with the Tripos exam, he enquired of the supervisor how soon after the start of the two and a half hour exam it was permissible to leave, and on being told that it was half an hour, Douglas duly stalked out, to a smattering of applause, leaving but sparsely filled sheets of paper behind him. But Douglas was rich and carefree and I was not. When faced with exam papers and pens and ink, I gave in. I had been at Oundle too geared to scholastic compliance, and was now too frightened not to make some sort of shot at suitable answers. Gradually, and with no fight left in me, I abandoned all thought of a career in the theatre, and knowing what

I know now, I thank both my parents and my lucky stars.

It was my mother who had, and rather brutally for her, delivered the final blow. I had felt that, theatrically at least, I held a trump card – Experience. It was then the fashion at schools for the female parts in plays to be acted by boys and in the early 1930s at Cambridge the convention still existed and male undergraduates togged themselves suitably up. Audiences sometimes gave an embarrassed and nervous giggle or two but then settled down and accepted the performances. At school, and at the time quite a slip of a thing, I had played the Confidante in *The Critic*, Kate Hardcastle in *She Stoops to Conquer* and Lady Mary in *The Admirable Crichton*. At Cambridge I had been equally fortunately cast and I wound up my last term by playing Lady Cicely in Shaw's *Captain Brassbound's Conversion*. Dadie directed us, and admirably too, Michael Redgrave played Brassbound, Humphrey Tilling was Drinkwater, Guy Burgess (presumably not by then enrolled) designed the sets and, after a very successful opening, we woke up to find that we had a smash hit on our hands. London critics praised us, Shaw himself wrote a letter, we appeared in gossip columns, the play was sold out, presents flowed in, the Duke of Kent arrived with a party and eventually and by popular demand we played a number of extra performances (I mention all this in order to increase the impact of my subsequent slap in the face). Why then, I asked my parents, did they not let me advance on London equipped with my excellent press notices and beard Cochran and Charlot and others, demanding recognition? My father, quite out of his depth, looked doubtful and unhappy, and my mother said crisply 'I do rather wonder, dear, what sort of welcome they would give to an amateur female impersonator. I think I'd keep rather quiet about it if I were you'. I always enjoyed those old *Punch* jokes which wound up with 'Collapse of stout party'. Well, I wasn't stout, but I sure as hell collapsed.

Kind readers, possibly worried about me and the effect on my character of all those female clothes, need not be anxious. The donning of the necessary underclothes and, usually, silk stockings, the dresses, the wigs, the make-up afforded me no pleasure in themselves and were merely a means to an end, that of acting. I got no kick of a transvestite sort (how bizarre it is when, say, a moustached bank manager decides to retire early and slops about all day in a daring negligée, buffing his nails and asking to be called Dulcie). The dressing up was pleasurable solely because it was the theatre, it was acting, it was make-believe, it was fun. For most female roles one's chest required attention and at school there were linen pouches stuffed with cotton wool and provided with shoulder straps. They were known as 'shapes' ('Please, Matron, we're going to need eight more shapes'). At Oundle, Mrs Hale had been wonderfully cooperative, entered violently into the spirit of the thing, put her entire wardrobe at my disposal (as Lady Mary, I had four changes) and that of her daughters, who were very slightly less enthusiastic on finding that I had ruined two pairs of their shoes.

My parents also held a trump card, and a higher one than mine, for when at the age of eighteen I left Oundle, Dr Fisher had let it be known that if, after Cambridge, I cared to return and join his staff, he would gladly consider me. We had always got on. Warmth has of necessity to be rare in headmasters but we had for some reason been friends from the moment I arrived as a boy. If I met him somewhere in the town or school buildings, he would stop and we, and it is the only word for it, gossiped. He liked to laugh and, heaven knows, so did I and before long he would purposely say something to make me giggle. We must have made a strange sight standing there, chuckling away. A constant joke was the names of the members of the music staff. They were Spurling, Tatam, Olley and Champ, and Dr Fisher (he was known to everybody as 'Bud' after the creator of the then popular Mutt and Jeff cartoons) would make me repeat them. The last two, Olley and Champ, sounded, to a boy of fourteen, especially risible and caused me to start to shake. Then the headmaster, head rather roguishly on one side, would say 'You're a very naughty little boy. Run along now', and we parted on a pleasurable note of friendship. Nothing, in the twenty-three years that I knew him, ever occurred to alter this relationship and I cherish nothing but happy memories of this unusual man.

And so, back to Oundle I duly went, quaking in my shoes.

It seems nowadays to be, among public schoolmasters, the fashion to chop and change jobs quite a lot, doing five years here and three years there, rather a rootless existence but doubtless rich in scholastic experience. And I gather that modern schoolmasters display, and why shouldn't they, a lively interest in creature comforts. Anxious about their amenities and the accommodation that will be available to them, they are apt to ask, at their interviews, searching questions. In my day, any question from the applicant was rare and to show an interest in whether one had or had not a bathroom to oneself (had not was the normal) would have been unpopular with a headmaster and would have sharply concluded the interview ('I didn't like the young man's attitude'). Nor was there much chopping and changing, except for those found to be unsatisfactory after a year or two. If you passed muster, you stayed put.

The ordinary procedure at Oundle was for a master to be appointed at about the age of twenty-two and, in those days invariably a bachelor, to do a stint as a House Tutor in one of the twelve boarding houses, subsequently, and after four or five years, marrying and smartly disappearing, like an eel, into the snug and seaweedy recesses of a lengthy thoroughfare called the Glapthorn Road. The Glapthorn Road in Oundle was the neighbourhood's Sargasso Sea, a sprawling domestic spawning area from whose fruitful depths masters eventually emerged complete with family and all ready, when their turn came, to take over as a housemaster. For a married master with, perhaps, by then four children (rather, in some cases, a thin spreading), to become a housemaster was more or less a life or death matter and not all masters were lucky. When I say lucky I am not referring to the work, which was killing, and in some sad cases literally so, for to go pop in your fifties was by no means unknown. But the luck consisted in the fact that, for the whole family, the accommodation and living expenses were, the whole year round, entirely free and part of the contract. And well deserved it was too for housemasters and, just as much, their wives led lives of worry, work and care that, as I have said, put paid to some of them.

The boys' boarding houses of Oundle School are divided between the so-called Field Houses and Town Houses and I found that I had been appointed House Tutor in a Town House called Laundimer. Although Laundimer was altogether more spacious than Dryden House for, having been originally Lord Lyveden's town house, it had an agreeable garden and a tennis court and looked out over countryside to the south, these houses did not adapt themselves very successfully to the presence of fifty boys and attendant servants. Once again I was to find myself disadvantageously housed. My study was a smallish room on the ground floor and as at that time it contained the house library books as well as me, privacy was not always mine. 'It will give you a chance to get to know the boys', encouraged the housemaster, Mr Ault. Well yes, I suppose so. The sole window looked out directly on to North Street, up and down which there rumbled day and night lorries from the prolific Peterborough brick fields. My bedroom, even smaller, was on the floor above and also provided sights and sounds of traffic. I shared a lavatory with Mr Ault (one coughed loudly on hearing hurrying footsteps approaching) and I was somewhat taken aback on learning that I could only have a bath three times a week, and even then in the boys' bathroom (they would at that time be elsewhere). These ablutionary excitements took place on half holidays between 6 and 6.30 pm. If I had lingered longer than 6.30, I would have found myself having a bath with the Matron, Miss Tomlinson, a nice, saintly person who would have been as startled as I. Miss Tomlinson had a dog which she had rashly christened Jerry, innocently providing schoolboy jokes ('Please sir, have you seen Miss Tomlinson's Jerry?'). The food, supervised by Mrs Ault, was first rate, the Aults welcomed me warmly and I soon settled in and managed to remain fairly fragrant with the aid of cans of hot water borne to my bedroom by the maids.

Before the boys returned, which was always on a Friday, there was a Masters' Meeting in the school library and there I met, and on an equal footing, most of those who had taught me (Mr Bray had, alas, retired). It was interesting to know them from, so to say, the other side. One thing was at once apparent: their virtue. The last word on the Oundle staffs of that time and of a later period (and, for all I know, now) was said by an old boy of the school who, after some time as a Cambridge don, returned to Oundle to teach. There was clearly a sharp contrast between his late Cambridge colleagues and those he found at Oundle for, after one such Masters' Meeting, he was discovered leaning against a wall, laughing weakly and saying over and over again, 'But they're all so *good*. They're all so good'.

It was no more than the truth. Probity, sincerity and conscientious endeavour were everywhere. A bright scholastic light shone. There was an urgency in the air and Sanderson's great principle lived on: the school must be made to suit the boy and not vice versa. There were countless Special Time-tables for boys who, for whatever worthy reason, needed to study a variety of subjects that fitted the set curriculum of no class. These time-tables entailed much extra work but nobody dreamt of complaining. Scholarship boys were tirelessly coached in long out-of-school hours but it would never have crossed anybody's mind to point out that in some establishments such extra work would be considered deserving of a cash reward.

Sanderson was Oundle's great headmaster, Frederick William Sanderson, an inspired and enthusiastic and splendidly ruthless innovator who brought, more or less single-handed, the teaching of Science and particularly of Engineering to public schools, opened every window, dusted down everything in sight (idle masters included, many of whom did indeed disappear in a cloud of dust), was loved and feared by one and all (as the ideal headmaster should be) and arriving in 1892, raised, and within thirty years, the school numbers from 101 to 532. He was affectionately known as 'Beans'. The nickname's origin is obscure but it seems possible that it is an amalgamation, so to speak, of 'to be full of beans' and 'I'll give you beans!' for beans in various forms were what he delivered. The school's continued prosperity, steadily increasing numbers and high standards would lead one to suppose that this exceptional man, genius even, was not barking up the wrong tree.

In games too there was hurry and bustle and drive. The school rugger XV, coached by a genius called Frank Spragg, rapidly became the scourge of the Midlands. Bedford fell before our boots. Uppingham crumbled. Rugby, who may have invented the thing but couldn't always win, succumbed. Haileybury hung their heads. Some of our easiest victories were over Stowe, an excellent school created by the famous Roxburgh but a school at which we liked to poke fun. We thought them, no doubt unjustly, a bit namby-pamby and unrobust and there was an illustrative story, perhaps apocryphal, from the rugger field. We were playing them in our customary, yearly manner and, in a sea of mud and flying feet, a loose scrum had formed over the ball. Here and there a player was lying prone. Suddenly from the base of the Stowe forwards, all pushing and shoving, there came a scream of agony and a voice was plaintively heard to shriek, 'Humphrey, for pity's sake, *you're standing on my hair!*'

It was with some consternation that I learnt that the first lesson at which I was to preside was Scripture. A class of twenty senior boys were, with me, to study St Matthew's Gospel and were subsequently and for what was then the Higher Certificate, to present themselves in the summer for outside examination. Oh my goodness! I was already struggling to map out my French and German lessons (I had to cope with five different classes) and to find myself landed with St Matthew was too much. I could spare no time for preparation and, apart from looking up the meaning of 'myrrh', decided to take the whole thing as it came.

Scripture was on Sunday and at midday, by which time everybody had recovered from Matins, and it lasted an hour. I vividly recall the apprehension, nay terror, with which, primly gowned and clutching mark book and Bible, I made my entrance and seated myself at the daïsed desk. I found facing me twenty docile scientists with Bibles and alert expressions. I asked them their names and carefully wrote them down in my mark book (well, it wasted a bit of time). We then tackled St Matthew. I invited the boy nearest me and in the front row to start reading. After a minute or two I said 'Next' and his neighbour started up. The minutes seemed endless and how dreadfully fast they read. Would St Matthew last out? Fortunately yes. And I had my final educational *bonne bouche* to give them. 'By the way', I heard myself saying in a nonchalant manner, 'some of you may have noticed that word 'myrrh' and wondered what it was. Well, it is a bitter, aromatic and transparent gum exuded from the bark of the Commiphora tree'. The information was received in a respectful silence, the parish church clock struck one and the lesson, if such it can be called, was over.

In those days there was, except in winter, a frightful class that began at 7 am and ended at 8. In the school houses rising-bells started clanging at 6.10 am. At 6.45 one hurriedly munched, while Matron supervised the boys ('Come *along*, Henderson!'), a digestive and gulped some slightly gritty cocoa. Then there was a hasty scamper to the school buildings, for the headmaster, dead nuts on puctuality, might be prowling purposefully, in order to be in the classroom on the tick of 7. And then what? Often and with senior boys we found ourselves battling with French literature in the shape of one of the many classical verse tragedies that French dramatists have so copiously supplied. As soon as you had finished one tragedy there was another one sitting up and waiting for you. The quills of Racine and Corneille ran quite disastrously on. Seven am is by no means the ideal time of day at which to encourage, for one tried to make the play come alive, reluctant and embarrassed schoolboys to rise from their desks and whisk themselves back once more into dear old Greece ('Now, let's see, which of you was Iphigénie last Wednesday?')

Picture then my dismay, nay horror, at finding that the 7 am Monday lesson was to be once again Scripture and I found myself facing faces which, though still polite, were less expectant than the day before. Once more we started reading St Matthew, taking up where we had left off. Not even the Last Supper aroused interest and after about ten minutes I could bear it no more. 'Oh do please stop', I cried, adding in the silence that fell, 'isn't this all perfectly ghastly? What *are* we to do?' We closed our bibles and just stared at each other for a time, the boys quite unaccustomed I think to such a candid approach. And then I said 'I tell you what. If you promise not to spread it abroad that we've dropped St Matthew, we'll read something that ought to interest you more. We'll begin next lesson. Have any of you ever heard of Aldous Huxley?' And so then, and in the years to come with this particular subject and form, we had a lively series of readings. We read *Brave New World*. We read and discussed H. G. Wells. We read *Cold Comfort Farm*. We read and acted *The Green Pastures*. We read, with great delight, the despised historical works of Lytton Strachey (such marvellous jokes). We read anything and everything that didn't bore and wasn't by St Matthew, fortunately a limited pen. News of my daring innovation reached Dr Fisher (I suspect one of the chaplains of sneaking) but he did nothing. In the Scripture Higher Certificate examination in July, several of the boys got o and I was told that one examiner had registered a complaint of blasphemy, but no Oundelian censure ever reached me. Dr Fisher turned the blindest of eyes and on I defiantly went in the face of the anger of the chaplain and the envy of my colleagues often condemned to a whole year of boredom with the *Acts of the Apostles* (far too few shipwrecks).

I only taught three periods of German a week, for my main subject was French and here I was helped in my struggle against boredom for it was possible to invent, for School

Certificate (O Level) forms, short scenes for boys to act – a tremendous row in a greengrocer's, say, about the cost of cabbages (*'Je refuse absolument de payer'*) or a scene in a doctor's consulting-room with a patient moaning *'Ah, que je souffre'* and a spirited death or two (*'Allez chercher le gendarme!'*). This improved their spoken French and they were more inclined to remember words and phrases learnt in such circumstances.

With older boys there was enormous pleasure and profit to be had from the short stories of Maupassant (we read his less saucy tales in a purified *Contes Choisis*: *Edition Pour la Jeunesse*), from the superb if hackneyed *Lettres de Mon Moulin* and from Mérimée's *Colomba*, full of Corsican feuds and vendettas. We acted some of that too and I insisted on portraying Colomba herself, making a fine ass of myself as a fiery lady ranging the maquis on horseback with murderous intent and absolutely no sense of humour. But here again, my idiocies and anxious falsetto screams helped them to remember vocabulary. In his *Lettres* Daudet often provides an obscure French word and I learnt not to mind being caught out in ignorance. 'I haven't the foggiest idea what it means', I would say, 'but if you really want to know you'd better look it up for yourself'. Far more sensible to be honest than to try to deceive, which is what I did at first ('Ah, I'm glad you've asked about that word. We're coming to it next lesson').

My theatrical leanings and yearnings and my disappointment at being professionally thwarted gradually died down and were assuaged for the simple reason that teaching is in itself a form of acting. As in the theatre, no good will come of teaching unless you give the public, in palatable form, what it wants and requires. Shut up for an hour in a classroom with thirty or so boys, one gave a sort of performance, for which one was perched up on a dais as on a stage. I was determined at least to try not to bore. Rather than see yawns and glazed eyes, I would have stood on my head (I used to be able to) and waggled my legs in the air. I don't for a minute think that I was always successful but the attempt was there. It was exhausting work. Four hours of teaching in the morning plus, three days a week, two in the afternoon (free periods were a rarity) hardly ranked as a rest cure, and that was very far from being the sum total of the day's commitments. Our communal meals required a show of animated conversation ('Isn't it about time that Bodger got his Colours?'), there were games to umpire or referee ('Off-side, Perkins!'), there was work to correct (thirty French proses took about 1½ hours) and lessons to prepare, there were parental letters to answer ('Do please be *completely frank* about Cedric's attitude'), there were monthly reports which required a comment on every boy one taught, there were meetings of the many school societies, there were this, that and the other thing and on Sundays, two, and sometimes three, Chapel services. The rest of the time was one's own.

There was at Oundle another theatrical outlet of a fairly unique kind in public schools. For a long time members of the staff had produced, every two or three years and at the end of the summer term, a home-made entertainment. There were songs, skits, sketches and a boisterous jollity everywhere. During my time as a boy there, I witnessed two of these affairs and I have to confess that they embarrassed me greatly for they were appallingly under-rehearsed and most of the material was feeble (it was thought to be funny if they all wore rugger jerseys and sang 'Blow the Man Down', none of which is in any way funny). The general jocularity jarred. Show-offs showed off. The more retiring, and nicer, masters took no part. There was, I shudder to recall, that most dreadful of audience participations, community singing. The boys, in holiday mood, were receptive and applauded everything and I suppose I was the only one to sniff in a superior manner and regret the number of missed opportunities and the small amount of trouble taken.

Now entrusted by Dr Fisher with the getting up of this entertainment, I set about, with a loyal band of supporters, the task of trying to improve it. I felt that at least it needn't be under-rehearsed (such an insult to an audience) and for a year we amassed material, tried out possibilities and assessed talent. At first the shyer staff members were reluctant to appear. They feared a diminishing of their authority and a decline in discipline. In fact the opposite was the case and those who took part were respected. Gradually the entire staff came to like the idea and agreed to perform and nobody wished to be excluded. It was easy enough to give everybody something within their compass and we arranged for each master to have his little moment of glory. It didn't need much histrionic talent or courage to dress up as a Matron, mount a tricycle and, in a market place scene, just pedal slowly across the stage, but the effect was stupendous and Matron had to cycle her way slowly back again as an encore. A good idea for providing moments of glory was to have a Kenneth Clark-type lecturer discoursing on various famous pictures which were then posed for by performers suitably rigged up and seen in an empty picture frame against a black background. 'The Anatomy Lesson' went well, and a rather timid physics master as the Mona Lisa ('Note the little half smile. She seems to know what you are thinking, eh?') scored a great hit.

There were no limits. We had a ballet, *La Tentation du Professeur*, with specially constructed tutus and I had quite a time persuading some of the cast that it would only be funny if we tried to dance it properly. No falling down. We had the Luton Girls Choir. We had WI members executing, quite seriously, a Country Dance. We had acrobats (The Gutz). We did a P. C. Wren-style musical playlet (it was called, I regret to say, *A Smack at the Blacks*) which was later used by the Cambridge Footlights and then found its way into a London revue, with Hermione Gingold and Michael Wilding.

I got permission to move the date from the summer term to the end of the winter term which, with Christmas then upon us, seemed more suitable and festive. There were in my time two finales of which I was very fond. One showed a wooden cut-out of the special train that the boys would be boarding next morning and the window of the only First Class compartment rattled down to reveal the face of the then headmaster, Graham Stainforth, angrily fuming at the train's late departure. The other showed the entire staff, 65 strong, massed upon the stage against a fir tree background. They were singing that pretty number from *State Fair*, 'It's a Grand Night for Singing', while snowflakes (shredded exam papers) fell gently. On the final note, every master pulled out a brightly coloured silk handkerchief, carefully concealed, and waved it and the sudden flash of brilliant colours among the falling snow was too much for me. It had succeeded so wonderfully that, at the dress rehearsal, I disgraced myself and wept for joy. The perennial name for this entertainment was *Masterpieces*. Well, we aimed high.

After a year or two of teaching it was borne in on me that I had taken to schoolmastering like a rather plump duck to water. Apart from the horrors of the Officers' Training Corps activities (there were dreadful ten-day summer camps at Tidworth and Strensall and Aldershot where the camp smells, mainly of earth lavatories and greasy food, induced wave after wave of nausea), I truly loved it all. I was unusually lucky in my colleagues and in the head of the Modern Languages, Hugo Caudwell, a nonpareil of efficiency, kindness and encouragement. On the staff there was still a sprinkling of austere greybeards appointed by Sanderson (remarkable man though he was, I cannot think that he laughed very much or ever led a conga line) but the Fisher appointments were of a different era and calibre and few of them were very serious for very long. Men reared in Victorian and Edwardian times would have found the use of Christian names very unacceptable and among the senior staff it was always 'Hale' and 'King' and 'Nightingale' (a genial Bacchus-like Classicist) but elsewhere this chilly approach was modified and in the 30s Christian names and nicknames came to be used. Friendlier.

Sanderson had not believed in cosseting his staff and some of his austerities lingered on. It will hardly be believed but until the mid-30s there was no masters' common-room (it was rumoured that Sanderson had so feared magisterial rebellion that he dreaded any communal meeting-place where discontent might breed). There was one remote and single-seat lavatory far away at the end of an upper corridor and life was certainly hard on the weak bladder. The sole mid-morning interval lasted fifteen minutes and was spent in the open or, on wet days, huddled with the boys in the so-called Cloisters, while the enuretics bicycled hurriedly home and back. There was no coffee or tea, for where could it have been served? If you were hungry and wanted a bun, you bought one of the boys' tuck-shop ones. Nobody resented the lack of creature comforts or paid much attention. We were all too enjoyably busy to grouse.

By 1933 I had managed to acquire a car, an Austin Seven of battered appearance but admirable performance and it enabled me, on the few evenings that were free, to motor to Cambridge, an hour's drive away and where I still had many friends and was steadily making more. It was the period when I was relentlessly performing my solo sketches and was beginning to be in some sort of demand at social gatherings. I had got to know Whitney Straight, then up at Trinity and, although American, soon to become entirely Anglicised with an English grandee wife and a life's work in various British undertakings.

And one summer's day at Oundle I received from Whitney a telegram that was as exciting as it was alarming: 'Hope you can come to a drinks party on Thursday at 6 o'clock. Brush up your turns. Ruth Draper coming'. Miss Draper's welcome practice was usually to be in England in the spring and summer, first doing two or three months (to full houses) in London at either the Vaudeville or St James's or Haymarket Theatre, and then to tour, coming for a week to the New Theatre, Cambridge and subsequently the Arts Theatre, an auditorium and audience that suited her perfectly.

Whitney then lived out of college and in spacious rooms in Trinity Street and there, appallingly self-assured in those days (confidence has long since deserted me), I performed to Miss Draper and the fifty or so people at the party. It was cheek, no other word for it, and all I can say in defence is that it was Whitney's idea. I had added to my schoolmistress sketches some others of a very English nature: a lady giving one of those dreadful Games Parties: a lady arranging a fête: a women's tea party, and so forth. Miss Draper was kindness itself and when all was over I was privileged to have a long talk with her about solo performing, how to look just over an audience's head without ever catching anybody's eye, how much an audience will accept in the way of absence of props, and so on. We were getting on so well that I was emboldened to say, and I blush to remember the impertinence, that I thought some of her sketches were now just two or three minutes too long. She ought (but her manners were perfect) to have struck me sharply in the face but instead she agreed at once, and seemed genuinely to do so. She said that all her sketches had started out as shorter pieces but that she had elaborated them over the years: 'I can remember exactly when and in which theatre I added this or that little section, and honestly I couldn't bear not to include them. I've become so fond of them all. But you're right. They are a bit long. And you see, with me the audience, if unconsciously, has to *work* too, and I dare say that by the end of the evening they're as tired as I am'. That is, in substance, what she said.

She had to leave early to prepare for her 8 o'clock performance at the theatre, whither Whitney and I and others later went to see her. She was, as ever, perfection. She did a sketch I had never seen before, 'The Actress', a flamboyant French-woman receiving a variety of visitors – a fat and elderly

American admirer, Mr Fuller Bumstead, a young poet who worships her and writes her a bad play, her manager, and many others. During the course of it I thought I saw at one point a slight hesitation, no more than that, and when we went round after to congratulate her, she said 'Wasn't it dreadful, I nearly dried up completely in "The Actress"! I couldn't remember which sketch I was doing or even which theatre I was in. When that happens, I just keep talking until I get on the right track again. Sometimes the clothes and props help me'. She had of course recovered at once and covered it over expertly and anyway, audiences are usually hypnotised and full of acceptance and notice very little. In my failed play, of which I shall be writing, dear Dame Sybil dried up completely on the second night at Brighton and, being her, just stumped over to the prompt corner and had a good look at the book. The audience was delighted. I think they thought it was intentional and all part of the fun.

Those who never saw Miss Draper at work (she died in 1956) may well wonder about her fame and may have in mind a kind of American Joyce Grenfell. There is really no comparison at all between the two. Although American, Miss Draper's various English accents were impeccable and she was at home in French, German, Italian, Spanish and a wonderful make-up language of her own, said to sound vaguely Polish. Because so much of her work had been in comedy, people's first reaction at the sight of Joyce was to smile contentedly. One did not smile at Miss Draper. It was a face of great distinction, dark-eyed and somewhat Jewish (a charcoal drawing by Sargent was a wonderful likeness), but which, when she performed, became superbly mobile and changing. Joyce, who could sing and act and was triumphant in revues and films, was certainly more versatile but there the matter ends. Her best sketches were brilliantly funny but they were lightweight and meant to be. Part of her attraction was a sort of amateur quality, a get-up-and-make-us-laugh thing. Her main intention was to amuse, and marvellously well she did it. Miss Draper could, heaven knows, amuse too ('Showing the Garden': 'A Class in Greek Poise': 'Doctors and Diets') but her longer sketches were wonderfully solid stuff and one of them, 'Three Women and Mr Clifford', was as absorbing as a three act play. Joyce Grenfell has loyally provided the last word on the difference between them. Talking to Miss Draper, and after a string of compliments, she said 'I don't know how anyone dares mention my name with yours'. Miss Draper's answer was brief. Just two words. 'They don't'.

Never having myself dared to be much of an eccentric, with odd clothes and unpredictable behaviour, I have always rather admired eccentricity in others, considering it rather dashing, and it must have been in 1934 that I first met Roger Senhouse and was happily, until his death, on the receiving end of his kindness and genorosity and interest. He was a bit older than I, had dabbled unsuitably in commerce after the war and then in the 1930s became a partner in the publishing firm of Secker and Warburg, books and writers being where his chief enthusiasms lay. Or part of them. He lived in beautiful if ramshackle rooms in Great Ormond Street, rooms from which no old newspaper or magazine had ever been banished (one might want to look something up). Items of food were apt to linger overlong in the kitchen area and become unacceptable. It was almost impossible to sit down for there were books on every chair. Letters and documents piled high, dust lay everywhere and it was unwise ever to bump into a bookcase or cupboard for it would bring down upon your head a selection of the Majolica objects which Roger collected and which he mainly kept, presumably with a mistaken idea of safety, out of sight and on the top of cupboards. And after the pottery, books would start to dislodge themselves and fall. Once, when staying with him, I turned in my sleep, touched something and received full in the face six volumes of *The Correspondence of Jonathan Swift*.

His full surname was Pocklington-Senhouse. I think. I add a note of doubt for one of the many things about this extraordinary character was that, in your dealings with him, the only certainty was uncertainty. For instance, staying one day at my London home from home, which was then the majestic Russell Hotel (13/6 a night, including vast breakfast), I received a morning telephone call. Roger.

'Are you alone?' I was usually alone at the hotel and I gave a tentative 'Yes'.

'I want you to have lunch. Just the two of us. I have something very private to discuss. Tell nobody. One o'clock at the Gourmet in Lisle Street'. This could mean that Roger had got into one of his periodical pickles. He was rather a one for pickles, amatory or financial as the case might be and often the former. Prepared to give what advice I could, I arrived on time at the Gourmet to find, not Roger but a mutual friend, David Farrer. He looked a little surprised and embarrassed and said 'I wish we could have lunched together but actually I'm lunching quite alone with Roger. Something's gone wrong. He told me to tell nobody'. The restaurant door opened and somebody else came in. Ralph Radcliffe. He saw us, gave a start and spoke. 'Have you seen Roger?' 'No', we said, 'but you're lunching quite alone with him, aren't you, and you aren't supposed to tell anybody, are you?' Unbelievably, two more friends, bidden to secrecy, appeared, followed by Roger, his customary 25 minutes late, arms full of newspapers and books and with all thought of private discussion gone. 'Oh, splendid! There you all are! Let's ask them to put these two tables together and we can all have lunch. What fun!' When we broke up he said (a) that he must go to the City, which lay to the east, (b) that he must go to Hatchard's (to the west), (c) that he must go to Rye (rather far off in the south) and he eventually disappeared, walking very fast, up Wardour Street (to the north). Such was the form.

We once went, in Roger's car, to Bournemouth: 'I have friends to see but they may be away', and of course they were. Roger's driving was, literally, a thing of hits and misses but we arrived for once intact and stayed at a hotel. Roger signed the register first and when my turn came I saw that I was apparently a fellow hotel guest of 'The Hon. Jasper Beauclerk'. Some fanciful, flowery and false address had been added. 'Why on earth haven't you put your real name?' 'Lower your voice. It never does to let these people know exactly who one is'. Another favourite alias was 'Ronnie Simpson' and for a time he blossomed out and ennobled himself with a peerage, I forget what.

I still have a characteristic letter from him, written in the violet-coloured ink which he preferred and which was also said to be used by elderly French governesses. The letter appeared to have been written in Switzerland though the postmark said Devizes and although undated I think we can assume a winter month and probably a severe one for there is much talk of chill winds, snow, ice and avalanche. The letter concludes with an account of a mountain walking trip, or should it be 'climb', for which the services of a Swiss guide had been wisely secured. The excitement gradually builds, and then 'On, on, on we went', the letter runs, 'ten, twelve, fifteen, sixteen, twenty-one miles into the very heart of the great glacier moraine'. Though admiring the jerky numerical progression of those figures, and the startling jump from sixteen to twenty-one is very striking, there is a suspicion in one's mind of something not quite adding up. If you walk all that distance into the very heart of the great glacier moraine, you presumably have in the end to turn round and walk a similar distance out of the very heart of the etc, and that seems to make the journey, and on foot, and over ice, forty-two miles. Oh well. Here all we can be sure of is that the letter was written on a sheet of Swiss hotel writing paper, and perhaps in Devizes.

He did eventually not only get to Rye but acquire a house there and live in it. It was no surprise to discover that the house had constructional imperfections. When I first went there, Roger kindly showed me round. It was a day of pelting rain and in some inner courtyard a gutter had broken loose and water was splashing everywhere, drenching us as we passed. 'Such a relief that the house is in such good order. As you see, everything works splendidly' proudly said my host, dabbing at himself with a handkerchief. Although he had already been there several months, nothing in the large sitting-room had been unpacked since its journey from London. 'Everything's fitted in nicely', said Roger, gazing serenely at the tea-chests and packages and boxes and cases that stood about, 'and look, Arthur, you can see my Duncan Grant'. I peered up a sort of alley-way through the unpacked conglomeration and there at the end and leaning against the wall was certainly a picture, which may or may not have been by Duncan Grant. On balance, I should say not.

Charles Fletcher-Cooke was invited to dine and spend the night and, after an enjoyable evening (Roger was the most lavish of hosts, though it didn't do to look too closely at forks and spoons), was shown to his room. Having unpacked, he retired to bed, put out the light and was composing himself for slumber when he became aware of something strange about the room – a sudden fall in the temperature, a waft of air, and a vague glimmer of some sort and, looking upwards, he saw immediately above what seemed to be a star twinkling at him. He was just thinking that it must be some trick of the light from the corridor, possibly reflecting on a metal object in the ceiling, when he saw another star, and then another. The night sky was indeed being revealed to him through a large hole in the roof which Roger had omitted to mention or, more likely, had never noticed. Charles prudently changed the position of his bed and no rain fell.

Roger was a handsome, manly fellow and had many admirers. He never married but one day, talking expansively about the past, he said 'Yes, it was during the time when I was engaged to Honey Harris'. Here was astonishing news! A friend hurried round to Honey to congratulate her, if belatedly, on having such an interesting fiancé, and also to ask what had gone wrong and ended it all. But Honey was just as astounded as everybody else. '*Were* we engaged? He never told me we were and I suppose I ought to have had some say. But what a shame! I loved him. I would have adored to be engaged to Roger'. Nor was Honey the only one who fell for him. I was having a late drink with him once in the first floor flat in Great Ormond Street when there was a scuffling sound at the door and an envelope was pushed under it by somebody who then went on up the stairs. 'Ah', said Roger, 'that will be from the woman on the top floor. She writes me a love letter every night'. He picked up the envelope and opened it. Not a love letter at all but an Account Rendered from Jackson's.

In 1935 and invited and encouraged by that fine writer and literary editor, Raymond Mortimer, I started to review books for the *New Statesman*. They were books of rather a specialist nature, namely girls' school stories. Every autumn publishers poured into the *Statesman* office a number of such books, for the demand for them was great and authoresses were not lacking, among the seasoned reliables being Miss Brazil herself, Winifred Darch, May Wynne, Elinor Brent-Dyer and many others. And so in every Christmas number up to the war, when such junketings ceased for the duration (I could hardly be found in the officers' mess eagerly reading the latest Brazil), I did a round-up review of the books. The stories were mainly splendid stuff and stood up well to having a little gentle fun poked at them. Often it was only necessary to quote a striking passage and I do so now as an illustration. It comes from Dorita Fairlie Bruce's *Nancy in the Sixth* and I regret to say that Nancy, mad keen to win the Woodford-Leigh Organ Scholarship, has, with a friend, abused a generous musical gesture made to help her. The music teacher lets fly:

When I asked Mrs Paterson as a very special favour
to allow you to use her organ, I gave her an undertaking — a solemn undertaking — that neither of you
would do it any damage. I told her that you could
be trusted — you were not beginners; I practically
pledged my honour that no harm would come to her
instrument — and what has happened? This morning
I get this note from her to say that she could hardly
get through the morning service yesterday because
some of her most important stops were completely out
of action.

Later on and little by little, I graduated to additional periodic-
als and to more adult books.

You cannot be a regular reviewer of books without getting,
from time to time, into hot water. I had met, when I was an
undergraduate, Godfrey Winn, at that time an actor and a
novelist as well as a budding journalist producing articles on
such thoughtful subjects as 'The daughter I would like to
have', 'Why the young are bad-tempered', and 'Have we failed
the dead?' My agreeable Cambridge contemporary, Geoffrey
Toone, and I went one summer's day, and daringly without
tutorial permission, to London to see a matinée of Dodie
Smith's *Autumn Crocus* (Geoffrey was to be an actor) and
afterwards we went on for a drink with Godfrey, with whom
Geoffrey had become friendly. Godfrey lived in Ebury Street.
He had, later on, a country house, a likeness of which featured
on one of those specially made coloured linen tea-cloths, a
cloth issued to mark the creation of the Godfrey Winn Rose
and which also showed Godfrey himself, the rose and a dog.
Have I misremembered the rose as being white with purple
patches? Very possibly.

We rang and were admitted and it became at once plain that
our host was out to dazzle us, two callow student princes from
Old Heidelberg. We were invited to seat ourselves and were
given sherry in glasses reminiscent of acorn-cups and of the
size from which one might imagine Pease-Blossom and Mustard-Seed sipping dew, though perhaps it wasn't quite the
moment for letting the mind rest on midsummer fairies.

While we too sipped, Godfrey twinkled to and fro and up
and down and, eventually twinkling right out of the room,
soon came twinkling back becomingly attired in two-piece

cerise pyjamas, the top half of which had one of those flaps which fold across the chest and are secured by a button high up in the neck and look vaguely Russian. Oh, I thought. He then made a tour of the room, showing off various possessions, among them a Staffordshire figure of a warrior-like female astride a chestnut horse. 'A present from Princess Pat', he kindly explained, and 'Oh' we said, the Princess being of royal birth. After that he produced a large folder containing several photographs of himself taken by the then fashionable Paul Tanqueray. We were invited to peer and admire. 'I told Paul to make me look eighteen'. 'Oh', we ventured, though I was longing to say 'What went wrong?' We escaped after an hour or so and as I was far less censorious in those days, I merely thought our host a little peculiar. But I would now supply, for it had really been rather too much in the field of egomania, an unkinder adjective.

Nevertheless, ever the jovial and just *littérateur*, I allowed no memory of this embarrassing parade to affect my judgment or cloud my views when required to review Godfrey's auto-biographical works. His publisher had considered him of sufficient importance and interest to enshrine him in three stout volumes, an adulatory estimation with the rightness of which Godfrey must have concurred. In the end only two of the books were published. In my review I begged Godfrey to stop calling London 'the Metropolis', to use 'to meet' instead of 'to encounter', and if somebody was very tired, just to say so rather than refer to them as being 'drained' or 'utterly spent'. I begged him to abandon the numerous foot-notes supplying titles for titled ladies. I begged him to stop writing about 'the whirligig of time'. I urged him to think twice, or even thrice, before putting down such a sentence as 'The sleeping land-scape crystallized under the aurora of the untarnished moon'. And I ended with a wailing cry of 'Does Mr Winn's ear tell him *nothing*?'

But I had hard luck, for against all this helpful advice, freely and generously given, Godfrey took, for some reason, umbrage. I got a waspish letter. When we chanced to meet in public, he snorted with rage (actually it came out as more of a squeak) and he turned, like some affronted Victorian hostess, his back on me. He tried to turn mutual friends against me and wrote to our beloved Adrianne Allen in Switzerland to say that if she didn't drop me at once he would have no more to do with her. Adrianne, I am happy to say, was at once on the telephone wires to relate details of this crisis and our cries of happy laughter nearly split the continental exchange in two. Perhaps what really upset him was my pointing out an idiotic mistake in an index, where Alfred Lunt appears as 'Mildred' Lunt, a misprint which gave Alfred enormous pleasure and for some time he signed his letters to me, 'Mildred'.

Brimful of energy as I then was, I found the time, in addition to my other literary activities, to dash off A. A. Milne-type articles for *Punch*, who briskly returned them with a polite word to the effect that the magazine already had an A. A. Milne. I never, and just as well, had either the nerve or the inclination to attempt a novel. I cannot now remember, my mind being so fully stocked with other valuable data, the name of the successful author who confessed that, early on and at one point in his career, he had been able, when in a wild and hysterical mood, to paper a whole room of his house with the rejection slips sent to him by publishers. Some of these gentlemen, kinder (and with more time) than others, supply, rather than a coldly printed notice of unacceptability, a short letter of regret and explanation, which might go something like this: 'Dear Mr Marshall, In returning to you the manuscript of your novel, *The Strange Quest of Adrian Babbington*, we would like to say that, although the Metropolitan Water Board background seems to us to be both authentic and finely sketched (we particularly enjoyed the light relief supplied by your crusty old tea-lady, "Mrs H"!) and the chapter in which a leak is discovered in the Staines Reservoir, with the town of Egham put at flood risk, is suspenseful indeed, we rather doubt whether the public is quite ready at the present time for a novel of 250,000 words in which a deprived water board employee struggles to "find himself"'.

A friend of mine called Richard Clowes decided in the 1920s and after an expensive public school education at Malvern College, to stay at home and, in the teeth of strong family opposition and disapprobation, become the writer for whom the world was waiting, providing an endless stream of matchless novels, plays, poems and belles lettres. And accordingly, and working fourteen hours a day, he settled to his task and covered sheet after sheet of paper and, as the manuscripts piled excitingly up on all sides, he sent them here and there for publishers' consideration.

They lived at Wimbledon and Dick's disapproving father was, as so many in those days were, something in the City and commuted thither every day down the electrified rails. Breakfasting with this forbidding presence morning after morning (his mother wisely had a tray in bed), Dick had to keep his ears cocked for the sound of the postman's boots crunching up the gravel, but however loudly he hummed a tune or clattered dishes or made frenzied conversation, nothing could muffle the gloomy and almost daily thud of a rejected manuscript being pushed through the letter-box and falling heavily to the hall floor. 'What was that, my boy'? his father used to ask, looking up from the *Morning Post*. 'I heard nothing', Dick lied, scuttling swiftly from the room and hiding the tattered brown paper parcel behind a curtain. He subsequently found, I am happy to say, a cosy and more suitable niche as a play reader in the world of the theatre, where he was much liked. Like many another, he found it easier and more restful to comment on the literary works of others rather than to have to provide them himself.

A schoolmaster's long holidays have often been a matter for envy by those confined to offices and granted three weeks in August, forgetful of their free week-ends, a blessing unknown to public school masters who in my day had to endure, in the winter term, ninety-one continuous days of labour. 'Just think of all your lovely holidays' has been the parrot cry from those who do not realise that holidays have to be paid for and the weeks got through on somewhat limited supplies of cash. However, those who, like myself, lived happily at home (I was ever made welcome and, as I grew older, my father cheered up no end), were in clover, especially in my case when flush with the extra money that the BBC and *New Statesman* were beginning to provide. The amounts involved did not require them to be delivered in an armoured van but for all that were helpful. Dadie was a keen foreign traveller and twice a year, and often with a party of friends, we went abroad, frequently to Monte Carlo where gambling, which we both enjoyed, and sunshine and tennis and entertainments (fine music and ballet at the Casino theatre) were available.

Among our fellow gamblers was almost always to be found the then Provost of King's College, Cambridge, Provost Sheppard who, the moment term was over, made a bee line for the roulette tables and provided a fine example of how not to gamble and often, indeed, of how not to behave. I think his principal pleasure lay in reaching forward and actually putting the counters and plaques on the numbers for he would frequently so plaster the board with stakes that, even if he could have chosen the number to come up, he would have won little or nothing. On most occasions the atmosphere in the Rooms resembled that of a church: voices were hushed, modest demeanours were encouraged and emotion was never displayed, except of course by the Provost, never averse to being the cynosure of all eyes. He roared, he moaned, he groaned and, with but a scanty knowledge of French, exited noisily and penniless with a cry of '*Maisong de voleurs!*' We then lent him ('Thank you, dear boy!') more money and pushed him back in again.

Had he ever looked like a young man? It would hardly appear so for he seemed, white-haired and hobbling along with a stick, to be extremely ancient although on occasion and when it suited him he could put on a fine turn of speed. A well-set-up St Catharine's undergraduate, passing through King's on his way to a lecture, was once much startled by somebody resembling a mad professor who came darting along, locks awry, and popped up in front of him with a heartfelt cry of 'My dear fellow! How nice of you to look so nice!' We know all this from the Provost's later and proud recounting of the incident when we were being invited to admire what he called his 'presence of mind'. He had, he said, at first been tongue-tied but then inspiration had come and he had lighted, for the young man was looking alarmed, on this tremendously suitable and complimentary form of greeting. 'Oh', we said. Another such episode concerned a visit to America and to Yale University and the occasion when he was invited, and as the sole guest, to dine with the Yale football team. He took the trouble to get a group photograph of them and then learnt all their names. 'And so, when I came to make my little speech of thanks', related the Provost, eyes shining, 'instead of just saying 'Gentlemen', I looked at each of them and said Mr This or Mr That and I got all their names right, every one, and they *loved* it. Oh it was wonderful, it was wonderful. You see, *I was the centre*'. Revealing.

The Provost was in no way stingy but his hospitable instincts were considerably greater than his ability to hold on to his money and one Easter in Monte Carlo there was expansive talk of a dinner which he wanted to give the five of us. As regards food and drink it seemed that the sky was to be the limit for the venue selected for this sensational beano was the Hôtel de Paris, than which there is none finer (or, then, more expensive). The date was fixed for a week's time and we all began keenly to look forward to the treat. The Provost continued to play roulette with abandon and in a day or two had started to wonder whether the Hôtel de Paris was *exactly* the right place for us. Would we truly be happy there? 'Do please say' but perhaps something smaller and less ornate might suit us better? The Hermitage, possibly? The next day we found that he had taken against hotels in general and had discovered a smallish restaurant ('Ideal!') in a side street. And then there came another change of plan. Why bother to go out at all? Why not dine, as usual, in our own rather modest hotel? They *knew* us there, and that always makes such a difference, don't you think? When the actual day came, the Provost spent a worried morning in deep thought but by tea-time had become once more buoyant. 'Everything's all right!', though those of us who thought this meant that he had acquired and held on to adequate dinner money were soon disappointed. 'I've just telephoned Smith'. Smith was a kind and long-suffering friend who lived along the coast. 'Smith's agreed to give us all dinner. We'll go by bus'. He then looked especially triumphant and cried 'I'VE GOT THE MONEY FOR THE FARES,' adding in a lower tone, 'only *there*, of course' before darting off for a few precious moments at the tables before we set off. Smith was as good as his word and gave us a splendid dinner of *blanquette de veau*, at which the Provost shamelessly acted as host. We went, as arranged, by bus and we paid the fares. Both ways.

In the years before the war, Dadie and I used to go and stay, before or after Monte Carlo, with Somerset Maugham in the famous Villa Mauresque at Cap Ferrat. Since his death his critics have, and without the aid of outrageous fortune, hurled so many slings and arrows at him, his character, his friend Gerald Haxton, his other friends, his marital misfortune, his life style and, when they couldn't think of anything else, his books and plays, that it is a pleasure to speak up in the defence of this much maligned man. Nobody would have had more contempt for the attacks made on him, not for their inaccuracy so much as for their vulgarity, and the attacks often came from people who should have known better.

Although we were friendly enough and were made very welcome, one of the main objects of our visits was for Dadie to give what universities call Tutorials in English Literature to our host. Willie, who was better and more widely read than most, used to complain that he was uneducated and needed guidance, though it wasn't put quite as baldly as that, and lunch would have been going for about five minutes when a tentative, stammering voice would say, 'D-d-d-adie, I have a notion that when George Eliot says in *Adam Bede* 'Our deeds determine us, as much as we determine our deeds', what she really meant to say was . . .' and there would follow some additional thought or comment of his own. Dadie would pause and cogitate and then reply, but if Willie's remark was something of a bromide (and bromides from his lips were by no means unknown, however portentously uttered), Dadie would just smile and nod and say 'Yes, Willie', upon which Willie would give me a sideways glance and just whisper 'I've b-b-b-been reproved'. I had little of interest or profit to offer but Willie never let me feel out of things and he was unfailingly kind and thoughtful and benevolent. He took enormous trouble over budding authors, answering all their letters, reading their manuscripts and giving advice. In his youth, nobody had ever bothered to encourage him but he saw no reason for treating that as an excuse for not himself bothering now.

The villa was everything that a guest could wish for. There was delicious food, breakfast in bed, a beautiful garden and pool, tennis, wonderful Riviera views, a yacht and a car and chauffeur to drive those who wished to gamble or shop. Willie's co-host, Gerald, was a lively presence, with his exuberance a fine contrast to Willie's basic shyness, and if, when officially supposed to be on the wagon but actually on the bottle, Gerald sneaked and drank a neat glass of gin when Willie's back was turned, that seemed to me to be nobody's business but his. Various literary grandees turned up, H. G. Wells among them and, to my great joy, Elizabeth Russell, the authoress of other things than the German Garden – *Mr Skeffington, The Caravaners* and, above all, *The Enchanted April*, of all books the one I think I have loved the best. Not only of hers. Of anybody's.

I make so bold as to reproduce here a short pastiche of Willie's style and vocabulary which perhaps represents what he might have felt and said of the hue and cry (the only words for it) that broke out after his death, with the snarling pack at his heels and with various literary persons speedily cashing in on this lucrative subject, among them being, and I regret to say it, his nephew Robin:

> I have a notion that when an old party dies it
> is as well to let him be. I am aware that
> certain persons have been preparing their
> recollections of me and that, anxious to publish,
> they have faced my death with fortitude. I can
> but think that the recollections are disobliging.
> Flattery does not sell. I do not blame them.
> It is not in me to judge my fellows; I am content
> to observe them. I am not a vindictive man
> and it merely amuses me to reflect that my stories
> will still be read when these persons and what
> they have thought fit to say are long since
> forgotten. They are small fry.

Meanwhile at Oundle happy term succeeded happy term with my salary increasing yearly by the princely sum of £20 so that by 1938 I was being rewarded to the tune of £390 a year (£15 extra, and I should hope so, for being in the OTC) and when my extraneous earnings were added on to that I found that that year I had broken the financial sound barrier of £500. It was de luxe living indeed for in the holidays I continued to be based at home, increasingly amused, and sometimes exasperated, by the rigid nature of our social life. My mother, as exasperated as I, was still required to accept and pay 'calls' and leave or receive those depressingly formal calling cards which piled up on a salver in the hall. Dreaded 'At Home' days ('Mrs Nyceley-Brown is at home on the second Thursday in the month') were things of the past but otherwise little had changed.

At Newbury everybody was fearfully anxious about whom it was possible to know and those who had to be politely avoided. Nobody was in the smallest doubt about their 'place' and sheep and goats weren't in it. I never understood why doctors were acceptable but not dentists and certainly not vets. Anybody remotely connected with retail trade was out, and here was a puzzle. It was apparently perfectly all right to be a City wine or tea shipper and sell the stuff, unseen, by the crate and chest, but if you just handed the bottles or the packets over the counter and received cash for them, you ruled yourself out. Neither were farmers, that pleasant and reputable lot, permissible and here there was sadness, for my brother, by then a chartered accountant, had been badly smitten by a nice girl who had been so foolish as to have a farmer father and it was firmly decided therefore that she could not be invited to Our Dance, a fearsome Christmas affair, claret cup and oyster patties and charlotte russe galore, in hired rooms in the town (my parents would not have minded but 'one had to think of The Others'). My father, himself at slight risk (there had been, three generations back, a prosperous tailor's shop in Bath), adopted a defiant attitude about newcomers ('Who *are* these Entwhistles, anyway?'). I liked, then as now, to know the widest possible range of human beings, finding all of them, now as then, attractive and interesting in one way or another and so I soon disregarded all the rules and raised eyebrows.

At Oundle everybody knew, naturally, everybody and as a result a happy atmosphere existed. Some staff members were, obviously, more life-enhancing than others and I had a happy moment at a Fisher dinner party for twelve when, standing as I was beside my hostess, of whom I was very fond, the door opened and a parlourmaid announced, in turn, the names of three totally righteous but not fully sparkling married couples. Mrs Fisher, a card if ever there was one, just turned to me and muttered 'Oh God! Oh Montreal!' Yes, it's Samuel Butler but originally uttered in a rather different context.

In the late 30s I had the great good fortune to meet the famous Oxonian character, Maurice Bowra, and, although he knew the whole world, to start a friendship which continued until his death in 1971. His numerous academic and administrative distinctions – Warden of Wadham and Vice-Chancellor, among others – sat very lightly upon him and he remained in many ways the brilliantly clever and funny and pugnacious Cheltenham schoolboy that he had once been. Nobody could have looked less like what he was and if Maurice had ever appeared, which God forbid for he would have startled them considerably, before the panel of the 'What's My Line' TV programme, whatever would they have made of this stunted and bellicose rotundity (there was a myth that when, after being knighted by the Queen, Her Majesty said 'Arise, Sir Maurice', the gruff reply was 'I *have* risen,

Ma'am'). What would their suggestions have been? A cattle salesman? A pork butcher (the eyes were rather piglike)? A seedy ex-boxer? Obviously aware of these physical imperfections, he sometimes had with him a photograph of himself at the age of eighteen and which he rather touchingly displayed to show The Glory That Once Was ('Not bad?').

He loved to poke fun and to tease, and chose to pretend (though it was uncomfortably close to the truth, given his own standards) that I was an amiable nitwit, not yet certifiable but just a little 'slow', don't you know, and if the conversation seemed, as it often in fact was, well above my intellectual head, he took time off to help me. 'We were talking about Greece, Arthur. Not the grease that engineers smear on axles but the *country*, Greece. It's spelt G-R-E-E-C-E and it's down the eastern end of the Mediterranean. Do you know where Gibraltar is? Well, not *that* end but the other one. Got it?' On other occasions he would just turn aside from the general chat and lower his voice and say 'Are you *all right*, Arthur?' All this was done mainly as a tease but there was real kindness and sympathy in it as well. I found his jokes hilarious, and showed it, and that is no despicable way into somebody's heart.

He also dearly loved to shock. His voice could be now a melodious coo with the head thrown slightly back and the lips pointed into an 'O', now a full-throated bellow, and the bellow was preferred when uttering indecent words in public places. Once when he was having lunch with me at the Reform Club, where decorous behaviour and lowered speech are the popular thing, we found ourselves next to a table with an inoffensive bishop at it. While he ate his pâté, Maurice gave his views on divines in general. 'Don't like bishops. Fishy lot. Blessed are the meek my foot! They're all on the climb. Ever heard of meekness stopping a bishop from becoming a bishop? Neither have I'. I wasn't sure how much of this our neighbour was hearing, but for the next utterance, Maurice inflated his lungs and boomed out in a rich and parsonical voice 'I expect to pass through this world but once and therefore if there is anybody that I want to kick in the crutch, I had better kick them in the crutch *now*, for I do not expect to pass this way again'. There followed a list of well-known names, the owners of which all qualified, it seemed, for crutch damage. By the end of it, I was relieved to see that our bishop had hastily munched up and gone.

Another time we were at a Sunday breakfast party in Dadie's rooms in King's. For many years at the universities, breakfast had been a recognised and pleasant social occasion and parties were frequent, continuing until wartime rations made them bleak feasts. Maurice was staying for the weekend, sleeping in a College guest room nearby, and to meet this celebrated figure Dadie had invited various undergraduates who, it was felt, would appreciate the visitor. As we sat waiting for his arrival, I wondered what my fellow guests were expecting, for Maurice was known as a name rather than a familiar physical presence. What might their picture of him be? A modest and white-haired *penseur* who would say something memorable that they could, that night, write down in their diaries? An Oxford ascetic who would nibble at a slice of toast and discuss Aristotle? What they were expecting can hardly have been what they got for after some time the door opened and Maurice, grubby, unkempt and unshaven, came shuffling into the room in a dressing-gown and looking displeased, remaining silent while Dadie introduced the various young men, by now a little nervous. Food was placed before him and, after staring gloomily at it, Maurice spoke. Just five words and not those of a really deep *penseur* but rather more showing his practical side. 'Must go to the lavatory'. Dadie gave a wail of dismay, 'Oh, Maurice! *Really*!' and the undergraduates flinched and twitched while we sat in silence and waited for the *penseur's* return. Soon he was back, in excellent spirits again. '*Most* satisfactory!' Everybody suddenly remembered essays that they had to write and the party soon broke up.

He was a great collector and digester of information, scandalous if possible, about public schools and when I made a motor trip anywhere near a school, he liked me to look in, lurk, linger, listen, test for 'tone' and subsequently send him a bulletin. Over the years, during some of which I was a schoolmaster and therefore well placed for investigations, I covered in this way Sherborne, Haileybury, Uppingham, Stowe, St Paul's and Bedford – each of them admirable. There was one however where all seemed to the practised eye far from well, and also to the ear (smutty talk and sniggers). The Headmaster was formerly at Oxford and known to Maurice and when I sent in my reluctantly adverse report, it was answered with 'Thought as much. Poor old Cloggers has let the place go to pot. I shall warn everybody to give it a miss. The *tone* sounds very poor: you can always tell'. He in turn wrote sometimes with news from Oxford, splendid letters with, after the greeting, no preamble but plunging you straight *in medias res*. 'Great excitement here. Case of incest recently discovered. A rather pi choral scholar found in bed with his sister. Great pity there isn't more of it. Keep it in the family'.

He was the most financially generous of friends and on a post-war Italian holiday (Naples, Positano, Amalfi, Rome) and when the foreign allowance of cash was small, he had managed to come by a good additional supply of lira and American dollars which he lavished on us, paying for rich meals well beyond our budget and hiring cars to take the five of us to Ravello and Pompeii and the temples at Paestum, all made even more agreeable and interesting by his knowledgeable discourse, loudly delivered and in short, staccato bursts (nobody knew better than he the virtue of brevity). Before we set off on these jaunts, a price had to be arranged with the Italian driver. Maurice would ask him how much he proposed to demand. The man, taken in by this seemingly gullible and genial Englishman, named a sum, always answered by such a wild bellow of rage, anguish, outrage and disagreement that the price was instantly halved and in we got ('Are you *all right*, Arthur?')

Every so often we bathed. Maurice's dive into the briny produced a tidal wave of impressive volume and some strange physical arrangement or errant centre of gravity meant that he swam upright and with both his head and his shoulders well out of the water and as though he were standing on a submerged and slow-moving trolley. While proceeding steadily along, he liked to sing snatches from the songs of the first world war, in which he had had a fearful time – 'Keep The Home Fires Burning' was a favourite, together with 'Pack Up Your Troubles'. In the water, one or other of us kept near him for there had already been some heart trouble. With the shore safely reached once more, he would hunt about in the shingle for small pieces of broken green bottle glass, rubbed smooth by the sea and referred to as the famous Bowra Emeralds, historical gems of considerable value and constantly at risk from continental jewel thieves, the whole collection being perilously housed overnight in a hollow in a rock.

As may be imagined, he was not, and certainly would not have wanted to be, everybody's cup of tea and one can but think that many of his Oxford colleagues found him alarming (so very awkward when you simply don't know what a fellow is going to *say*, what he's going to come *out* with. Well, don't you agree, Jocelyn?). Although his friends had to mind their p's and q's (unpunctuality was unpopular), his loyalties were fierce. Nobody loved and appreciated him more than Noël and Gabriele Annan. They met constantly and, when Maurice came to London, they would arrange this or that dinner party for him. Sometimes, when two or three talented and distinguished guests were suggested, Maurice would, apparently, say 'No thanks. Don't feel in the mood for them. Let's just have poor old Arthur'. Forgive this sad little boast but the happiness of finding oneself to have been among the chosen has been a great one.

His body lies in an Oxford cemetery and when they are in the neighbourhood, Noël and Gaby visit their good old friend, and stand and remember and say a loving and grateful word.

SCENE VI

Little Toy Soldier

And then, on September 3rd, 1939, and after years of what are sometimes dyspeptically referred to as 'rumblings', the long foreseen war did actually break out and all was changed. And yet, was it? In a sense, nothing was changed. A 'Carry On' film of the time might well have been called *Carry On Normally*, though 'normally' is hardly the adverb for those filmic goings-on.

For the first few anti-climactic months I remained a master at Oundle, commissioned and awaiting call-up. Though in our remote corner of Northamptonshire we were of a quite negligible interest as a bomb target, we were no great distance from the immensely important and visible iron works at Corby, and the Oundle town council, rightly feeling that we should all be alert and on our toes for any enemy action that mishits at Corby might spill over on to us, decided to arrange various surprise tests of civic initiative. I was still an assistant housemaster in a boarding-house situated in the middle of the town itself and when, very late one night in November, 1939, the front door bell rang, I seemed to be the only person up and about and ready to answer it. I like to think that I was conscientiously correcting French proses and preparing my thoughts on Racine for the next day, but I was more probably reading yet another of my favourite stage autobiographies of the As -you-see-they-seemed-to-like-me-well-enough-in-Bradford kind, to a soothing background of Henry Hall on the wireless.

It was nearly midnight. Who could it be? The bursar come to inspect a cracked basin, or with a new, patented cockroach deterrent? Prudently dousing the lights in the hall and abiding by the blackout regulations, I opened the door and shone outwards the beams of my torch, carefully directing them downwards in case some wily Jerry airman was silently circling above in his Dornier, sinisterly waiting his chance to come zooming down and put paid to me, for such was the common expectancy in those naïve days. Just visible in the dim light was not the bursar but a diminutive female figure. She spoke, and she spoke lugubriously. 'I'm a high-explosive bomb', she said.

She was, of course, no such thing. I recognised her at once as an assistant in one of the town's two drapery establishments. She had taken, fittingly enough, a leading role in *Our Miss Gibbs*, that melodious musical about a shopgirl that had recently been staged, regardless of expense and in open defiance of Hitler, by the town's amateurs for a week's performances in our Victoria Hall. However, swiftly reacting to the challenge brought by this council emissary, I asked her if, as a bomb, she was supposed to have already gone off, or to be on the very verge of going off, or if we were to regard her as being, in the mind's eye, embedded in the roadway, categorised as 'unexploded' and just about to be railed off and forbidden access by the general public. She said that she was sorry but she did not know. 'They' had not told her.

The night was chilly and this menace from the skies looked forlorn and frail standing there, so I asked her if her duties permitted a break for refreshment in the shape of coffee and biscuits. Instantly deserting her post, in the carefree and lackadaisical military manner of 1939, Miss Gibbs stepped briskly in, swiftly downed two cups of 'Camp' and a handful of oval Maries, and then went off again, reinvigorated, to bring her dreaded rain of horror from above to other sleepy sections of the town. It was never made clear to me what I was expected to do when discovering high-explosive positively on the door-step. It was generally felt, on discussing the matter with colleagues, that coffee and biscuits was as good an emergency measure as any.

Those people who had spent part of their childhood playing the delightful game of Charades found themselves at quite an advantage when joining up. It helped considerably, and here an experience of amateur dramatics too was a bonus, to feel that you were merely acting a minor role in a rather long-running play (*Journey's End* springs to mind or, on a more fanciful note, *Chu-Chin-Chow*), especially at moments when the realities of war were being particularly disagreeable and alarming. To enjoy being on the receiving end of dive bombers must be an acquired taste. Such a frightful *noise*, apart from anything else.

A sense of humour however feeble, as in my own case, was also a comfort. It didn't mean that one wasn't taking the war seriously but it made life easier and one's sympathies went out to the very few one met who seemed to have been caught behind the door when the good fairies were handing out fun. Early in 1944 I found myself with a major to whom fun in any form had never found its way. All my attempts to make him livelier were a failure and he thought me both odd and irresponsible, in one of which estimations he was correct. On one occasion he gave me a deeply depressed look and said, 'Everybody in this outfit seems to be using Christian names. What's yours?' I have three initials and the first is 'C'. 'It's Cynthia', I replied, wishful to lighten the gloom. '*Cynthia*? That's a bloody silly name for a man!' 'Yes, isn't it?' I said. However, for a week he called me Cynthia loudly and rather defiantly and until I had to beg him to stop. 'People', I said 'are talking', but the little joke passed him by, alas, and he just thought me odder still.

I had been for some seven years a markedly reluctant member of the Oundle School Officers' Training Corps. I wasn't really what is called officer material and I looked a bit bizarre in uniform (I once, absentmindedly and on a wet day, went on parade with an umbrella) but Dr Fisher, on considering me for the Oundle staff in 1931, had made it clear that an offer to participate in the OTC would be favourably viewed. He didn't actually say '. . . or else' but the words hovered in the air, so up I joined.

On formal occasions we wore, almost unbelievably, swords and there was a, to me, highly complicated and baffling drill for wielding the wretched implements. Among my fellow wielders at that time was the Rev R. W. Stopford, known to all as 'Stoppers' and later to be such a genial Bishop of London, though Liverpool would have suited better the strongly regional accent which he retained through life. The swords' bluntness made them unsuitable even for slicing a Hovis loaf, let alone a Jerry head. Would they be sharpened for warfare, one wondered? What was the German for 'Surrender at once or I will cut your head off'? Time alone would tell.

Although my Uncle Wilfred had been at Sandhurst we were far from being a military family and in 1939 my parents, partly proud of my call-up and partly apprehensive, wished for a pleasing likeness of me in uniform and despatched me to London and to the then modish Howard Coster who took snaps, and favoured cabinet size, in Essex Street and who advertised himself as being a 'Photographer of Men', which rather limited his range. It was before the days when photographers clicked in such a currently lavish and spendthrift manner and Mr Coster restricted himself and me to six poses ('Let's now try a little half smile, shall we?') and a fine, fearless and false job he made of me, but it gave satisfaction in the home that I was shortly to leave.

The War Office document summoning me to the colours on such and such a day contained a thoughtful proviso. If, it comforted, I were to find myself indisposed in any way on the appointed date, 'not to worry' (though this cheery reassurance was implied rather than actually stated) but just let them know at a department called FORCEDLY TWO. The capital letters were impressive. Was there perhaps also a FORCEDLY ONE (snuffly colds and tummy upsets) and a FORCEDLY THREE for terminal matters? My own FORCEDLY I took to mean influenza or anything manifesting a temperature.

Schoolmasters with a knowledge of French and German were often enrolled in the Intelligence Corps and here I found myself, in January 1940, being groomed for stardom at Mytchett, a hutted camp near Aldershot, a camp which numbered among its supporting cast a bright button called Sgt Malcolm Muggeridge, vocally rather weird and difficult to place and already a bit creased facially but taking a refreshingly detached and amused view of life in general and of Intelligence in particular. Here we were lectured to at length and every day, were informed about the Security branch of the Intelligence service, were closely examined on what we had learnt, were separated into sheep and goats and finally, initiated, indoctrinated and inoculated, were inserted into battle dress and packed off to various parts of the BEF in Northern France.

In addition to FORCEDLY TWO, the War Office Calling Up Notice had kindly given wise advice on clothing and equipment. If, for example, I were joining up while wearing 'breeches, knickerbocker' or 'breeches, mounted pattern', I would require field boots and leggings. The document tended to harp on people being mounted. Were there then, and

Heaven help us all, to be horses? I was also counselled to obtain a canvas bucket, a 'cap comforter', whatever that might be, a housewife (ho! ho!), a whistle, 'grease or vaseline' (for chapped lips, perhaps, and how thoughtful), binoculars and, very mysteriously, 'a collapsible lantern'. One's eyebrows rose! Whatever would sentries think if, on going my Florence Nightingale rounds at night, my lantern were to collapse? One was already and even *sans* collapsing lanterns at considerable risk as a figure of fun.

At first and until I evolved a way of dealing with them, I found staff officers and generals very startling stuff. They alarmed me. I dare say it was the red tabs and the medal ribbons and the moustaches and the aura with which high rank seemed to hedge itself. However, and because of my admiration for Angela Brazil, I chose to imagine that we were all in a vast girls' school: Headmistress, Miss Gladys Gort: School colours, Khaki and black: School motto, Don't Look Back Or You Might See Something Nasty. All the junior girls were dead nuts on that new and dashing little hockey mistress, Miss Brenda Montgomery, and with this phantasy, the tensions gradually eased. Forgive the apparent idiocy, inspired by personal need and inadequacy rather than by disrespect.

It was the fledgling Miss Montgomery that I met first. We were based among the flesh-pots of Lille and I was in command of a Field Security Section. It consisted of a Sergeant-Major, a dozen or so trained NCOs mounted on, though not all the time, motor-bicycles, a small Ford car, and me. Our object was to thwart enemy attempts at espionage, sabotage and propaganda and it required close cooperation, at that point freely given, with the French authorities. As we were there more or less on sufferance, our training had emphasised the importance of the friendly approach, *savoir faire* and the display of whatever charm one could muster. At first we were known as Field Security Police, but the word 'Police' scared people and was subsequently dropped.

We lectured to British troops on the vital importance of secrecy (Be Like Dad. Keep Mum). We cross-questioned alleged spies. We investigated the countless reports of lights mysteriously flashing at night and with, for me, memories of a wretched Oundle master with the unfortunate name of Hornstein. He, during the first world war, was suspected of signalling to Zeppelins up the chimney of his lodgings. Nobody bothered to wonder what had led the Zeppelin to the wilds of Northamptonshire or just what sensational news, school or otherwise, he had been so skilfully passing on. The result of a rugger match, perhaps: Oundle 49, Uppingham 3, an item sufficient to cause excited comment ('*Gott in Himmel!*') in the gondola as it swayed its way back to Heligoland.

A Field Security Officer was something of a novelty in the army and the fiction that one was fully in the know about spies, preferably big-bosomed and female (Mata Hari and all that) made one a, to some, intriguing object. Our company, if not actually sought, was not always considered displeasing. Operating as we were in his Divisional area, I had to present myself to General Montgomery and explain what we were up to. He was kind enough to appear interested in our activities and while he asked me various questions I became fascinated, inconsequentially, by the elegance and length of his nose. Could all of it possibly be real? I met it again some years later when its owner came to lecture at Oundle and I sat next to him at lunch, when all the old wonderment returned. Dare one give it an investigative tweak? Better not, perhaps. He was a pleasant man to meet in private and when in relaxed mood, but in public and when lecturing one wished him otherwise, for the boastful victor and really rather sad braggart emerged, a cut below the Churchills and Alexanders and Eisenhowers of this world.

Is it now remembered that although the outwardly impressive Maginot Line actually extended only to the area south of Sedan, that valuable and vulnerable point previously exploited by the Germans for a break-through, the Line was frequently and reassuringly shown on newspaper maps as reaching to the coast near Calais. So, on arrival in France, I looked about on the Belgian frontier for the sight of impregnable fortifications but was merely greeted by some barbed wire and a few ditches that may or may not have been devilish tank-traps: and the more one looked, the more they just looked ditches. Similarly unrewarding was a search for a satisfactory array of tanks, armoured vehicles and guns. Divisions too were known to be pretty thin on the ground. Lonely, one felt, and never more so than when, in the early hours of May 10th, 1940, and in time to ruin my thirtieth birthday (it must have been deliberate) the balloon went, as we phrased it, up and the phoney war was over.

A number of things then happened, all of them unpleasant. Much of the army pressed forward into a Belgium that, though welcoming now, had previously been entirely uncooperative. The Belgian forces were seen, with their largely horse-drawn artillery, to be only rather vaguely geared to modern combat: and their troops had a, to put it mildly, listless look. The fog of war swiftly descended and before long it became difficult to locate our formations and units. When one was given a map reference for a headquarters, it really only meant that the headquarters wasn't there any more. Offices, hastily abandoned, still often held documents valuable to an enemy and which had to be burnt. Meanwhile the roads filled with cars, mattresses strapped to their roofs, carts, horses, bicycles and humans all hurrying westwards. The fleeing columns were relentlessly bombed and machine-gunned from the air.

By now we had acquired a truck, usually full of suspects (the more suspicious of them blindfolded), and our journeys hither and thither were interrupted by the necessity to leave our vehicles and take prudent cover in a ditch. Once, driving along an exposed highway somewhere near Oudenarde, we became aware that shot and shell were passing rather close overhead and discovered that we had driven happily along, a target as splendidly visible as those ducks that judder by in a fair's shooting gallery, between the advancing Germans and the speedily collapsing Belgian army. Fortune evidently favours the foolish as well as others. Another time, my sergeant-major and I had mounted a hillock, the better to view the landscape o'er and to see what was happening. Becoming aware of a swishing sound from behind, we turned and observed a German aeroplane gliding towards us and although I emptied, as they say, my revolver into it, it kept right on, dropped two bombs, covered us with earth and stones and killed a cow.

There was spy mania everywhere. Whole nunneries of devout ladies (the rascally Boche in disguise, of course) had been seen parachuting down, their bloomers doubtless filling with air and easing the burden on their silken canopies. On alighting, they disappeared, for none were ever found, into thin air, habits, boots, bloomers and all. A curious civilian bystander had only to cast one enquiring glance at a tank to be instantly arrested and brought to us for interrogation. There were three methods of dealing with a suspect. There was the British one, which was to question him and then, in our customary and just manner and for want of solid evidence, release him. There was the French method, which was to question the man and then shoot him. And there was the Belgian, which was the same as the French only without the questions.

There was another problem. German Jews who had, in the 30s fled from persecution and worse in their own country, had often found refuge in Belgium. Arrested and interned on the outbreak of war, they had now been liberated by the Belgians and left to get away as best they could from their fellow countrymen. Jabbering away in their native tongue and normally without any means of identification, they too jammed the roads and hurried to the west. They were genuinely suspicious persons and fear had made many of them, I am sorry to say, both arrogant and demanding, but one did what one could to help. The French, however, held the old-fashioned opinion that the only good German was a dead one and we tried to avoid hearing the sad sound of shouts and remonstrances and then rifles firing behind a wall.

Quite soon, food became difficult to find and, much worse, drinking water was not always available. Wine isn't much help to a raging thirst. Formations moved mainly by night and sleep was hard to come by. A German tank suddenly appeared from nowhere and opened fire on us, while another Field Security officer, driving his car at dusk out of a side road, joined a column of vehicles moving north west and found, to his surprise, that they were German. Nobody seemed to notice him and he was able to make his departure ('*Gute Nacht*') up the next side road. And when the chaos was at its height, the Belgian and French authorities considered that the ideal moment had arrived for opening all their prisons and asylums and releasing the inmates: murderers, thieves and poor loonies, strangely attired in, of all things, green corduroy, thronged the roads, wildly pilfering and grimacing. All, I need hardly say, were at once arrested.

One of our pre-Blitz tasks in France had been to report on civilian morale, even then pretty low, and to this end and during a rare moment of stability, I opened conversation, in a deserted and badly damaged Roubaix estaminet, with the proprietress, a large and apathetic lady with a husband in the forces. She wanted only peace, and no matter at what price. France was done for, so why go on? Her thoughts then turned to Hitler. Was he married, she wondered, or was he, as the rumour went, not fond of women and required more awkward physical diversions? *'C'est un goût comme un autre'* she said, moodily polishing glasses that were soon to know different customers.

At one point in the general confusion I was given some crisp orders by a very trim and military Lt Col called G. Templer, later to be a Field Marshal. He was smoking a cigarette in one of those long black holders so popular with Eton-cropped ladies in the 20s, though there the resemblance ended. Cool as a cucumber, he urged me to nurture my car ('Your life, Marshall, may depend on it'), a statement which so unnerved me that, on leaving him, I drove straight over one of those raised and circular traffic humps in French towns and nearly broke the front axle. The bearing of senior officers was throughout very splendid and an example to all. On my way one day into the headquarters, located for once, of 2 Corps, I saw approaching me, as though emerging from a routine Roedean staff meeting, Miss Gort, Miss Brooke, Miss Barker and Miss Montgomery (apologies again). I gave my best salute, never up to much, and was duly saluted back. Although evacuation was but ten days away, they looked as quietly confident as if they had just been deciding to introduce a new type of gym-slip and to increase the cocoa ration, and one's grateful heart went out to them. I could, and how very astonished they would have been, have hugged them.

One afternoon, having momentarily lost touch with my section, I heard what was, for that time, a strange sound – the strains of a violin and, following it to its source, I found, as I peered into a quiet courtyard, my lance-corporals gathered hungrily round a roast fowl, while a professional violinist, bribed no doubt with English cigarettes, was giving them a selection from *Madam Butterfly*. It seemed to me a fine example of initiative and I did not disturb them. During much of the time after May 10th, the Army Post Office contrived, in some miraculous way, to continue to function and letters, although weeks late, managed to reach us. Their contents showed that the writers were, naturally, somewhat out of touch with current events. 'Have you visited the Maginot Line yet?', they said, or 'Why not spend your leave in Paris?'

Soon life became really very difficult indeed but the various built-in-mechanisms of the human body supply an antidote to unimaginable disaster. A blessed sense of dreamlike unreality descends. And I had one great advantage. I had taken part, both as a schoolboy and as a master, in many school field days, all of which had ended in turmoil. Blue Force had failed to find Green Force. Red Force had not linked up with Brown Force. The CO (sometimes the school chaplain and known as The Church Militant) had fallen off his horse. And so now, in the rather bemused state brought on by lack of sleep and food, I felt sure that, rounding the next corner, we would find the school tuck-shop van and trestle tables and currant buns and a steaming tea-urn and people saying 'Well tried, anyway'.

In due course we were instructed to abandon our non-portable possessions and immobilise our transport (we put bullets through tyres, but matches and petrol would have been more effective) and make for Dunkirk, all too visible as it blazed away on the horizon. And once there, we moved from the inland chaos and sense of failure and despair into a relatively orderly world, for the Navy was present in force, the dark blue uniforms radiating calm. There were destroyers and other ships out at sea, and various boats lined the one remaining mole (badly damaged but usable). The acrid smell of burning hung in the air, and drinking water was still nearly impossible to find (a hardship, and an extraordinarily unpleasant one, that had never come my way before). There was by now no food. Occasionally an abandoned car was found and the radiator could be drained for the water it contained.

From time to time, bombs fell and the enemy had got our range with mortars, an unlovely weapon because its shells, like George and Margaret in the play, take so long to arrive and are fully audible throughout. Absence of food, coupled with exhaustion, made the nights (we had two of them) seem unusually cold and there is little of comfort, save protection of a sort, to be found in a sand dune. One's childhood love of sand and beaches disappeared in a trice.

The long lines of troops waiting to be rowed out to the destroyers and other ships stretched down to the sea and into it, and calm prevailed. Tiredness had induced a mood of quiet acceptance (English towns, ceaselessly bombed, were subsequently to experience much the same thing). I got some disapproving looks for, occasionally, smiling. Smiles were rare, but when things are very bad, my nervous reaction (I think it must be due to my theatrical tendencies) is to wear a look of inane cheerfulness, quite horrible to behold but when the star of a show has broken her leg back-stage, the cast, wildly smiling, attempts to conceal the fact.

There was another attempt at concealment by a very conscientious Major who, distressed by the scene of devastation presented by the seashore, with its littered stores and equipment and webbing and greatcoats (people swimming out to boats aren't going to bother to take such things with them), went round trying, in his own phrase, 'to tidy the place up a bit'. We gave him a hand, as it was something to do while waiting, and we made little piles of uniform here and little piles of webbing there, but I cannot think that the Germans (known to everybody as, and with surprisingly little hatred, 'Old Jerry') were deceived. '*That's* better', said the Major, giving a final look. But it wasn't.

We came home via the mole and on a small cross-channel French steamer, its decks already jammed with troops. We found, with difficulty, inches of space in corners and, lying down, fell instantly asleep, and thus we missed seeing the armada of small boats that was already setting out for Dunkirk on that soul-stirring rescue mission. We missed too the white cliffs, the sight of which is always so reassuring to a returning traveller.

The organisation at Folkestone, where we put in, was beyond all praise. Food, water, cups of tea. Welcoming faces. Kind WI ladies dispensed sweets ('How about some chocky?' one kept saying, red-eyed, as we filed past). The trains left every twenty minutes or so, bearing us away to army camps all over the country, and as we set off, the windows of houses all along the line were open and were filled with people waving and cheering and shouting. Children stood on embankments and fluttered flags, cars blew their horns. 'Good heavens', somebody said, 'whatever would they have done if we had won?'

Some three months later, and for reasons unvouchsafed to me by the War Office, never much given to explaining anything, I was promoted to the rank of GSO 3, or Staff Officer Captain, and ordered to Northern Ireland and to the headquarters of the British troops there. I had spent the intervening time with a Security Section on the Cumbrian coast in the vicinity of two towns with misleadingly pleasing names, Maryport and Whitehaven, neither of them very strong on beauty, though inland things improved. En route to the Lakes, we had stopped off at a somewhat bleak Blackpool where, as the section had had no food for some time, I ordered them fish-and-chips in a café. Attempts later on to extract from the military branch concerned the sum disbursed for this simple but sustaining feast met with failure. The men, I was informed, should have been tucking in to 'the unexpended portion of their day's ration'. What ration? Our farewells at what was then the Chatham depot ('Send us a post-card!') had included no mention of rations. Not so much as a biscuit had changed hands. If the War Office now cares to have a change of heart, £1 18s 4d would about cover my outlay, and I sportingly waive the matter of interest on that sum.

At about the same time I was coping with the financial claims that we could officially make for items of clothing lost at Dunkirk. There was a schedule of permissibles (I hunted in vain for collapsible lanterns) somewhat on the lines of a school clothing list: battle-dress, 1: boots, 4: prs. socks, 3, presumably on the principle of one on, one off and one in the wash. It said 'handkerchiefs, 6' and so, having lost all but what I stood up in, I applied for 6 but sure enough back came my claim changing 6 to 5 and pointing out that 'one handkerchief should, at the time of the evacuation and unless the applicant had had entirely to disrobe, have been being carried on the person'. But of course! I do see. Silly me.

Our Northern Ireland HQ was at Lisburn, some eight miles to the south-west of Belfast and consisted of a converted country house (senior officers, for the use of) surrounded by Nissen huts (us), with sleeping quarters and messes dotted here and there in small red brick houses intended, in peace-time, as married quarters for regular officers. With our army rations supplemented by irregular goods from Eire, living was comfortable and I merely wondered why on earth we were all there. With us there were eventually, if memory serves, three divisions, a Corps HQ and a mobile Brigade. To what end?

Gradually, however, a solution offered itself. The officer in command of our Intelligence Section was Major S. E Buckley, MC, who, in World War One, had distinguished himself by an especially skilful escape from a German P.O.W. camp, a deed excitingly described by a fellow-escapee in his book *The Escaping Club*. Our commander was also from the BEF, Lieut-General Sir Henry Pownall who had been Gort's Chief of Staff. Other senior officers had also, it turned out, been in France and had been blooded in the shambles. We were there because, it was discovered, we were all alleged to have had, and one can but give the surprising words capital letters, Battle Experience. So that was what it had been! Long on Experience, certainly, but a bit short on Battle.

There was at the time an opinion, held high up somewhere in Whitehall, that the enemy would invade Eire and use it as a base from which to attack, and eventually invade, Britain. The German army had of course reached Brest long since and from there and other French ports it was, to panicky imaginations, but a step to Cork. This took no account of the 300 miles of frequently stormy seas, let alone the British Navy or the certainly hostile reception that the neutral Irish would accord sea-borne visitors before, as was envisaged, calling on our aid. On the assumption that we would then be required, our cohorts gleaming in purple and gold, to pour down into Eire from the north, intelligence and operational officers in civilian clothes and feeling rather dare-devil, went south and measured roads and bridges and drew up plans for the battle that never was.

Events in France and Belgium had at least taught one lesson: the importance to everybody of speed and mobility. To be potentially nippy was the thing and to that end we had all to learn how to ride a motor-bicycle, a machine which, though docile enough (for the seasoned wheelman accustomed to bicycling) when proceeding along at a stately rate of 20 mph, scorching up to 25 if in the mood, developed when halted and at rest a rebellious life of its own, lurching heavily and unexpectedly to right or left, throwing you on to the road and then pinning you painfully down. Our sergeant instructors were kind and helpful but perked noticeably up when the lesson was over.

We also practised firing revolvers and it was really quite agreeable to draw a bead on a motionless Jerry officer obligingly awaiting death in plywood silhouette. And, just in case of real trouble, we learnt how to throw live hand-grenades and here one's past cricketing days were, rusty though one might be, of value, particularly with those of us who had restricted our bowling activities to lofty lobs. Immense precautions were taken to avoid mishaps in the butts. If you or an instructor dropped a grenade prematurely, they urged you not to wait to apologise or to cry a mocking 'Butterfingers' but to dart behind the buttress, where there was room, I hoped, for two.

Apart from anxious worries about loved ones getting bombed in England, I cannot claim that the year and a half that I spent in Ireland was anything but a refreshing spree. Once everything was prepared for the dash south, there was little of importance to do. Social life was vigorous, enthusiastically led by Lady Pownall, a great encourager. ENSA companies visited Belfast and us and, though some were markedly better than others, I would never subscribe to the ungrateful view that the letters stood for Every Night Something Awful. And best of all, we were allowed, provided we had civilian clothes, to spend our periodical 48 hours leave in neutral Dublin, a concession that few can ever have been in a position to enjoy in wartime.

Here was another world, a brightly-lit demi-Paradise (for some) which offered both the Abbey Theatre and the Gate Theatre, coupled with superb cooking at Jammet's famous restaurant where one sometimes found oneself at a table next to members of the German embassy, gassing away in their unlovely tongue. It was only military decorum and British dignity that prevented one from leaning towards them and startling them with a loud 'BOO!', followed by 'Who's losing the war?'

Can it have been my good old Battle Experience, now wearing decidedly thin, that wafted me one happy day in April, 1942, to Combined Operations and its London headquarters? Mystery again shrouds my appointment there, with the rank of Major, as SO (M) or Security Officer (Military). The 'M' was required to distinguish me from my naval counterpart, or SO (N), the delightful Lt Cdr Gerald Williams, formerly MP for Tonbridge (Conservative) and all that one could wish for in a colleague, and together we slogged away to make the HQ in Whitehall's Richmond Terrace reasonably secure and also the various commando establishments scattered countrywide and in hard training for raids on Europe.

It was clearly important to keep to a minimum the number of people who needed to have detailed knowledge of any particular raid that was being planned and to achieve this a system was evolved. Those officially connected with a raid (let us imagine the codename CLOUDBURST) were issued by us, after ascertaining the applicant's bona fides, at the security office with a printed card for CLOUDBURST. Those so

equipped could then only discuss the raid with other CLOUD-
BURST card-carrying officers. There was a sort of collector's
mania and Happy Families element in the subsequent use of
the cards. One officer would say to another 'Have you got
CLOUDBURST?' to which the other might reply 'No, but I've
got SCARECROW and SWIFTSURE *and* BLAZING!' He
didn't add 'So there!' but there might be a hint of it in the air.
Some of the senior officers applying to us for cards often
looked, as well they might, over-worked and anxious and it
was frequently my custom, as they left the office and wishful to
raise their morale, to say 'Oh by the way, sir, everybody tells
me that you're doing *simply splendidly*'. This was apparently
an unusual procedure for it caused surprise in most ('Oh really,
Marshall?') but pleasure in many. Well, why not? The HQ
officers represented the three services and were mainly pretty
senior. It had been my habit, when called upon to answer the
telephone in the BEF in France, to remember the impressive lilt
of 'Kitchener of Khartoum' and 'Lawrence of Arabia' and,
jolliness itself, to announce myself as being 'Marshall of Lille'
but in CO HQ the caller might well be Mountbatten himself
and so I had to be a shade more circumspect and sober.

'There was a shine on us' was Noël Coward's autobiographical way of describing his and Gertrude Lawrence's
success (not to speak of that of Adrianne Allen and a young
man called Laurence Olivier) in *Private Lives* in 1930 and
there was a similar sort of shine, in 1942, on CO HQ. We were
all basking in the reflected glory of the immensely courageous
raid on St Nazaire when, in the early hours of March 28th,
HMS *Campbeltown* burst through a hail of enemy fire and
rammed the gates of the lock that could shelter the *Tirpitz*.
Three VCs had been won and a great many Germans had been
killed or blown up (a delayed-action bomb on *Campbeltown*
had exterminated forty or so senior German officers who had
been rashly inspecting the damage and going, in German,
'tut-tut'). Meanwhile the Commandos had landed and were
doing great damage to port installations, not to speak of Hun
soldiers. And further to confuse the enemy and to mask the
sound of approaching ships, bombers flew low overhead. A
combined operation indeed.

The dashing Mountbatten was himself a histrionic character
– it was always said that he and Noël would have liked to
change places and the latter's performance in *In Which We*

Serve bears this out. Amphibious warfare on a big scale was still a relatively new idea and at the headquarters there was a refreshing breeziness and a feeling that at last the war was getting somewhere. In that largely Navy-orientated place, briskness was the thing.

I had sometimes to report, quaking a little, to Mountbatten himself. A succession of orders and instructions were crisply rapped out (there were never any repetitions to make sure that you had got it right), followed by that sensational smile and the words 'Now, Marshall, will you run along and do that for me?' One departed in a haze of hero-worship, a worship that was common to the entire headquarters. I once had to spend twenty minutes with Mountbatten while we decided where the marine sentries could stand so that they would be out of a draught, although draughtless nooks and corners tended to mask their field of view and diminish their usefulness as sentries. We tried this place and that ('Stand over there, Marshall. Now, are you in a draught?'). The sentries looked on, nonplussed by this quite unusual care for their welfare.

The naval officers with us behaved as though we were, though only in an aquatic sense, all at sea. Offices were cabins. To go upstairs was to go topsides. Messages were signals and the floor was the deck. One tried not to smile for smiles were not always welcome. I have to say that the reputedly good manners of all officers of the Royal Navy were not always exhibited to their inferiors and especially if the inferiors were in military uniform (the RAF, saviours of us all, seemed to pass muster). But at least the army didn't victimise its amateur officers by allotting them different insignia. The Wavy Navy could be instantly picked out by the regulars and were sometimes treated less than well. There was a very grumpy and fault-finding Commodore who, possibly frightened of the Security Service and also scornful of amateurs, took against Gerald and me and conducted a mild persecution. Of the two of us, he disliked me more and the cut of my jib failed utterly to please. One day, finding myself alone with him in the canteen, I plucked up courage, smiled ingratiatingly, as I hoped, and said 'I say, do stop being horrid'. The insubordination, and the lack of the word 'Sir', and the use of the word 'horrid', so astonished him that from then on things got a bit better.

There was, however, a lot to be amused about. The CO canteen itself, in a palatial annexe of CO HQ and which was formerly Montagu House, was run by upper-crust ladies and staffed by beautiful and engaging girls with only a very remote idea of commerce. The food was delicious (odd that lobsters, now such a costly rarity, were then relatively plentiful. Frightened inshore by the numerous explosions at sea? I put it forward as a thought). On being handed, say, a plate of lobster mayonnaise for lunch, one asked the radiant *serveuse* how much one owed for it, but she seldom knew. 'My dear, I simply haven't the faintest. I'll just ask Caroline'. A lengthy and muttered confab then took place, after which she would return and say 'We were wondering if ninepence would be too much'. I was happy to be with quite a few people who liked to extract from the daily happenings whatever fun they might contain. Just along the corridor from us was the office of David Astor, then Foreign Editor of the *Observer* and the CO press representative, no light task as Mountbatten lived, not unwillingly, in a blaze of publicity. Barely a week passed by without David coming bursting in, smiling happily and saying 'Just guess what's happened now!' It was usually something highly peculiar, as it might be a request from a Duchess that, if there were ever a raid on Le Touquet, would the raiders please bring back her golf-clubs, left in locker 47 ('They can't miss it. It's got my name on it. *Too* kind'). Or possibly Princess Marina, calling on Mountbatten for a cup of tea, had wandered by mistake into the MOST SECRET map room and had had to be led out blindfolded. And CO HQ was also my first experience of the well-known words so familiar to all staff officers – 'Haven't you heard? It's all been changed'.

A dismaying social occasion awaited me. All officers in the HQ were invited, usually in pairs, to have lunch with the Mountbattens in their house in Chester Street. They could not have been easier or more welcoming and they made one feel that this had, for them, been the Treat of the Week. But the occasion to which I refer was a dinner given by Mountbatten for about ten of us and at the distinguished Senior Army and Navy Club in Waterloo Place, an austere club full of likewise members. The dinner itself was extremely pleasing but after it was over and we had moved for coffee to the large smoking room, where we were surrounded on all sides by high-ranking officers busy digesting their food and reading newspapers, Mountbatten said 'Now, Marshall, I hear you do comic turns on the wireless. Get up and do one for us'. Horrified at the dreadful suggestion, I protested vigorously but no notice at all was taken of my objections. 'Nonsense. Up you get and start at once'. So there was nothing for it. Our little group responded merrily and loyally to my botany mistress taking her girls for a nature walk, complete with mild indecencies, and to mock chapters from Angela Brazil, but they could not see what I could, and all too clearly see, a look of total horror on the faces of generals and admirals scattered around. Only Mount-batten's presence and prestige prevented a public outcry. A very alarming experience.

A more enjoyable one was to come in the shape of a royal visit and inspection. We were told what to do: do not give the King a hearty handshake but just hold fingers: do not speak (as if one would) unless spoken to: do not bow from the waist but remain upright and jerk the head sharply downwards, a manoeuvre which we practised assiduously on each other ('It's my turn to be the King. *Bow*, Arthur. Now tell me, Marshall, what do you fellows do exactly?'). His Majesty, who turned out, as with many public figures, to be shorter than one had thought, arrived in naval uniform and had a sunburn which, I was fairly sure, did not owe itself entirely to sun. We were lined up on the terrace of Montagu House and as the King moved slowly along, Mountbatten effortlessly rattled off our names and ranks (he could do the same with the NCOs and always congratulated them on their promotions). When my turn came and I almost jerked my head off, I had an impression of great warmth and, if I may say so, friendliness. Few of us were required to speak. Three cheers were given as our visitor left and if only we had been a school he would certainly have asked for an extra day's holiday.

Holidays were, in fact, rather few and far between, and where best to go when one got them? It is strange now to remember how deserted London was in those years. Looking down Piccadilly from the Circus, there was sometimes nobody at all to be seen. By 1942 bombing raids had become spas-modic, though fearful devastation was still everywhere visible. Disagreeable smells of various kinds hung about. I became a member of the Reform Club, mercifully undamaged though the Convervative Club next door had been destroyed, and I shared a flat in Yeoman's Row (handy for Harrods, which occasionally had cakes) with Noël Annan. We frequently dined, if such it can be called, in and Noël became and of necessity a gifted cook and was able to encourage powdered egg to give of its best though I could never get him to peel potatoes in any way but as though sharpening a pencil. We wondered then, as I wonder now, whatever became of wartime onions. Few came our way and they would have jollied things up no end in the *cuisine*. Noël was the kindest and most unselfish of companions though his habit of reading the *Daily Mail* in the bath and sogging its lower half into complete illegibility was trying. He too was militarily occupied but was also writing for the *New Statesman* the series of brilliant articles that partly led to his becoming a Fellow of his old Cambridge college, King's, and to high office there and elsewhere.

We were looked after by a characteristic London charlady, Mrs Beatrice Honeyball. She lived in Battersea, soon became 'Honey' to us, and turned up by bus every morning at 8 am, no matter how daunting the night had been. Buzz-bomb time was especially discouraging and one dreadful night all her windows were blown out but there she was with us next morning, on the dot and uncomplaining, if understandably a bit tearful ('It's nothing that a cup of tea won't put right'). She was a dear, and when our rations ran out she would turn up with some of her own. Placed upon the stage, and perhaps played by that fine actress, Gladys Henson, she would have seemed an exaggeration, so typical of her splendid type was she. She had no light hand with breakables and when there was to be heard the sound of a loud crash of crockery from the basement where the kitchen was, her voice would invariably come floating up to us with 'Never mind. Jesus loves us!' She was also always ready, on arrival and on a cold morning, with 'Lazy wind this morning. Won't go round you. Goes through you'. Her bomb stories from 1940 and 1941 were legion, each starting from the moment when the enemy planes were approaching and she found herself being nudged awake by an alert Mr Honeyball, urging her to listen to the engines' drone with the words 'Ark, Beat!'. To discourage such enemy aircraft, the barrage balloons hovered high above and one frosty night the unworldly John Gielgud, walking home after the theatre, was heard to say sympathetically 'Those poor fellows must be so terribly cold up there', his mind not having yet moved forward from the first world war's observation balloons.

Although CO HQ was demanding in time and energy, I too

had a part-time occupation and early one week in 1943 there came from the BBC a crisis call for help. Richard Haydn, then appearing in a weekly comedy series called *Take It From Here*, a title made famous later in other and wittier hands, had fallen ill with jaundice and they were stuck for somebody to fill in for him at the following Sunday's recording (the programme went out on Tuesdays). The producer was David Yates Mason, an old and very talented Cambridge friend, and he suggested that I should be a hearty and bossy nurse come from the hospital to report on Richard's condition, and thus it was that Nurse Dugdale, with her opening cry of 'Out of my way, dear', was born. The BBC officials, perhaps more given in those days than they are now to worry about offending listeners' sensibilities, were anxious. Might not a bouncy nurse making boisterous jokes about kidney dishes and nasal probes and swab cupboards upset those working or languishing in hospitals? Fortunately the public and critical reaction showed the opposite to be the case and so we were given the go-ahead signal for further series. David and I wrote the scripts and in due course the title changed itself to *A Date with Nurse Dugdale*. An attempt to call it *Nurse Dugdale's Doings* was sat upon, the BBC censors pursing their prudish lips and producing the damaging adjective 'suggestive'.

We were lucky indeed with our fellow performers and enormously helped by a cast which included Elizabeth Welch, Alvar Lidell, John Slater, Jack Jackson (and his band) and, most of all, Marjorie Westbury, a vastly gifted and versatile radio star who could also sing like a bird and who played the dithering Sister Parkinson. We did the show to an audience of about 300 and I dare say that the sight of me at the microphone in Major's uniform and flanked by Marjorie who is five feet nothing, added a certain piquancy to the undertaking. The programme appeared to hold a fascination for army officers of senior rank and one evening I noted that our audience's front row was entirely occupied by red-tabbed figures, with Generals galore and Brigadiers two a penny. Strange.

The most important, though non-existent, member of our cast was Matron, an imposing figure who never spoke and remained a brooding background presence of whom everybody in the hospital was scared stiff, a realistic person and one to be found, I am told, in hospitals the country over. Gradually other characters established themselves: poor old Mrs Muirhead who was for ever, and for unspecified reasons, fusing her electric blanket: scatter-brained Probationer Muspratt getting into a muddle with Miss Medlicott's tourniquet ('Oh dear, she's going ever such a funny colour'): and larky Canon Baldwin for whom the BBC dance programmes, relayed to the wards, proved much too exciting and who was discovered 'out of bed and locked in a frenzied beguine with one of the bronchials'. We were perhaps rather too fond of ending each programme with disaster involving noise – Matron disappearing with a crash through some temporary floorboards in the nurses' rest room, or an emergency in one of the endowed beds, or, during an important meeting of The Board, the tea-urn exploding all over Sir Timothy's agenda.

Sometimes there was a celebrity 'spot' and we were kindly joined, honoured indeed, by people such as the famous boxer, Len Harvey ('Might I trouble you, Mr Harvey dear, to bulge your biceps for poor old Parky: she gets so few treats'), Deborah Kerr already launched on that brilliant film career, Stuart Hibberd and Robert Helpmann (pioneer, or so we alleged, of the patented *Splitproof* tights). It was all for me a very happy period though some of my mocking friends have never let me forget that when the distinguished theatre impresario, Emile Littler, was with us, he encouraged me, wildly over-estimating my potential, with the words 'You could play Dame at Leeds tomorrow'. From then on, and after having to refuse a lunch or dinner invitation with a friend, 'Off to Leeds, I suppose' was a phrase to which I had to get accustomed.

I used, in my character as Nurse, sometimes to chide Sister Parkinson (a bit inclined to let her tongue run away with her) with the words 'You're like the war, dear. You just go on and on'. It did indeed do just that, and at too needless a length in the opinion of some. How sadly ill-informed were, in the summer of 1943, those SECOND FRONT NOW protesters who chanted, in Trafalgar Square, their calamitous slogans. An invasion then would soon have ended in total disaster, such was our lack of proper craft and equipment – a Dieppe raid on a very much larger scale and with a dangerous lowering of morale.

By the end of the year, however, invasion plans and preparations, with 1944 in mind, were going smoothly forward and a number of us were transferred from CO HQ to what became SHAEF HQ and we changed from Richmond Terrace to

Norfolk House in St James's Square, a minor benefit for me being its close proximity to the Reform Club in Pall Mall. Here we were integrated with American officers on a fifty-fifty and share-alike basis and the air rang with cries of 'My land!' and 'Sakes alive!' and 'I'll bet you four bits to a quarter'. One might have been in a Hollywood film. The post-Pearl Harbor Americans had first arrived in Northern Ireland during my time there but had remained fairly remote and in separate formations and so SHAEF HQ was my first chance to observe them closely and at first hand, rather than via the novels of Sinclair Lewis, Edna Ferber and Scott Fitzgerald, in which almost every male American is shown to be, at heart, a fairly tough cookie.

Not so. All wrong. Naïve is what I found them to be, and kind, and uncomplaining, and in every way generous, and I formed then for them a deep admiration and affection that I have never since had the slightest occasion to change. They are, after all, the only great nation ever to have bothered about anybody else and in a disinterested manner, Great Britain's philanthropy down the years not standing up very well to close scrutiny.

Soon, General Eisenhower arrived to command us, the headquarters steadily increased in size and before long we all moved to a vast hutted camp in Bushy Park, Twickenham, not to be confused with the North West suburb of Bushey. Here the difficulties of keeping secret the fact that the invasion was aimed at Normandy were very great. The number of people who had to be in the know was alarming and we passed agitating days and nights. We were fortunate, however, in our enemy, for the Germans seemed ready, though we didn't then know the full extent of their gullibility, to gobble up every item of false invasion information that was, by various means, fed to them. Bamboozled they were and the stupid, plodding Boche of World War One lived again.

Bushy Park turned out to be situated in what became known as one of the Buzz Bomb Alleys and we had some near misses, one of which blew out the windows of our hut and drew blood from the finger of an American secretary, winning her a Purple Heart medal for being Wounded in Action. Oh well. Another time, and in cloudy conditions, a buzz bomb's engine cut out overhead as I was outside and awaiting transport, with another officer, at the camp gate. 'Do you know', he said conversationally and peering upwards, 'that I've never yet actually seen one?' 'Well then, now's your chance', I cried, witty as ever and diving under the nearest hut where, even on the ground and relatively protected, the blast blew my cap off. 'Happy now?' I said, genial to the last.

Shelters had been constructed underground and dotted about, for the huts in which we worked offered little protection and there was some anxiety that a bomb in the centre of the closely packed huts would wipe out a very large number of officers. Some of us were very far from being irreplaceable but we did have a good bit of experience and knowledge between us and it would have been, to put it mildly, a nuisance to find and train substitutes at that late hour. And so a notice went up, signed by Eisenhower himself, pointing all this out and announcing that when the siren went we were all to make for the nearest shelter and that he, Eisenhower, would be the first in – this plainly by way of encouraging everybody and removing any guilty feeling of our being funks.

Hearing one day the warning, I dutifully made for a shelter, entered and sat down and saw, in the darkness, another seated figure who, when my eyes got accustomed to the gloom, revealed himself to be Eisenhower. Silence fell. Nobody else came. No buzz bomb. No All Clear. No nothing. We had been there for five minutes or so when the General spoke. 'Well,' he said, 'as long as I keep sitting here, they can't ask me to sign anything'. Then a buzz bomb could be heard approaching. It passed overhead and went off into the distance and eventually there was a dull explosion. 'You know,' said the General, 'every time I pray "Oh Lord keep that engine going", I feel kinda mean'. It is small wonder that he was so liked, respected and admired and in all my 1½ years in SHAEF (in the end I had become, in the G2 or Intelligence Section, the Oldest Inhabitant) I never heard a sharp or critical word said of him. Sad it was that Montgomery should have made himself such a vexatious thorn in his side.

On June 6th, 1944, the invasion began and later the huge SHAEF HQ went lumbering after it, moving from Avranches to plushy surroundings in Versailles and thence to Rheims and, finally, Frankfurt, always a comfortable distance behind the places where the action was though our official address, which was 'Advanced SHAEF PO', convinced my mother that I was perched up in a forward observation post, with my father's opera glasses sweeping the horizon for signs of Jerry, glasses previously trained, from the dress circle, on Gertie Millar and Gladys Cooper.

Nearly a year later I found myself in Flensburg, the Baltic port where the German high command had finally halted. I was with a delegation from SHAEF, flown from Frankfurt to acquire, and send hastily to London, the German War Diary (our only means of knowing exactly what troops the Russians had), and also, in my case and as I spoke German, to try to discover where Himmler was. The Germans expressed a perfectly genuine ignorance of his whereabouts and he was later caught by a Field Security section and, thus saving everybody a lot of trouble, obligingly did away with himself.

We were lodged on Hitler's commodious yacht in Flensburg harbour and it was odd, on one's way to and fro along the quay, to pass Jodl or Keitel, summoned for interrogation on board. Courtesies were exchanged. We saluted, and the Field Marshal baton was raised in answer. They both looked as calm as though they were just out for a morning's stroll. Once more life became dreamlike.

We ate in the yacht's dining saloon, down one end of which there were some German naval personnel engaged on a course of lectures on submarines and torpedoes, a course which continued because, and could anything be more nationally characteristic, nobody had yet told it to stop. In the centre of the saloon was a bust of Hitler mounted on a pedestal and one day during lunch a couple of German workmen appeared with a saw. They got to work at once and, with expressionless faces, sawed their way through Hitler's throat, the head soon falling, with a noisy thud, on to the deck. They scooped it up, popped it in a sack and exited, not to a round of applause but to, from us, a stunned silence, though some of our Russian allies (they had turned up rather late and had missed the War Diary) were inclined to provide guffaws.

I was paired with a distinguished Oxford don, also by then a Lt Col and in the more active side of Intelligence, and soon we had to summon to the yacht, for interrogation, those who amounted to our opposite numbers in the German High Command. We were both in battle dress and we cut defiantly unmilitary figures. We had no batmen with us and we looked dishevelled, with bulgy blouses and dull boots. The interviews were to take place in one of the larger cabins and, at the hour arranged, there came a knock at the door and after, from me, a warmly welcoming '*Herein*!', there entered, with a lot of noisy heel clicking, four German officers of equivalent rank to ours. They were immaculately turned out in their best uniforms. Everything that was supposed to shine, shone. They were freshly shaved and utterly spick and span and as I made, gushingly, with the social niceties ('Who's for a cigarette?' and 'Do take a pew' and 'Will you be comfy there?'), I saw them staring at us with a look of total disbelief on their faces. Whatever is this riff-raff, they were thinking? What on earth went wrong? How could we possibly have lost the war? Thinking it over later, I found I was as perplexed as they.

SCENE VII

Of Cabbages and Kings

I did not emerge from His Majesty's Forces, as did some who had fared much less comfortably and well, with the feeling that I had wasted six years of my life. I wouldn't, in one way, have missed it for anything. I had enjoyed, if that be the verb, some strange experiences. On a night of pea-soup fog in Whitehall I had wandered, groping my way towards Trafalgar Square as I thought, into Downing Street and had got cannoned into by Churchill. He muttered 'Shorry!' and blundered on, pursued by two detectives who saw me and shouted 'Oh my God, we've lost him. Which way did he go?' It was a short, even a brief, encounter but I felt inspirited to have brushed shoulders, and literally enough, with greatness. I was very far from averse, as in the theatre, to having dealings with Big Names and one morning I was bidden to accompany Mountbatten to a high-powered security meeting where the subject under discussion was one very familiar to me but not to him. He displayed, for once, uncertainty, even nervousness. 'I tell you what', he said as we set out, 'you sit opposite me and, if you approve of what they're up to, just nod. And when you nod, I'll nod too', and quite fairly strange we must have looked, nodding away like two of those carved figures that pendulate sedately to and fro, bowing to each other. Between the nods, he winked, which did me no good at all and my sober demeanour slipped. And in addition to unusual experiences, my life had been enriched by numerous friendships many of which have continued to go bouncing happily along down the years and will I hope do so until, if I may so phrase it and remembering my military days, the last great Stand-To.

My actual demobilisation took place partly in Yorkshire where, finding myself one morning the senior officer present, I had to take a parade and then march a large contingent of men to the railway station. I had not marched anybody anywhere or raised my voice on parade for more than five years and I was, to say the least, rusty. Words of command came from me sluggishly and, I fear, inaccurately. I was still forming fours, a ritual which had been, unknown to me, abandoned. There they all were, lined up in threes and it is difficult to make threes into fours, but they had clearly known officers' muddles before and accepted me and my inefficiency philosophically. Eventually, and as so often ('Carry on, sergeant-major') I was rescued by an NCO. The final parting happened in London's Albany Street barracks where I was given a macintosh, a not very wearable suit, shoes, a hat mainly constructed of cardboard, sweet rations and, later on, a cheque for £180. And later too there arrived a very handsome SHAEF document thanking me effusively for what I had done. Many people, though not I, have such documents framed and then hang them, moved by who knows what Freudian urge, in a lavatory.

My brother had long since married and left the nest but I continued to be based on Newbury until, at the end of the war, we changed houses and counties. Our departure from Berkshire and arrival in Devon was brought about by so many happy chances that those who believe in predestination would consider it proof that the entire thing was Intended. In 1944 my mother was 62 years old, not an ideal age for up-anchoring, nor had she at that time any intention of doing so, despite the fact that the fields near our Berkshire house were being increasingly built upon and it was clear that in the end we would be entirely hemmed in by dwellings containing people some of whom would need to be called on and, eventually, given tea and buns and conversation.

One November week-end in 1944 my mother went to stay with my Cousin Madge in Ilfracombe and finding on the Sunday the *Observer* unobtainable, they settled instead for the *Sunday Times* (let us call that Fluke No. One). Madge liked to read a newspaper from cover to cover and front to back and, still perusing it at tea-time, announced that in the property section there was a charming-sounding house for sale in a South Devon village – four bedrooms, two bathrooms, three sitting-rooms, kitchen etc, barn, garage and four acres of orchard with a stream running through, and all going for £4,500. The fact that she should have noticed this and read it out rates it as Fluke Two. My mother said that it all sounded very attractive, and that was that.

Madge was due on the Monday to accompany my mother back to Newbury, changing trains on the way and pausing at Exeter to consult her lawyers about her mother's estate, recently inherited. They paused, they left their luggage in, where else, the Left Luggage, they taxied from the station, they saw the lawyers and, having completed their business, repaired to the Clarence Hotel in the Cathedral Close for lunch, only to be told (Fluke Three) that the First Sitting was full and they would have to wait for the second one. The day was fine and they took a stroll. There are at least five exits from the Close, but they chose (Fluke Four) the one that leads out into the pleasant and formerly residential area of Southernhay but by then taken over by, and ideally suited to, the offices of lawyers and accountants and architects and such like. Madge, gazing about her, suddenly said 'Look, there's that house agent, Cherry, who was advertising that village house. Why don't we go in and look at any photographs they've got? It will pass the time till lunch'. We are now at Fluke Five. They entered the office, to find Mr Cherry there in person. He was, he said, motoring out to the village, Christow, that very afternoon. Would they like to come too? Yes, it was really a very attractive house and there were several people interested but nobody yet had actually Signed (Fluke Six).

As though in a trance, and by now plainly Guided from Above, they abandoned their luggage, they abandoned the train to Newbury, they abandoned the Second Sitting. I have the feeling that, had it chanced to occur that afternoon, they would have ignored the Second Coming ('Please don't bother us just now'). They drove out of Exeter and up the hills to Longdown, with its spectacular views of Dartmoor. They drove along the beautiful Teign valley and then turned up a side road and drove into the village, its very name a plus mark. They noticed the church and the hills around and in which Christow so neatly sits and quite soon they came in mid-village to a stone wall and a gate and two yew trees and a cobbled path leading down to a pretty white house about three hundred years old. And by the side of the path there happened to be some violets in full bloom and, impossible though it may seem, there were primroses too. 'Thank you', said my mother, 'but I really don't need to see anything more'.

They did, of course, see everything and, on returning to Exeter, my mother signed, virtually unread, every document that was placed before her (Mr Cherry was kindness and reliability itself) and she and Madge, exhausted and dazed but triumphant, spent the night at the Clarence, who obligingly sent down to St David's Station for their luggage. Where are we now with those Flukes? Perhaps the biggest one of all was that my mother, who had never bought a house before, was able to summon up the courage, for she knew, or suspected, the fuss that her Trustees were going to make.

And she was not mistaken. Her trustees were her two brothers-in-law and both of them were lawyers, trained to depress clients and to be generally awkward. The law may or may not be an ass, but what it is, and for certain sure, is a soulless and dilatory machine and extremely expensive to operate. Only madmen go to law and it irks me that in order to die tidily you have to have recourse to the law. I am reminded of the mother of a schoolfriend, a splendidly comical lady, who had also an aversion to and distrust of the law. She wanted to leave, not a Will, but an instruction that, immediately after her death, all her possessions were to be competed for by her relations, the competitions to take the form of athletic events on the lawn. 'Line up for Dorothy's grand piano, and after that it's the egg-and-spoon for her diamond clip'.

When next day my mother informed the Colchester office of what she had done, there were no encouraging cries of 'But how very nice it all sounds'. There was no warmth but instead, a chilly barrage of questions. Had the house a good 'title', a word unknown to her in this sense, her thoughts flying to Chatsworth and Blenheim, but which seems to mean title deeds and proof of ownership and so on. Was the water supply from mains or a well? She hadn't the slightest idea, though there had *been* water (the courteous owner had made them a cup of tea). What did the surveyor's report say? There wasn't time to get one. Well then, of what did the drains consist, and here my mother, vexed by all this badgering, said that she assumed that at some point during the house's long history a nasally sensitive owner had been sufficiently reckless with his cash to install proper drains. To their final, horrified squeak of 'But you surely haven't *signed* anything!' she replied that of course she had: she had signed everything in sight: if asked to do so, she would have signed Mr Cherry's driving licence. Eventually, but only after a year or so, they had to agree that she had done well, but their questions so disturbed and worried her that she fell ill and had to take to her bed for a spell. The house is still there, of course, and as attractive as ever. Its name was originally 'Two Yews' but we got so tired of receiving letters addressed to 'Two Jews' that we changed it to Yew Tree Cottage.

In the upsets and difficulties that occurred and which her firm religious faith helped her to endure, my mother was greatly comforted and supported by the presence in the house of Elsie Elizabeth Jane Appleton. She had come to us as a maid in 1931, speedily revealed a wide range of talents (gardening, tree felling and log cutting, cooking, rug-making, carpentry, chicken rearing, washing and ironing) and was brimful of energy from early morning until nightfall. From my father's death on she never left my mother's side and she died in her arms. Elsie is here still, though nowadays she fells fewer trees. In 1931 she came to us on January 6th, the Feast of the Epiphany. It also happened to be her birthday but one on which she provided, rather unfairly, a magnificent birthday present for us.

After demobilisation and a final BBC series of Nurse Dugdale in early 1946, I returned to Oundle at the beginning of the summer term to find a new broom hard at work, industriously sweeping out corners, and only occasionally getting into a muddle and sweeping where no dust was. This was our new headmaster, an exemplary glutton for work. It was a considerable sadness to me that Dr Fisher, who had retired in 1945 and to a village near by, had almost immediately died – so often the case with people who suddenly change vigorous activity and the strenuous life for complete rest. I had greatly been looking forward to renewing our friendship and laughing as before, though Mrs Fisher happily for us stayed on and was an ever welcoming hostess. Dr Fisher's successor was Graham Stainforth. He came to us from Wellington College, where he had also been a schoolboy, and he carefully concealed behind what seemed initially a slightly bleak exterior, the kind of acute sense of humour that no headmaster can really afford to have. As he increased in confidence with the years, he dared to reveal more and more of his sense of fun and his end of term speeches contained jokes so bright and witty and apposite that the boys cheerfully applauded them as in a music hall. He did great good and rates the highest marks.

The difference between Fisher and Stainforth was very

pronounced and is well illustrated by their attitudes to the School Fixture List. Under Dr Fisher, this list was one that supplied details of fixtures that it was fairly confidently hoped were going to take place and which quite often did. However, there was nothing absolutely cut-and-dried about it. One must remain flexible. Pity to be too rigid, and if Canon Smalley-Law's sermon eventually took place on the last Sunday in November as opposed to the first Sunday in October, as advertised, who was spiritually any the worse? Stainforth, on the other hand, preferred rigidity. A fixture was a fixture and as immovable as Christmas. He was such a worker and took such limited holidays that there was a general fear for his well-being. Would he, perhaps, Break Down? Once when the matter of his health was being discussed by somebody with the school secretary, the wholly excellent Miss Crowe, admired by all, there was a suggestion that such a devotion to duty might lead in the end to a nervous collapse. Miss Crowe gave a short, sharp laugh and said 'But he can't collapse. It's not on the fixture list'.

In 1947 I was offered a housemastership and, though feeling in many ways inadequate and knowing well that I was hardly the conventional type, I accepted it. It meant a welcome increase in salary and the elevation would, I knew, please my mother, and my father's ghost, and so in the summer I set about preparing in various ways for my installation in September. The business of engaging a Matron for a school house had, in the Fishers' day, been undertaken by Mrs Fisher, a keen-eyed and very experienced chooser. But under Stainforth this task was delegated and became one of the many that fell to the housemaster and to which I duly addressed myself, spending quite a lot of time in the interview rooms of a well-known scholastic agency. In my years in the army I had had to interview a number of people for this or that purpose and to attempt to sum them up in that stressful ten minutes of mutual contemplation, trying to remember that they may not like the look of you either or your impertinent questions ('Why did you leave Hopcroft and Snodgrass?'). In this connection, there was a pleasing episode in the career of a Cambridge friend of mine. Considering at one post-graduate stage a life in journalism, he went, supplied with various glowing testimonials as to his writing abilities, for an interview with the editress of a glossy ladies' magazine. She was large and cheerful and in her conversation went in quite a lot for diminutives. These can certainly create a pleasingly informal atmosphere ('Do make yourself comfy!') but he was momentarily taken aback when, after the first preliminaries were over and she was wishful for some solid proof on paper of his excellence, she leant forward, smiling, and said cheerily 'And now, dear, let me have a peep at your testies'.

A fictional interviewer once figured prominently in the dear old School Certificate, a scholastic examination hurdle that will be all too familiar to a number of middle-aged and older readers who will recall that in this severe test of ability, a broad spread of subjects was required and all of them had to be passed or you failed the Certificate (dreaded maths floored dozens). One of the requirements was 'a language' and in many cases the one chosen was French. The examination was in five sections. There were some terribly depressing sentences for translation ('Whatever you do, and whichever course you choose, I shall never believe you'). There was a fairly simple bit of English prose to turn into accurate French. There was an Unseen, to test vocabulary. There was a brief oral examination, which some might consider the most important part but which carried with it ('*Je m'appelle Marshall et j'ai quinze ans*') deplorably few marks. But the *pièce de résistance* (see how the phrases come tumbling back!) of the whole affair was something rather interestingly called Reproduction and at which many might have shone but which turned out to have no biological connection whatsoever.

Reproduction here consisted of a very short French story of an anecdotal character usually ending up with a surprise or a mini-joke. This was twice read out by the master concerned and then had to be reproduced in, more or less, their own words by the alarmed candidates, who were given a thin synopsis to keep them on the right track. Thus, if the anecdote were King Alfred and the Cakes, the synopsis might be '*Roi seul en voyage – chaumière – vieille paysanne – gâteaux – le roi s'endort – pourquoi la paysanne est-elle si furieuse?*'. Kings appeared frequently in these tales, usually quite alone and incognito and in the middle of a wood. '*Mais je suis le roi*' was normally the pay-off line, astounding one and all; but the interviewer story of which I write was on different lines.

Here a bank manager, with his deputy, was interviewing prospective bank clerks and, on choosing one of them, was taken to task by the deputy. 'Why on earth did you choose that one? He had no letters of recommendation!' 'Ah,' swiftly replied the manager, 'how wrong can you get (*Que vous avez tort!*). He had many (*Il en avait beaucoup*)'. There then followed a long list of praiseworthy matters which the deputy had, of course, overlooked. The applicant had neatly brushed hair. His shoes were brightly polished. He was respectful and went to church every Sunday. His clothes were clean and, most telling of all, he had picked up a pin which the wily old manager had left on purpose (*exprès*) on the floor. 'These', summed up the manager, 'are worth all the letters of recommendation in the world', thus unerringly choosing what sounds like a really frightful little prig.

I left no pin on the agency floor. It was not necessary, for the duds announced themselves soon enough. One of them gave a cry of dismay and asked, for it was a sunny day, whether she might sit with her back to the light, a request which I granted and which she followed by asking me if I were married. One of them asked whether she would be allowed to arrange numerous bowls of flowers. One wanted to know whether she would be free at week-ends. One said that she had no experience but 'just loved boys'. Eventually and when I was near despair, there arrived Miss Margaret Rope, a splendid person in every way – experienced, efficient, uncomplaining, brisk and, as it turned out, almost as keen on the London theatre as I was. It was very refreshing to be greeted at breakfast with 'I see they've got another flop at the Vaudeville'.

The Oundle house to which I was appointed was the so-called New House, paradoxically by far the oldest building in the school, it being a rambling Elizabethan construction of considerable attraction. It straggled its length down the side of a hill, had a pleasing garden leading down to the placid River Nene and, as the house stood on the town's edge, it afforded wide and beautiful views (if you discounted the town cemetery) of the countryside stretching away to Stoke Doyle and beyond. Cromwell, on his way to make a nuisance of himself somewhere, had once put in for a night and a plaque on the wall of the Cromwell Room bore witness to this remarkably dull fact.

The house must have made in past centuries a pleasing home for a family of perhaps a dozen or so persons and a staff of six and it was now hard put to accommodate 52 boys by day (some of them slept in an annexe), three masters, a matron, a cook and, if we were lucky, a staff of four. The school had acquired the premises in 1907 during the fruitful Sanderson expansion period and the three previous and long-serving housemasters had all been married and were fathers of families. It had always therefore been regarded as what we called 'a married house' and, stepping in as I did as a firm bachelor and ahead of one or two married masters who had been expectantly waiting their turn, there were, here and there, signs of discontent and envy.

The discontented would possibly have been less envious had they known some of the difficulties. However, the least difficult aspect of my task was the boys themselves. They were kind enough to welcome me warmly (I was already teaching a number of them), to overlook my oddities and, for all of my time there, they were entirely cooperative and helpful. Discipline was never the smallest bother and I like to think that we all lived together *en*, as it were, *famille*. All one could really do was to try to create a nice atmosphere and hope for the best.

In return for all their help one naturally wanted to do the best possible for the boys, particularly in such matters as food, but the wartime rationing was still very much in force and was to continue for all of my time there, and both quality and quantity were sometimes poor and inadequate for growing boys – nobody's fault but Hitler's for the staff struggled away to achieve palatable results and often worked wonders. There were also on occasion wonders of deception for unpopular vegetables, more or less rejected at lunch (I never forced them to eat what they didn't like, but anything taken and placed upon a plate had to be finished up), reappeared, heavily disguised by potato and gravy, as an appetising supper dish and got happily gobbled up. Our cook, the diminutive Miss Dixon, was a model of competence and ingenuity and, even on the bleakest days, radiated contentment, chuckling away in a semi-basement kitchen not ideally suited to the preparation of food for sixty or so persons, food that had then to make a perilous journey down passages and up several stairs.

There were other impediments to gracious living. What training is given, I wonder, to school bursars? Is there a Dehumanising Cabinet (patent applied for) in which they spend an hour a day? I can but think that during their instruction there is at least a week devoted to the subject of

How To Make Difficulties. Perhaps prizes are given to those who dream up fresh frustrations. Like lawyers, trained to curb and thwart and create confusion in the mind, bursars have, I suppose, to curb and thwart anything that is going to end in expenditure. Applying for, perhaps, a new set of crockery for one's well-earned cup of tea (hastily gulped down between refereeing rugger and attending afternoon school), one was made to feel that this modest demand savoured of a woefully *de luxe* style of living and was clearly the thin end of a sybaritic wedge that might lead to further excessive requests (extra cushions, who knows?) and must be discouraged. In the end I took to buying a number of household things myself to avoid the distasteful wranglings. In private life our bursar was the most friendly of men, but then not all life is private.

I mentioned previously the strain and exhaustion of a housemaster's life and the sometimes unfortunate outcome for some. At Oundle there was a tradition of diligent service and when I heard, from a very reliable source, namely his head boy, that a Malvern housemaster used often to go off for a week-end and fish, I was much astonished. With us it was a 24-hour-a-day job for you could be got at at all hours by anybody who cared to invade you and one's only privacy was when in the bath or in the lavatory – both rather limited periods of seclusion. And on top of care of the house, your ordinary classroom teaching continued unabated and with the large amount of paper work that it too entailed. And every so often there was a *Masterpieces* to dream up. It was no picnic.

From my father's death to her own in 1961, my mother kept all my letters to her. Although serious things happened from time to time, I did not burden her with them and concentrated on, if such it can be called, the lighter side. A few short snippets from the letters will give the lay reader, who perhaps has not experienced a public school, some idea of the vast kaleidoscopic panorama, the warp and woof, the ups and downs, the ins and outs, the fair days and the foul of life in an unfrequented corner of Northamptonshire:

'Two boys managed to be sick during the Carol Service, and with the Duchess of Gloucester present. *Not* very tactful . . . We have a new "daily" called Miss Barley, known to us, because of *South Pacific*, as "Barley High" . . . There are nine confirmands and so I have heard nine Catechisms and delivered nine talks about Life . . . The houseman, our invaluable Clipston, known to all as "Pa", called me very early and asked me to come downstairs as the gardener was sobbing in the kitchen! . . . New potatoes for lunch: great excitement . . . We've been inspected by the Board of Education and, unless my old eyes deceive me, at least two of the inspectors are obviously Failed Schoolmasters . . . Miss Dixon has invented a new austerity breakfast dish – two slices of fried bread with Marmite in between and called Savoury Sandwich: not bad at all . . . We have had to have a school Governor to stay for two nights, the one who grunts all the time, doesn't listen to a word we say, and fails to leave a tip for Pa . . . Housemasters have no entertainment allowance. CAN THIS BE RIGHT?! . . . Some mildly indecent photographs have been found by an unruffled Miss Rope in a handkerchief drawer: not easy to look sufficiently shocked . . . John Betjeman came for morning coffee after his brilliant Tennyson lecture last night: wildly funny about schools in general . . . 12 letters to write yesterday, all of them long ones, and even more to do today . . . A tiresome epidemic of streptococcal throats, but that chicken pox case turned out to be heat rash . . . The masters' wives' new Speech Day hats as gloriously hilarious as ever . . . Casualties everywhere – one bronchial asthma, one stomach chill, two waters-on-the-knee, one sprained ankle, a threat of pink eye and a dislocated shoulder to be sent by ambulance to Peterborough to be put back again . . . The dailies are giving trouble – here one minute and gone the next: am contemplating lecturing them on Loyalty . . . The fees are up again to £315 a year . . . Siegfried Sassoon called unheralded and talked about himself for an hour non-stop while staring at the floor . . . We have had a black Professor from Africa wished on us for two nights, and not a Cape gooseberry to be had! . . . Leavers' party tonight and mounds of sausage-rolls whichever way you look . . . My study becomes more like Charing Cross Station every minute . . . Ground hard as concrete and so no rugger . . . Miss Dixon has housemaid's knee after kneeling so often on the stone floor to get at the oven and Pa is in bed wth a septic toe . . . After I had explained to two new parents that if their son falls ill we write every day to report progress, the mother said "Oh please don't bother about that. Just send us a post-card if he's dead": splendid people!'

And thus, more or less, it went on for seven long years towards the end of which time I began to yearn for a complete change. Much as I loved, and love, Oundle, I had been going there off and on for thirty years and I was not by nature a Mr Chips and had no wish to finish my life scratching away short-sightedly on the blackboard and making, an object of friendly derision perhaps, the same tired old jokes. But where to go and what to do? I let it be known among my friends that I felt unsettled and was 'available for offers: anything considered' and soon there came a suggestion from, of all attractive places, Cambridge and from Victor and Tess Rothschild, both of them very old friends. Would I like to go to them for a time as Private Secretary? It was an answer to prayer (not to mine, for I had long since abandoned prayer as being unprofitable, but to my mother's, who knew well my predicament and hopes) and I hastily accepted before they could change their minds. I am not much given to quoting Shakespeare but if I were, the words 'for this relief much thanks' would be appropriate. Francisco, you will remember, has been on sentry duty on the Elsinore battlements, my own duties being at times not dissimilar. I greatly dreaded the numerous happenings inseparable from a leave-taking after so many years – explanations, apologies, letters, parties, speeches, gifts, packing, tidying up and handing over – but my feelings of liberation and joy carried me through. On top of it all, and perhaps to make full use of me up to the final moment, I was asked to produce a last mini-*Masterpieces*, half boys and half masters, and early in August, 1954, I arrived, an exhausted ex-schoolmaster wreck aged 44, at Merton Hall.

It was a large, ancient and beautiful house perched on the Cambridge Backs with a garden leading down to the Cam and just opposite St John's College, which has since jumped the river and invaded the grounds. I had my own small and pretty cottage (one up, one down) next to the Hall. We were a secretariat of three, housed for work in a roomy hut and consisting of Miss Brewster (Margaret), Mrs Thomson (Ann) and me. There were, if memory serves, over a thousand correspondence files dealing with assorted subjects, for Victor had a large family and extensive scientific and banking interests and was at that time Chairman of the Agricultural Research Council. Bells, buzzers and telephones were everywhere and promptly at 9 am they started pealing, buzzing and ringing, often all together and frequently catching poor Margaret, running breathlessly and two minutes late up the drive, on the hop. We would exchange a smile as she went flying past my window and into the house and Victor's study, the main centre of operations or, in cyclone language, the heart of the storm. It was at once apparent to me that the two ladies possessed, and it was essential for survival in the sometimes rather feverish surroundings, acute senses of humour.

I was hardly the ideal secretary but Victor nobly accepted my shortcomings. It is true that I soon became quite skilful at protecting him as much as possible from the outside world, from mad inventors requiring cash, from (repeatedly, and what toads they can be) the cheaper press requiring gossip and scandal, from bores, from climbers, from chance callers and from the many who thought how nice it would be if Victor were to give them a cheque for £100 ('I am sorry but Lord Rothschild is in Paris . . . Lord Rothschild is in America . . . in the House of Lords . . . the Outer Hebrides . . . the bath') but my shorthand merely consisted of abbreviated longhand ('th' had to stand for the, that, those, theirs and, rather rarely, thine) punctuated by gasps of 'please don't go so fast'. There was also a dictaphone in the car with a microphone attached to the dashboard so that any fugitive and valuable *pensées* that came to mind while driving could be recorded and subsequently deciphered through the noise of gear changes and tootings and achieve permanence on paper, to be considered at leisure later, though in fact leisure was something that Victor seldom allowed himself.

He and Tess were sweet to me and I was treated with immense consideration by the whole staff. The butler, Sweeney, was tireless with trays of food and Irish twinkles. Mrs Prentice was a cook in a million and kindness and goodness personified. Mrs Peck kept my cottage spick and span and provided, while dusting, wise comments on Life ('Who that Bevan thinks he is I really don't know'). The gardener, Jordan, brought me flowers and fruit and advice on my own little plot. The unflappable chauffeur, Wally, all his life with the Rothschild family, smiled genially the long day through. Once, after having done what he had been expressly ordered not to do, he received, and rightly, the most tremendous wigging. Was dismissal threatened? Possibly. At all events, thinking an hour or so later that he might be feeling rather shaken and shattered, I ventured in with friendly oil to pour. It was not needed. Never was water less troubled. I found him seated happily, munching cake and with a steaming tea-pot before him. 'Well', he said, 'when in doubt, brew up', – as good a maxim for life as any. It was a great joy to find that all these splendid people also had such bright senses of humour. Laughter was everywhere.

But not, and how could it reasonably be, always. With somebody as clever, industrious, intelligent and painstaking as our employer (whom we all loved, no matter what, for his charm was irresistible), there were good days and bad days. We of the secretariat were members of no union and could call no strikes but against such an ebullient and sometimes over-demanding personality we had occasionally to take protective measures of a mild kind. One could, I suppose, call them sanctions. There was no collusion but a sort of mutual and unspoken agreement that the time had come for each of us to get busy on our own. Margaret's strong line was to sigh and assume a harassed and almost distraught look, while Ann sometimes closed the study door a shade more firmly than it required. Neither of these abnormalities went unnoticed or failed to register ('What on earth's the matter with everybody this morning?') My own 'thing' was to gaze solemnly, not into Victor's eyes but at a spot about three inches above his head ('And what's up with *you* today?'). The failure to meet some-body's eyes, if prolonged for an hour or so, is extremely off-putting and discouraging and I warmly recommend it as a weapon. Our combined ploys generally worked and soon a calmer atmosphere descended on Merton Hall. And before long we would all be smiling again for Victor's jokes were first-rate. And there was the simple fact that almost everything he did was directed towards the good of others in some way or other.

I already had a number of Cambridge friends (on many joyful occasions I dined at the King's high table) and happily made more. In addition, Binkie Beaumont and John Perry had bought an entrancing and fairy-tale-like thatched cottage, mainly for week-end use, about ten miles off and on the borders of Essex and they moved in at about the same time as I arrived on the Backs. The house was called Knots Fosse and was much larger than it looked, with six bedrooms and three bathrooms and at week-ends it was full, and often with famous names. It stood in five acres of beautiful garden (both owners were enthusiasts) and in course of time it sprouted a tennis-court, a croquet lawn, a covered and heated pool, and a sauna. Almost my first private telephone call at Cambridge was from Binkie inviting me over on a Sunday and from then on I was made most kindly welcome and urged to go over as often as I liked. And ten miles away and in another direction, there were further welcomes. Through Combined Operations and David Astor, I had come to know his brother, Jakie, who lived in another beautiful house, Hatley Park on the borders of Bedfordshire, and there too I was a frequent guest. I was everywhere surrounded by kindnesses and have never known happier years.

At Knots Fosse one never knew who were to be one's fellow guests. A car would crunch to a halt on the gravel and out would step the tall and elegant Margaret Leighton (John Perry, after a lifetime in the theatre and no respecter of persons, used to call her, affectionately, 'Lofty'). Or it might be Diana Wynyard, or Emlyn Williams, or the much loved Adrianne Allen with her daughter, Anna Massey. From time to time it was the Oliviers, with Vivien looking, as real beauties sometimes do, lovelier each day. One afternoon I found myself upon the croquet lawn and as partner to Noël Coward, who loved the game and wielded a very keen mallet. Our opponents were Joyce Carey and Keith Baxter and Noël kept up a constant rattle of encouragement and admonishment in tones so characteristic that, if one turned one's head away, it might have been one of his many imitators. If I managed to do a good shot, the slightly adenoidal comment was 'You are a complete and *utter* darling'. On the other hand, a bad shot was not very popular. 'You are a very very silly COW!' Both of the comments made it hard for me to clutch my mallet, for giggles resulted.

John Perry and I were ardent tennis players and enjoyed single after single. We played an old-fashioned game and modelled ourselves on a past lady champion of very much yesteryear, a lady with the euphonious name of Dorothea Lambert Chambers. We both remained firmly anchored to the base line and just concentrated on returning the ball with sufficient length to prevent the opposing player from, as they have it, 'storming the net', as though either of us would dare. Our rallies, therefore, went on for quite some time. I think the record for this is held by a splendid woman called Phyllis Satterthwaite and stands at 5¼ minutes, but John and I must have run her close. We were not the only players and on one occasion we had a doubles match and I partnered John Gielgud against John Perry and Ralph Richardson. At the time Sir John, his mind elsewhere, was busy casting a play that he was to direct and it was disconcerting, after I had called out '30-15' and was preparing to serve again, to hear a voice say loudly and to nobody in particular, 'I *won't* have Martita Hunt' or '*Why* won't Binkie let me have Pamela Brown?' Sir Ralph's absent-minded forte was to serve when he happened to be ready. If the opponent didn't happen also to be ready, well, hard luck and 15-0. To add to the air of unreality, a thickish mist suddenly descended on us, Knots Fosse standing on the only eminence for miles around. Sir John, seen through swirls of misty vapour had a look of the Prospero that he had so brilliantly played, while Sir Ralph and John became totally invisible beyond the net, though an occasional and distant shout of 'Play!' warned us that a ball might soon be expected. Neither of the knights dreamt of stopping the game, and seemed indeed not to have noticed the adverse weather conditions. But for John and me, all was merriment and confusion.

After four years at Cambridge, I abandoned bells, buzzers, files, telephones ('Lord Rothschild is in Israel . . . Africa . . . Penzance') and my truncated longhand and, on hearing a rumour that the streets of London were paved with gold, I hurried thither to scoop up my share. Since our Barnes days, I had longed to return to live there (my two wartime years in the capital hardly ranked as a treat) and so here was my chance. Victor kindly let me keep on my cottage and sportingly continued to pay me my salary (in all my time there I never knew an ungenerous gesture) and for a year I shuttled contentedly to and fro by car between Cambridge and Rugby Street, WC1, where I had a part share in a flat with Mr and Mrs John Wyse. It was a Box and Cox arrangement for the Wyses had a pleasant Berkshire farmhouse where they preferred to spend their week-ends and so I installed myself on Friday afternoon and then removed myself by Monday lunchtime, a shuffling convenient for all. John was an established actor who had run the Boltons Theatre in Kensington, and Mrs Wyse was known to a wide public as Jonquil Antony and her achievement was to have created *Mrs Dale's Diary*, the wireless series that gave such enormous teatime pleasure to millions of listeners anxious for the latest hot news of the good doctor and his family – Bob and Jenny and Mrs Freeman, not to speak of the pulsating social life of Parkwood Hill.

When I came to Rugby Street the Diary was being written by a team of three. Each of the three writers took it in turns to supply a week's scripts and it was Jonquil's custom to complete her stint of five episodes in one 24 hour Herculean (labours of) period. She started at 9 am one morning and emerged from her task, pale and shaking, at 9 am the next day. Then she was, to put it ungraciously, shot of the thing for a clear fortnight. Although the main story line was, as with all such serials, decided on in advance and by a committee and had to be strictly kept to, it was naturally possible to twist events a little bit this way or that and it was Jonquil's delight, in the last of her five episodes, to land the Dale family in some sort of mess or muddle or crisis.

Let me hasten to reassure you. The Dale crises bore no sort of relation to the family crises experienced by those who appear in such things as *Dallas* and *Dynasty* (have you ever noticed that the last two syllables of the latter form the adjective 'nasty'? I just mention it). Parkwood Hill knew, more or less, how to behave itself and such failings as drunkenness and infidelity never touched the hem of Mrs Dale's herringbone costume. The Dale crises were of a minor nature and tended to be domestic. Perhaps Mrs Dale's sister, Sally, and that peculiar husband of hers were coming to Virginia Lodge for Sunday supper and there was insufficient food, the strain of it all being clearly heard in Mrs Dale's agitated voice: 'I've just come from the larder, Jim, and there's only enough cold mutton for two. Oh what *are* we going to do?', followed by that twanging harp and the entire listening public distraught and on tenterhooks until the following Monday. Or, failing inadequate mutton, Mrs Freeman's octogenarian cat, Captain, could go missing and be found next week nailed down under the floorboards by electricians come to re-wire the first floor. Nailed down by mistake needless to say. And still alive.

After a month or two of this agreeable and motorised shilly-shallying, Binkie and John Perry, ever mindful of my welfare and the staunchest of friends, put a pleasant literary job my way. H. M. Tennent were then providing for ATV a fortnightly television play of what might be called a prestige nature, for they often featured famous performers under contract to HMT. The organisation responsible for this Tennent offshoot was called Globe Productions, was saucily known in the profession as 'Binkievision in glamorous Perryscope' and was housed, under the command of a model of taste and efficiency and niceness whose name was Cecil Clarke, in a Queen's Theatre office. Into the office there poured daily, sometimes sent by agents but more often just sent, a cascade of TV play scripts written and submitted by the hopeful. There were a number of professional and established playwrights already under contract and producing excellent material, but somebody was needed to examine the unsolicited plays in case a Rattigan or an Ayckbourn was lurking within the suspiciously dog-eared covers. It was what seemed an interesting task, and it fell to me.

But alas, I was lucky if one script in a hundred made stimulating reading, or if one script in two hundred was worth drawing to Cecil's attention. Knowing what high hopes came with them, I never, in the five years in which I tackled about 30 scripts a week, skipped anything. It seemed unfair to do so even though, early on, I had learnt to recognise some of the danger signals that showed that onward progress was likely to prove unrewarding – 'To the left of the cocktail cabinet': 'To the right of the french windows': '"Thank you kind sir" (and Cynthia drops him a mock curtsey)'. There was also occasionally some technical jargon mugged up from a text book ('The camera pans and favours Hildebrand'). Because of the high hopes, I could not bear just to return a script with a bleak rejection slip and I always wrote a letter and tried to inject into it some crumb of comfort: 'Your play begins strongly and the brutal landlord, Silas Carver, is splendidly conceived but we did feel that the dramatic tension falls away a little after Silas has been accepted into the lay brotherhood of that Surrey community, fine though the repentance scene and subsequent breakdown are (I know you won't mind my mentioning that there are two p's in "appalling"). We all greatly liked your prior, rosy-cheeked old Boniface, and the comic "business" with the doughnuts in Act IV caused many chuckles here! We now look forward to reading any further scripts that you may care to send us'. Perhaps it would have been kinder in the end to discourage. Who can say?

As might be expected, an eccentric or two popped up, one of whom bore the distinctive name of Harry H. Wimbley. From him we received a regular flow of unproducable plays accompanied by some impressive printed writing paper which had at the top a large heading which read HARRY H. WIMBLEY PLAY PRODUCTIONS LTD. PRESIDENT – HARRY H. WIMBLEY. The letter began 'Dear Mr Marshall, I have pleasure in sending you the latest comedy by Harry H. Wimbley'. There was then a printed signature at the bottom of the page, HARRY H. WIMBLEY, which Harry H. Wimbley had signed, naturally, 'Harry H. Wimbley'. And at the very foot of the page there was a line which read – AGENT FOR HARRY H. WIMBLEY, HARRY H. WIMBLEY.

There was also a not very literate male with harmlessly licentious leanings, a passion for young parlourmaids and an inability, when excited, to control in his prose the letter 'h'. He sent in two or three plays a year and they varied little in content and were centred round the home life of Mr and Mrs Brown, who sometimes appeared, to give the thing a lift, as Mr and Mrs White. The happy pair were always 'discovered' at breakfast.

Mr Brown:	What are you going to do today, dear?
Mrs Brown:	I thought of changing my library book.
Mr Brown:	What a good idea.
Mrs Brown:	And then I might have a cup of coffee at Benton's.
Mr Brown:	That's nice for you, dear. They speak well of Benton's coffee. As you pass Boots, could you get me some more bunion plasters?
Mrs Brown:	Of course, dear.
Mr Brown:	How about another grilled sausage?
Mrs Brown:	No thank you. I have had sufficient.

And so forth. At first I wondered whither all this lively chat was leading but I soon came to know that what it was leading to was the parlourmaid Jane. After about twenty pages of dialogue, Mrs Brown exited and – and this was the author's big moment – Mr Brown pressed the bell. Enter, after a pause, Jane.

Mr Brown:	Good morning, Jane.
Jane:	Good morning, sir.
Mr Brown:	Why has this room not been dusted, Jane?
Jane:	Oh but it has been, sir.

Mr Brown:	No it hasn't, Jane. See, I can write the words NAUGHTY JANE in the dust on our side-board. You mustn't tell fibs.
Jane:	Oh no, sir.
Mr Brown:	And that was a fib, wasn't it?

(Jane looks frightened)

	Do you know what happens to naughty little girls who tell fibs?
Jane:	No sir.
Mr Brown:	They get spanked, Jane.
Jane:	Oh sir.
Mr Brown:	And lazy little girls who don't dust rooms get spanked too.
Jane:	Oh sir!
Mr Brown:	So do you know what I'm going to do, Jane?
Jane:	No sir!
Mr Brown:	I'M GOING TO TURN YOU HUP AND SLAP YOUR BUM.

(Jane screams and runs out of the room. Enter Mrs Brown)

Mr Brown:	Oh there you are again, dear, did you change your library book?
Mrs Brown:	Yes I did, dear. The girl suggested that nice life of Mr Chamberlain.
Mr Brown:	Oh, that's nice, dear. You always enjoy a nice life.

And so on. The key lines never changed. Prefaced by talk of spanking, hup remained hup. Jane remained Jane. She screamed to order and a good time was had, if not precisely by all, certainly by one.

One day, while reading some play submissions (I collected them in batches from the Queen's Theatre office), I came upon an American novel sent in by the distinguished agent, A. P. Watt, with a view to its adaptation as a television play, a novel which was to provide for me a humiliation and a disappointment which lasted for several years and even now has power enough to produce yet another twinge of regret. The book's title was *Every Third Thought* (in case you've forgotten, it is a quotation from *The Tempest*, and Prospero saying 'And thence retire me to my Milan, where every third thought shall be my grave'.) Its author was the American writer, Dorothea

184

Malm. The British publisher was Peter Davies and the publisher's teasing preamble had me at once hooked for it told of two elderly sisters who live with their brother in Minneapolis and who invite to stay every Christmas their great-niece and her husband, neither of whom they like and whom they rightly suspect of being after their money. The book ends in a killing. All this against a falsely jolly Christmas background seemed to me to be full of dramatic possibilities. Miss Malm's dialogue was admirable and would, I felt, sound well on the stage.

Full of enthusiasm, I asked for, and received, Binkie's permission to go ahead and adapt it for the theatre. I slogged away (it was much harder work than I had imagined) and after a lot of re-writing and discussion with John Perry, the wisest of counsellors and himself a successful playwright, I produced a script that appeared to be possible and which everybody enjoyed reading. And that was the trouble. It *read* too well (the credit is Miss Malm's, not mine). The title that I chose for it was an ironical one, *Season of Goodwill*, and Binkie decided to take the plunge.

Because it read well, it attracted three considerable star performers – Sybil Thorndike, Gwen Ffrangcon-Davies and Paul Rogers. Our director, the excellent Vivian Matalon, was also, I suspect, hypnotised by the words and we went into rehearsal in a 1964 heat-wave in a room at the top of the Queen's Theatre. Dame Sybil was, of course, 'Dame Sybil' to us all until, within twenty-four hours, checked ('Just "Sybil" dear, please: it's *easier*'). It became at once clear that the three principals (the young people hardly appeared at all) were going to give admirable performances, the designer, Michael Annals, designed us a perfect set, the director splendidly directed and after six weeks off we went to Brighton for a five week pre-London tour that was also to take us to Cambridge, Leeds, Newcastle and Oxford.

The day that I left London for the Brighton try-out was a Saturday (dress rehearsal, Sunday, first night, Monday, a first night that I saw, to my horror and embarrassment, was described on the bills as 'World Premiere') and Joyce Carey kindly gave me lunch before I departed. In addition to being a much admired actress, she had herself also been twice a playwright, with one resounding success, *Sweet Aloes*, to her credit. She had been through try-outs many times before and knew all about them and as we separated after lunch she gave me a long, affectionate and searching look and said, 'I'm sure you know what you're in for, and I'm sure you'll be equal to it'. I did not at the time understand what she meant. I was very soon to find out.

Those out on a pre-London tour become unwilling Aunt Sallies for everybody connected with the theatre, everybody not connected with the theatre, for friends, acquaintances and complete unknowns. After a performance, an assortment of these comes flying through the stage door, bursts upon you unannounced and unexpected and lets fly. Without any sort of polite introduction, I had to listen to such sentences as 'Did you *have* to have Sybil? . . . You realise that Paul is much too young . . . What a shame that Gwen didn't sing – that *lovely* voice . . . Your set is very badly lit and so depressing, my dear . . . *Can't* you improve the first act curtain?' If they couldn't think of any more individual criticisms, they just sighed and then said something along the lines of '*Whatever* possessed you to have anything to do with it in the first place?' We were, at Brighton, not without august visitors. Joan Plowright came early in the week, was kind enough to like the piece and returned on the Saturday bringing with her Laurence Olivier. We had a talk and he was very encouraging but was worried about the cast's American accents. They rang, to his ear, false. Could anything be done? I promised to tell Vivian. Larry then went to see Sybil. I do not know exactly what transpired between them but she was displeased. When, at supper, I said how good it was of him to come and take an interest, I found her to be not in agreement. 'Larry's a *pick*,' she said, unusually crossly for her. 'But he was so helpful', I said. 'No! He just loves to criticise. With him it's pick, pick, pick all the time'. In view of what was to happen to us, I see that he could with advantage have picked a good bit more.

When we went north, the vast and half-full theatres in Leeds and Newcastle in no way helped our delicate little play. Everybody told everybody else that it was the glorious summer (it was August) that was keeping people out of the theatre. There were, of course, a few happy theatrical moments. In Newcastle and in Act I, Gwen suddenly tripped up, fell over and disappeared completely from view behind the sofa. Sybil, concerned for her well-being, instantly abandoned her accent, leant over the back of the sofa and said, in bracing English tones, 'Are you all right, dear?' Gwen, struggling up and realising that the play must at all costs be got back into America at once, supplied some invented dialogue of her own and said 'Ah sure am, honey! Ah didn't hurt mahself none', thus smartly removing the action from Minnesota to somewhere in the deep South. Sybil replied 'Oh good' and the two ladies struggled nobly on.

Sybil's husband, Sir Lewis Casson, came with us on the tour and was throughout a helpful, calming presence, though on one occasion he did rather agitate me by saying that in places (and they had become legion) where things seemed a little slow, 'Sybil can always make some of her funny faces'. Dearly as I loved Sybil and greatly as I admired her, I had, at Cambridge, seen some of her funny faces when she arrived at the New Theatre with a farce called *Madame Plays Nap*, a thinnish piece featuring Napoleon and his washerwoman. There was also the really alarming photograph of her squinting comically at the audience in Herbert Farjeon's *Advertising April* (the play's alternative title was 'The Girl Who Made The Sunshine Jealous'). But Vivian was firm and Sybil reluctantly left her funny faces in her dressing-room. We all stayed in the same hotel and it was delightful to see the Cassons at breakfast downstairs on the stroke of 9, with Sybil opening her letters and passing the information they contained to the slightly deaf Sir Lewis – 'Oh good, Freda's going to have another baby. Hooray! . . . Here's a nice post-card from that girl who does such marvellous work for the Blind . . . The Mayor of Hemel Hempstead wants me to open a swimming-bath . . .' Once when I was lunching with them and a few others, we happened to be talking, quite happily and serenely, about Death, and Sybil boomed out 'I hope to goodness Lewis goes before I do. He'd be perfectly hopeless on his own'. Lewis was aware that he was under discussion but had missed the subject and the words. 'What did Sybil say?' he said to me, and I had to shout 'SYBIL HOPES TO GOODNESS THAT YOU DIE BEFORE HER'. He nodded contentedly. 'She's quite right, bless her'. And so it fell out.

We got to London, we opened and we speedily closed. Nobody booed us, and at the first night I distinctly heard somebody cheer, but it was all a disaster. The reviews weren't rude, merely depressing and discouraging. They complained, all of them, of inaction. They complained justifiably. Nothing really happened until the murder, by which time the play was on the floor and it was all my fault. The cast behaved like angels throughout, and Binkie, as solid in failure as in success, spoke comfortingly. The kinder people were, the worse I felt. My idea. My writing. My ambitious project. I was entirely responsible, as all playwrights ultimately are, however much they may complain about actors and directors. I blamed only myself and I sadly do so still.

My script-reading activities meant frequent discussions with Cecil Clarke and after a time he let it be known that he would prefer me to be permanently stationed in London and available every day and so I sadly abandoned Cambridge and my Box and Coxing and looked about for accommodation. In the next twelve years I was extremely lucky and, to start me off, John Gielgud very generously lent me his charming house in Cowley Street, Westminster, where Big Ben obligingly told one the time. He was doing a play in America and would be away for about six months, which would give me plenty of time to look about. The house was one of those tall and thin London ones which have a single room on each floor and, attractive as the rooms were, much of a resident's time was necessarily spent upon the stairs. As I was still on the right side of 50, just, this was no hardship and everywhere one looked there was a treat for the eye – a theatrical painting, a Cecil Beaton stage design, a pleasing piece of furniture or china or, as a result of John's and his family's long service in the theatre, some important stage prop or personal relic (the ever irreverent John Perry said 'Don't open a drawer or Ellen Terry's false teeth will fall out') And when and for me Cowley Street came to an end and John returned, I moved into the top floor, miraculously empty, of the Chester Row home of Coral Browne and her husband, Philip Pearman. It was in SW 1 and handy for Sloane Square and Peter Jones. If ever I felt uncertain about the country's future or the world situation (it was the time of 'the wind of change' and President Kennedy's assassination, and riots here and civil war there) it was my custom to go and have a cup of coffee in Peter Jones's admirable roof-top restaurant. And there, surrounded on all sides by everything that was most wholesome and good and solid and respectable in the way of British womanhood, fresh from shopping and blooming with good health, I felt that, at the very least and in the confident words of the song, there would always be an England. And in the lift one sometimes heard pleasing fragments: 'Where are you going to go now, dear?' 'I'm going into the casseroles, and I may linger'.

Coral Browne needs no introduction – she was then at the Haymarket and in the smash-hit *The Pleasure of His Company* – and Philip was a one-time actor and then a theatrical agent in the considerable firm of MCA. I had known him since Cambridge days for he was a schoolfriend of Ronnie Hill, host of that Party That Never Was. It cannot be easy having a paying guest in the house, sharing a staircase and a front door and having to listen to assorted noises overhead, but the Pearmans were saints of kindness and goodness and in all my four years with them they never registered even so much as a half-frown. I had a lovely time and when they had finally to decide to swop the house for one in Brighton and a small London flat, the Rothschilds came once more to my rescue for, with an eye to the future of their elder daughter, Emma, then a schoolgirl, they had bought for her a house in Radnor Walk. As she would not need it for some time, they suggested that I live there, first of all at a peppercorn rent and subsequently with no rent at all and just fulfilling the far from arduous role of 'Housekeeper'. Eventually I was there for six years. Radnor Walk was off the King's Road in Chelsea, a road which in those days still had nice old-fashioned shops – grocers and fishmongers and greengrocers and itinerant barrows – and hadn't yet been invaded by the little army of modish dress-sellers who provide canned music which blares forth from their pullulating boutiques and makes life, for the middle-aged and elderly who remember sedater periods, difficult to bear.

Binkie and John Perry were apparently undeterred by the elaborate and expensive lack of success of *Season of Goodwill* for in 1967 they suggested that I take part in another stage venture. Incidentally, when the curtain has finally fallen on a failure and you have faced worried looks and next day's damaging notices in the newspapers, your *via dolorosa* has only just begun. There are the evening papers. There are the Sunday papers ('A woefully dull evening . . .'). The weekly magazines were more in number then than now ('These spineless goings-on . . .'). There were the monthly magazines ('Happily we have now said good-bye to . . .'). At Christmas there are the round-ups of the year's plays ('Bottom of the list, and sadly so because of the presence in it of Dame Sybil, we must place . . .'). And at last and when you think you have endured all, a biography appears of one of your leading players ('We shall never know what madness seized her when she agreed to . . .'). To this day, a normally kind friend and one who should know better refers to 'your flop'. So be warned. When strolling up or down Shaftesbury Avenue, I fixed to my face a look, carefully practised at home, of serene detachment but nobody was for a moment deceived.

My new task was again a literary one. The French comedy, *Fleur de Cactus* by Messieurs Barillet *et* Gredy, had achieved a triumphantly long run in Paris, after which, transformed into the American language, and with an American setting, by Abe Burrows and now called *Cactus Flower*, it had been equally successful in New York. Its producer was David Merrick, responsible for *Hello Dolly* and much else besides, and he and Binkie decided that *Cactus Flower* was right for London. But it had now to be de-Americanised and made verbally acceptable to English audiences. Binkie had first offered this job to Paul Dehn, but Paul was far too busy writing his excellent film scripts, James Bond ones among them, and so in the end H. M. Tennent fell bravely back on me. I was invited to translate the original French version, some of which Abe had thrown out, into English and then marry it up with the considerably altered American one. Happy as a lark, I got to work.

The play's main theme concerned an amorous dentist who, to avoid being forced into matrimony by his young mistress, pretends to be already married and coerces his reluctant and spiky dental assistant (the 'cactus' of the title) into playing, on occasion, the part of his wife. In the end, of course, she bursts into flower and blossoms and he falls for her instead. In America the assistant had been played by Lauren Bacall and Binkie had managed, at his most honey-tongued and persuasive, to secure Margaret Leighton for London. It took some doing for Maggie was not by nature or wish a light comedy actress and preferred to be in heavier (in the best sense) and more substantial plays. The dentist was to be played by Tony Britton, that most skilful of actors with the lightest of touches and brilliant command of timing. Abe was to come over to direct and we were to open 'cold' (no tour) at the Lyric Theatre which had the great advantage of possessing a revolving stage, for the play made use of four sets which had to be changed at lightning speed or the play's impetus was gone. The revolve had not been operated for about fifty years and it was a relief to find that it revolved, worked by stage-hands toiling at a winch beneath, as smoothly as ever. Maggie's dressing-room had to be on the revolve itself, for there was no time between scenes for her to get to her proper room, and she and her dresser had, as they speedily made her changes, quite a vertiginous little time of it.

Abe Burrows arrived (he was everybody's idea of an American play director and could have stepped straight from a Hollywood film) and rehearsals began. It was a great relief to discover, and fairly soon, that Abe and I were going to hit it off and have an amicable relationship as he disapproved of many of my alterations. Before long he didn't like me to leave his side, teased me ceaselessly about being so English and when once I had to absent myself for an afternoon's BBC recording, I never heard the end of it. When one of our textual arguments began, it was amusing to find that Abe was immediately supported by, on his right, his son, and on his left, his assistant director, a nice man by the unusual name of Biff Liff, these two yes-men adding their voices in the discussion. One of our differences concerned the word 'doctor' as applied to a dentist. They simply could not take in the fact that no English person refers to his dentist as 'the doctor'. But I too had my supporters in the loyal shape of Maggie and Tony and the rest of the excellent cast. They backed me up, and anyway had learnt my words and weren't going to change them.

Still badly stage-struck, I found to my great satisfaction that we were to rehearse in a number of theatres – the Globe, Queen's, Prince of Wales and, of all unsuitable auditoriums for a light comedy, Drury Lane. Here, in my script-reading days, I had had a room allotted to me in which to interview and encourage potential TV playwrights and one day, hearing raised voices on the stage, I tip-toed into the back of a box and heard Moss Hart, the original director of *My Fair Lady*, rehearsing, and a miracle of tact and patience and expertise he was, James Hayter who was to take over from Stanley Holloway as Dolittle. And then, in mounting excitement, *Cactus Flower* had a week of the by then fashionable previews at the Lyric and in March, 1967, opened. I stationed myself in an upper box, unoccupied because it contained some of the lighting, and, feeling fairly confident, watched unobserved the audience's reactions. At almost any first night, the first six rows of the stalls are so much dead meat (and dead meat would be more rewarding, for you could at least eat it) but further back they were all having a jolly time. I had inserted, all on my own, quite a good comedy line for Maggie (as it concerned the seamier side of Hyde Park, Abe had failed to understand it) which got a laugh and, some nights, was applauded. Cheers greeted the curtain and we all went contentedly to bed.

The reviews next day were, as we all expected, sniffy (audiences laughing and having an enjoyable evening often seem to upset some critics) but on the second night, Binkie darted into the box-office and emerged smiling and saying 'We're going to be all right'. It was a cheering experience to see, night after night, queues at the box-office (I was on a percentage) and to be able to go through the stage door and stand in the wings and watch the revolve revolve. One night the lights came up too soon (there was a blackout between scenes) and Maggie was revealed, seated at her desk and being rapidly whirled away into outer darkness. The audience loved it, audiences being always happy when something has clearly gone wrong. Abe stayed with us for a time. He had, on the first night, been here, there and everywhere, joining in the laughter from the back of the stalls and, to my slight dismay, shouting hoarse words of encouragement ('Hit it, Tony!') from the wings. And after the performance, it was enjoyable to go and sit with one of the cast and discuss ('Did you feel that I *pressed* too hard this evening? Do please be frank') the evening. We ran for seven months to packed houses and might still be there but for the sad fact that Maggie had contracted herself to America and a Tennessee Williams revival and there was nobody who could possibly replace her.

In other literary ways I was fairly industrious though I responded better to direct requests for reviews and articles and broadcasting material rather than to any inner urges to scratch, say, a thousand words on some subject that might be of use later ('New Ways With Cold Bread Sauce'). From its inception the BBC's *Woman's Hour* had welcomed me warmly and I have been, down the years, a frequent contributor, ready to drone away for three or four (the preferred length) or even eight minutes on such subjects as games parties, 'elevenses', tennis, shower-baths, telephones, amateur theatricals, matinées, 'The Child I Was', treasure hunts, overworked words, Shakespeare, speed, Speech Days, boredom, handbags, gluttony, nostalgia, diaries — quite a wide range. My own diversionary frivolities apart, can there ever have been a more helpful, valuable, intelligent, conscientious and better organised wireless programme than *Woman's Hour*? I very much doubt it. The dozen or so women who at any one time run it are dedicated, quite simply, to doing good in various ways. The programme flinches at nothing, from talks on abortion to advice to mothers not to worry if their twenty-seven year old son doesn't seem to be noticing girls yet. They have even taken VD on the chin (an unusual seat for it). They inform, they provide sympathy and encouragement, they suggest, they are classless and non-political. I have the greatest possible respect for this admirable institution and for the women who have devoted their working lives to it.

In the twelve years that I lived in London my social life was busy and front doors swung hospitably open, and no door swung more often open than that of Jamie and Yvonne Hamilton, resident in, appropriately, Hamilton Terrace (Jamie liked to be near Lord's). 'Jamie' is Hamish Hamilton, the distinguished publisher, and, totally unaware of the fact that socially Things Had Changed, the Hamiltons continued to give regular dinner parties for twelve, with the men in fullish fig (Jamie would have preferred white ties but had to make do with black) and the ladies in their finest array. The sexes divided neatly up, half a dozen of each, and if ever a prize were to have been given to The Hostess Least Likely to Flag, it would have been scooped up year after year by Yvonne, the very soul of spirited animation, happily flapping her fan at one end of the table, with Jamie a debonair host sometimes in elaborate Highland rig and radiating bonhomie at the other. Impeccable food and drink resulted in bright faces and vigorous chat.

Fellow guests were very far from dull. If your luck was really in there would be Nancy Mitford, so elegant and witty and crisp and loving to laugh ('Oh I can't bear it, I can't bear it' was her customary reaction to any joke that she found especially fetching). There might be Diana Cooper, refusing all food. Or Malcolm Sargent, not the shyest of talkers. Or a Princess. Or a nice American Ambassador called Bruce. Or Vivien Leigh. Or the supremely gifted Kathleen Ferrier, headed for such a tragic end. Or a sprinkling of agreeable Americans (for me, disagreeable ones do not exist). There used to be, early on, Roger Senhouse, until the arrival of last-minute and improbable telegrams locally despatched ('Very sorry. Delayed in Hong Kong') revealed him to be an unreliable guest (The Man Who Didn't Come To Dinner) and he got himself black-listed. And sometimes, and to everybody's delight, there was Joseph Cooper who could usually be coaxed to the piano to provide 'Kitten on the Keys' in the style of Mozart, or some such musical treat.

It was Jamie Hamilton who, with his partner, Roger Machell, had bravely taken a chance on me in 1953 with my book, *Nineteen to the Dozen*, and they have been the most faithful of supporters ever since. The book was a collection of short stories and literary articles (I fight shy of the words *belles lettres* though it might be jolly to baffle chance visitors to my tombstone to find on it the brief description 'Bellettrist'). Roger's door in Albany was another that seemed to be ever open and here again there might be Nancy Mitford, or the Lunts, or Margaret Lane and her daughter, Selina Hastings, or our American actress friends, Margalo Gillmore and Brenda Forbes (neither of them the most serious of ladies), or Joyce Carey, or a scribble (for want of a better collective noun) of writers, all basking in Roger's warmly friendly aura and in the peace and quiet of the most beautiful backwater in London and just one hundred yards from Piccadilly. And no record of my social life would be complete without mention of Paul Dehn and Jimmy Bernard, ceaselessly entertaining callers in their Bramerton Street house which, though on the small side, seldom contained fewer than ten persons, and at any hour of the day or night (rings at the front door bell were answered by 'Come on in, whoever you are') friends were being cosseted in one way or another with comfort, food, advice, money if needed, coffee and gins and tonics of jumbo proportions. And when they moved to larger premises in Tite Street, it merely meant that there would be twenty people where before there had been ten. By all of these friends I was thoroughly spoiled.

Binkie and John Perry, living side by side in Nos 14 and 15, Lord North Street, were wonderfully generous hosts and their theatrical evenings were a joy (Noël Coward once sang, from memory, the entire score of *Our Miss Gibbs*). They had also been, for many years, kind suppliers of tickets for first nights, one of which resulted in my receiving a well-deserved rebuff. It was while I was still at Oundle and I had been invited to the highly memorable *première* of *Oklahoma* at Drury Lane, when the tumultuous cheering and applause became an extraordinary, solid wall of sound and even disillusioned critics were seen to be weeping for joy at the cascade of beauty and freshness and melody that had just overwhelmed us. In all my years of theatre-going I have never known anything to compare with it and, with this marvellous experience still in my mind, I returned three days later to Oundle for the summer term. Wishful to pass on something of my glow to my colleagues, I was holding forth in the common room to what was, I thought, a charmed circle, only to find that one of them, a resentful teacher of mathematics, was a good bit less than charmed. I finished my boastful discourse, to tepid oh's and ah's, and he opened his mouth. Just three words. 'But why *you*?' he said. Why indeed? I slunk abashed away.

Another first night, that of *My Fair Lady*, provided the only occasion on which I ever saw Binkie's steel-like control give a lurch, a wobble. Normally his face, whatever the provocation, was serene and revealed nothing. A pleasant smile gave nothing away (if he had been to a play, and you asked him for his opinion of it, the reply never varied. 'Lovely!'. No more, and no less, and that way he could neither be quoted nor misquoted). But so much hung, financially and artistically, on *My Fair Lady* that a wobble is fully understandable. We were together in a box ('Why you?' again) with Irene Selznick and her son. Everything had gone splendidly and we were just coming to Freddie's great number, 'The Street Where You Live', perhaps the best in the score, and I do not forget 'I Could Have Danced All Night'. Freddie achieved the verse excellently and was just starting on the first chorus when, for a moment, there was a small croak in the voice, a roughness, followed by the slightest of hesitations. Fearful that the actor might, from nerves, be going to crack, Binkie rose quickly from his seat, rushed to the back of the box where he would be out of sight, knelt down and put his fingers in his ears. If there was going to be a disaster he wanted neither to see nor hear it. But there was no disaster, the roughness vanished, the song continued and I was soon able to give Binkie the thumbs-up sign and back he came.

I had, since the war years in London, been a privileged recipient of Hester Chapman's warm friendship and enthusiasms and here too was an open door at various addresses in the W1 area. Hester was by then the admired historian and novelist, Hester W Chapman, and I had known her since 1932 when, with her first husband, Nigel Chapman, she ran an unconventional prep school called 'Spyway' on the coast near Swanage. She was a fascinating person who was firmly determined to be, in everything, unusual. 'Can't you be more ordinary?' Nigel used to moan. Not a hope. Her hair was sometimes a mass of golden curls that hung down round her shoulders, and sometimes it transformed itself into a grey cone-like construction which stuck up a foot above her head and contained, or so Emlyn Williams laughingly announced, her press notices. She had a cackling laugh that cracked china. Whenever she sat down and remained seated for any length of time, her 'fallout' spread itself upon the floor around her – a conglomeration of hair-pins and biscuit crumbs and cigarette ash and pieces of hair and face-powder. Impossible to over-look such a card but, being rather short-sighted, I doubt if she ever took in the surprised glances that came her way when in public.

Hester bravely stayed on in London during the entire war (she was quite fearless and paid no attention whatever to bombs or their nuisance value) and most sportingly used to save up her rations and give every fortnight, with her second husband, Ronnie Griffin, a sustaining dinner party to which one was frequently bidden. They were nights to remember indeed, particularly when the AA guns were firing and there were thuds and explosions everywhere ('Darling, you *must* have another anchovy egg'). Ronnie was a gentle, frail banker of great charm and on these occasions was in charge of the drinks. 'Ronnie's just coming up with the drinks' Hester used to say and the sound of bottles clonking in the basement indicated that Ronnie was at work, the continued clonkings, as the minutes ticked by and throats became parched, tempting one to think that, when they came, a goodish percentage of the drinks were going to come up inside Ronnie. Well, why not? Host's privilege after all, and there was always heaps for everybody. Between them they developed the happiest and most relaxed of atmospheres, their dinners were oases of delight and one always left after midnight, perfectly ready to face a blackouted walk home.

Hester was in some ways like an enthusiastic schoolgirl of twelve for she developed old-fashioned 'crushes' on people, though never on the games mistress but rather on men in trousers. At the end of the war and during the run of *Perchance to Dream* at the Hippodrome, I took her to a matinée and we went round after and I introduced her to Ivor. Incidentally, the business of 'going round' can be a very trying experience but Ivor always made it easy as he undertook most of the talking – '*Didn't* you love it? *Isn't* it all Heaven? Didn't you *adore* the music? Isn't Roma a *dream*? *Aren't* the sets perfection?' One just nodded one's head off and everybody was happy. Between Ivor and the swooning Hester there was an instant sympathy, a platonic love match and she and Ronnie were frequent guests at Ivor's country house, 'Redroofs', near Maidenhead. At times, when the worshipping and adoration became rather intense, he might refer to her as Hysteria W. Chapman, but he appreciated her properly and when he died she was passed on, as it were, to Noël Coward, who relished her equally and cherished her. Noël especially enjoyed her well-known theory that Queen Boadicea lies buried under Platform 7 at St Pancras Station and the recital of her unsuccessful attempts to get British Rail to allow archaeologists to start digging ('There are plenty of other platforms for them to use').

I am deeply grateful to Hester for many happy introductions which led on to friendships and among them I was lucky to count Rose Macaulay, the sharply satirical authoress and critic who pounced like a female leopard on the numerous follies and idiocies of the age and tore them, though always in a restrained and polite manner, to shreds. I had particularly enjoyed, in 1934, her novel, *Going Abroad* in which she made fine fun of the Oxford Group and I warmly recommend it (the book, I mean).

The last occasion on which I saw dear Dame Rose (I had known her for some time and was allowed to drop the Dame) was at a *New Statesman* party given for contributors and friends and in, of all places, Londonderry House in Park Lane. I suppose that this must have been some time in the 50s and lavishness hardly describes the outpourings of champagne and other drinks, the toothsome canapés (I distinctly spotted caviare) and the elaborate flower arrangements. I saw no sign of guilt on any of the faces present, no hint that they felt that we ought properly to be drinking beer and eating corned beef sandwiches and discussing existentialism in a run-down town hall somewhere south of the Thames. Best bibs and tuckers were everywhere to be seen except, of course, on dear Rose.

Though always fresh as a daisy, she was by no means what is sometimes called a dressy person and she often looked, in Dorothy Parker's vivid phrase, as though she was on her way out of a burning building and had snatched up the first garments that came to hand. We had a happy chat for she liked to laugh and, gazing about us, there was much to please that splendidly witty and uniquely gifted lady.

I did not like to ask her if she had come by car for she would certainly have offered, in her kind way, to run me home and I had had already a dozen or so years before, the traumatic experience of being her passenger. It was in London and during the war and the Blitz and the blackout and when few, luckily, were awheel. We had been fellow guests at dinner with Hester in Percy Street, off the Tottenham Court Road, and my destination was, on that occasion, Pall Mall and the Reform Club. Emerging from dinner and into the pitch-black night, we climbed into what must have been something like a Baby Austin, Rose settled herself confidently at the wheel and we were off. I forget now exactly when I realised for the first time that we were progressing not upon the road but upon the pavement. There had certainly been a bump and a lurch, after which the lamp-posts, looming up in the very feeble light that was all that was allowed from the slotted head-lamps, were appearing on the right hand side of the car rather than on the left. Meanwhile Rose chattered away amiably about the extraordinary difficulty of buying onions in wartime London and what an added excitement, and a much needed one, they would impart to Woolton Pie. I would not have upset or wounded her for the world and it was fortunate that the darkness in the car concealed the fact that my eyes were from then on tight shut throughout further lurches and bumps, for I am not stout-hearted enough to wish to see death approaching but would prefer it to come, as come it will, as a complete surprise. But she got me there in the end, and I was full of gratitude for her kindness and the lift. I was grateful to her too for life itself.

In London I was fortunate to be able to do my reciprocal entertaining at the Reform Club in Pall Mall, a club of which I had been a member since 1943. The club's telegraphic address may be ONWARD, LONDON, but in point of fact BACK-WARD, LONDON, would be more in tune with the splendours of Barry's masterpiece (he architected the Houses of

Parliament too) with its look of being a Roman Palazzo of two centuries ago and its generally Italian air within. I have had, and for forty years, nothing but kindness from the staff and members and my membership has been one of the most rewarding experiences of my life, though here, and once more, I suffered a rebuff. I was staying in the club for the Coronation and, as the day wore on, I saw that a member who had clearly been loyally toasting Her Majesty to very good purpose and for quite some time, had decided to lie down and rest awhile, choosing for this healthful repose the mat just inside the street door and in the entrance hall. Not the ideal spot, perhaps, but any port in a storm. After he had been resting for about two hours, I felt that perhaps something should be done and, rather officiously I suppose but with good intentions, I approached the Secretary and informed him of the member's predicament and present whereabouts. 'Is he breathing?' asked the Secretary. 'Well, yes', I said. 'Actually he's snoring rather loudly'. 'Well then, is he being a nuisance to anybody?' I said that people had to step over him when going in or out but that hardly rated as being a nuisance. 'In that case', said the Secretary, 'I shall do nothing. If a member wishes to lie down and go to sleep in any part of the club that he chooses, he is perfectly at liberty to do so. Good day to you'. I had been ticked off, and serve me right.

SCENE VIII

Indian Summer

I left London in 1970 and in a way was glad to go for the running of two establishments was both exhausting and expensive and my Christow house seemed increasingly to need attention and to be cared for. I had moved from my mother's house and had renovated and done up three old mill-workers' cottages in the same bit of land, a fairly inaccessible residence at the bottom of a narrow lane but still in the middle of the village and conveniently placed. Quite attractive, really. And in 1975 I became an Old Age Pensioner though the official beasts responsible for dishing out the cash refused to give me my pension (some tale of my earning too much) until I was seventy. However, having arrived at the great age of sixty-five, I had accustomed myself to the idea of gently vegetating, of sitting in the Devon sun on my terrace and reading Dickens, of gathering apples from my orchard, of watching the trout in the stream, of taking an occasional motor-trip with my dear old Cousin Madge and her friend, Ruth Toller, to Wales, and of gradually fading away, perfectly happy and contented, into obscurity. But then quite suddenly a number of things happened and three telephone calls plunged me overnight into an Indian Summer of a quite startlingly bright effulgence.

The first one came one Saturday evening shortly before Christmas, 1975. It came from Anthony Howard, then editor of the *New Statesman,* and it was to say that Auberon Waugh, who was contributing the First Person column, had been, and at very short notice, lured away (apparently with offers, and what could be more acceptable, of increased cash) to the *Spectator* and would I consider taking his place. Tony named a sum of money that seemed to me to be just about right. The time was 8.15 pm and so I asked how long I could have to ponder this flattering offer. 'I must know first thing tomorrow morning. I'll ring you at 9'. Luckily, Peter Kelland was staying with me and I had the benefit of his wise advice and, fortunately, encouragement. We finished our dinner and I went early to bed, prepared for a fairly sleepless night.

I knew and liked Tony and for some time he had been kindly urging me to take on more reviewing work for the paper than I was doing, which was roughly a review every five or six weeks. The books sent to me were mainly biographies and autobiographies of the lighter sort, very often concerning theatre people, and as some of them were not very good, I was expected to make a little not very cruel fun of them. But apart from the Nurse Dugdale scripts, I had never been brave enough to commit myself to a regular and weekly output of work. I felt ill-equipped and doubted my competence and so, when Tony rang, I asked whether I might not perhaps alternate with another writer, or even two others, and thus produce a column every two or three weeks. 'No', said Tony. 'People buy a magazine like ours expecting to find the same features and writers in it week after week'. This was of course true. For years I had been enjoying the 'This England' section, the Diary, the competition and, indeed Auberon's 'First Person' and would have resented their absence or alteration. And so, after further discussion, I agreed to take it on, anyway for three months or so while they thought of somebody else, a three months that was to be in the end nearly six years.

When I recently asked Miles Kington how he managed to provide his remarkable daily piece for the *Times*, he just smiled and produced a one word answer. It was 'Fright'. All journalists will know what he means. If it were not for the deadline, no journalist would write a word but it is a happy fact that the dreaded moment of *having* to produce the material, produces the material. To do my weekly article of 1,400 words (no 'Away on holiday' either), I knew better than to sit myself down before a blank sheet of paper, biro poised and the face puckered in concentration. Such antics discourage a Muse from dropping in. Inspiration will come when it feels like it and not before, and daily chores – washing up, cooking, answering letters – are the moments when inspiration is most likely to pop up its welcome little head. I was very lucky. In all those six years, I was never once at panic stations. Perhaps you wonder whether I had in reserve and as a safety measure an all-purpose article which I could use in a backs-to-the-wall situation. No I hadn't.

I do not know how other journalists proceed but I used to write the articles in longhand first, then I typed them, subtracting or, more likely, adding this or that phrase, then re-typed and made further alterations and additions and so on until I felt happy about the piece. My sentences tended to be long ones, the above procedure inevitably resulting in verbosity. I knew that it was important to give the reader some idea of my life and background and where I lived and to that end I wrote of my experiences as a schoolboy and a schoolmaster, of my six years in the army, of my peaceful life in Devon and of the village residents. These, like the village itself (I called it 'Appleton'), were heavily disguised. My house I called 'Myrtlebank', a name which I found comical and which used to be popular in the old-fashioned boarding-house world, along with 'Bella Vista' and grand names, with inverted commas added, borrowed from elsewhere: 'Chatsworth', 'Blenheim', 'Glamis'.

Some of my partly fictional village residents became popular with readers – Canon and Mrs Mountjoy (a timorous lady whose Christian name was Berenice), Miss Entwhistle (a pillar of the church) and our smart set, Giles and Bunty Bultitude who inhabited a large house complete with heated pool and rumpus room (ping-pong), cried 'Cheers!' and 'Bung-ho!' and 'Chippertipip!' on every possible occasion, had large cars and wintered abroad (post-cards used to come saying 'Don't you just *adore* Cannes?') and were ceaselessly generous ('Crash on up to us for a snifter!') and defiantly extrovert. People used to write to me and ask for the latest news of them and many letters, often with foreign stamps on them, were addressed to me at 'Myrtlebank' and 'Appleton'. As the writers usually added 'Devon', the letters ended up in the Exeter sorting-office, where my name was sometimes recognised locally and the letters got sent on with TRY CHRISTOW on them.

Weekly exposure in the pages of the *New Statesman* revealed to producers and editors that I was alive and kicking and living in Devon and caused before long a brisk resurgence of interest in what, if anything, I had to offer and one of the more agreeable results was an appearance (there were in the end to be three) in the Michael Parkinson BBC TV Show. It was the programme's practice to send, well ahead of D Day, a researcher, usually a pleasantly bright girl, to extract from the subject a skeleton life history. This was then broken down for Michael into areas of possible chat that might prove lively and productive on the box. About an hour before going on, one met Michael and he said that he thought of starting with this or that subject, or would I rather prefer that or this subject, and a sort of running order was agreed on and everything was made easy and comfortable. You then practised in the studio coming round that corner, giving a slight bow and then negotiating those rather shallow steps (really the evening's severest challenge) without falling flat on your face. For when safely seated opposite Michael in that little pool of light, it was simple enough to forget the cameras, the audience in the studio and the wider one outside and just gossip away to this receptive and pleasant chap. He had the virtue that so many interviewers lack: he knew when to shut up and let you jabber away. On my first appearance, Michael asked me a question and like a volcano I erupted and talked non-stop for about five minutes. After which he said 'Good God, whatever would have happened if I had asked you a serious question?'

Two years later and in 1977 there came another telephone call, this time from the features editor of the *Sunday Telegraph*. When I was next in London, could I possibly drop in for a chat? I could indeed and duly dropped in and was speedily cheered by the niceness and gentle tact of Desmond Albrow and the editor, John Thompson. They said that they had heard a rumour (inaccurate at that time) that I was unhappy at the *New Statesman* and would I consider switching to them instead? I corrected the rumour and explained that I would find it too agitating to do two regular columns a week, but how about a fortnightly one for them of about 800 words? This was happily agreed to and there, at the time of writing, I have been ever since. They have been unfailingly helpful and considerate and, if I am short of a faintly topical subject, are always ready to suggest one.

My departure from the *New Statesman* had its interesting features and piquant moments. In August, 1981, there arrived, out of the blue and with no prior warning, a letter from Bruce Page, the then editor, giving me the sack. When I say that it was a letter from Bruce Page, it was one of those 'dictated by Bruce Page and signed in his absence' ones and so it lacked that warm personal touch that can make all the difference to the sensitive. The letter was politeness itself and it thanked me for 'the very great pleasure' I had been able to give readers and for my 'conscientiousness and co-operation'. But it was time, which I well understood, for 'a wider selection of voices' to be heard. I was asked if I would like to be gradually tapered off – a monthly article for a year, perhaps – or go straight away. I don't care for taperings off and I chose to go pretty well straight away for that held an attractive inducement. If I were to choose the straight break 'we would try to make some reasonable offer by way of compensation'.

Here was handsome talk indeed for I had never in all my forty-five years with the magazine had any written contract or formal arrangement, save an (in that case) rightly styled gentlemen's agreement with Tony Howard in 1975. But what compensation? Would it be a three or four figure amount I asked myself, excitedly and in the mind's eye purchasing several saucy new shirts from the Army and Navy Stores and an air ticket to Cannes. I waited patiently for six months (time for Bruce and The Board to add on a few delightful noughts to the sum they had decided on) and then wrote again to Bruce asking for details of what was happening for the end of the financial year was approaching and I needed to Know Where I Was. But the letter received no acknowledgement, much less an answer. I was full of wonder, and my wonderment by no means ended there.

Before I actually left, a kind mention had come from a staff member of what was apparently a general wish to give me 'a present'. What would I like? I had been fond of everybody there, and still am of most, and so, for one must consider expense and my suggestion would work out at about ten bob a head, or 50p if you like, I asked for a copy of the new Oxford Dictionary of Quotations, in the front of which those who felt so disposed could write their names. I would treasure it equally with the one given me in 1954 and signed by all the boys in the last form I ever had at Oundle. But alas, nothing ever arrived. No present. No book. No names. Nothing to treasure, and we aren't out of the wood yet.

To mark my final departure, two letters were printed in the magazine's correspondence section, one in favour of my departure and one against. The latter was by an old friend, and friendly indeed. The other was not. It was a Good Riddance letter of a wounding kind and I asked myself (it was plainly no good asking Bruce) whether at that particular moment it had been really necessary to spit on my white hairs and provide a nasty letter of any sort.

The third telephone call was to waft me into a different world. It came from Frank Muir and it brought sad news, namely that Patrick Campbell, the very popular, stammering captain of one of the BBC's *Call My Bluff* TV teams, had bad heart trouble and couldn't carry on. I had, and luckily for me, been a friend of Paddy's for many years, ever since we used both to write, from around 1948 onwards, for that pleasing little publication, *Lilliput*. On one occasion and after we had had a heartening and somewhat prolonged lunch at the Reform, we had gone to the private showing at the Royal Academy and I had been able to dissuade him from attacking an offensively awful item of modern sculpture with his umbrella ('One really g-g-g-good wh-whack and I could have its head off'). And I had been a member of his *Call My Bluff* team for two programmes and was therefore known to Frank and the then admirable director, Johnny Downes.

Frank said that a number of possible names to replace Paddy were under discussion by the BBC and that one of them was mine. What did I think about the idea? I was flattered and frightened in about equal measure and felt, as usual, inadequate. However, I did have one small advantage of a negative kind. It was Availability. I had no commitments which would ever prevent me from attending the week-end recordings (we do two programmes on Saturday and two on Sunday) while most of the other names were simultaneously busy in other directions. I was therefore almost the only one who was unlikely to fall between two stools (such a very unfortunate phrase, I always think, for anybody involved in the nursing profession). And so in the end and *faute de mieux*, they settled for me and what was to be a very cheerful experience began. Paddy kindly rang from his French home to wish me well, Frank was helpful in every possible way. Johnny gave me valuable advice (I was inclined to tease too much when extracting the BLUFF card), Robert Robinson was good enough to beam encouragement, and in 1979 off I went. The first programme was a memorable one for I proudly led my team to a disastrous 8-0 defeat. Oh well, I thought, from now on it can only get better and I roared with laughter, which seemed to be the natural thing to do.

Come to think of it, I have been laughing at most things all my life.

Index

207

A Grain of Truth

Jack Webster

In this autobiography by one of Scotland's best known journalists Jack Webster writes vividly of his childhood in Aberdeenshire, of golden hairsts and feein' markets, of honest toil and twinkling humour – the beginning of a route which took him from the *Turriff Advertiser* to the *Scottish Daily Express*.

He writes of his meetings with the rich and famous, from Charlie Chaplin to Mohammed Ali, and of his coverage of great events. But through it all Jack Webster remains a man of the North East, firmly rooted in his origins and their very real values.

FONTANA PAPERBACKS

Fontana Paperbacks: Non-fiction

Fontana is a leading paperback publisher of non-fiction. Below are some recent titles.